WHITEWORK EMBROIDERY

TECHNIQUES AND PROJECTS

Auburn Claire Lucas

WHITEWORK EMBROIDERY
TECHNIQUES AND PROJECTS

THE CROWOOD PRESS

CONTENTS

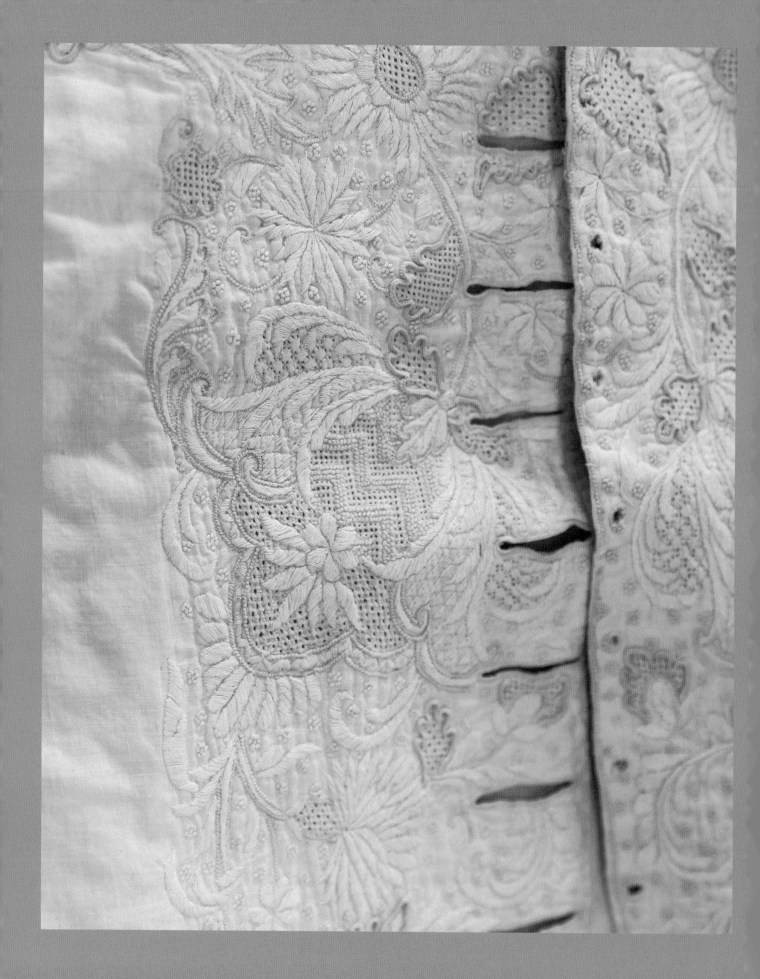

CHAPTER 1

INTRODUCTION AND A BRIEF HISTORY OF WHITEWORK

Whitework is an exquisite and ever-changing form of embroidery. The term whitework, in its broadest sense, covers any piece of embroidery that has been stitched in white thread onto a white fabric. However, there are certain techniques and stitches that are specific to whitework embroidery. There are many of these techniques and stitches. To attempt to include all of them in one book would be a lifetime's worth of work, and if I had included everything, this book would be a weighty volume indeed.

The whitework techniques and stitches featured in this book are a mixture of those that I was taught when first learning whitework, and those that I have researched and experimented with for fun and for professional development. These techniques and stitches are what I and many of my contemporaries consider to be some of the basic and key whitework techniques and stitches. The chosen techniques are pulled thread, drawn thread, cutwork, eyelets and ladder stitch and shadow work.

Within these techniques, again, I have not been able to include every stitch and its variations because for some techniques, such as pulled thread, the opportunities are endless. For each technique I have therefore included a range of core stitches that covers the basic stitches for beginners, leading to more advanced and intricate stitches for already practising embroiderers.

I have also included some standard surface embroidery stitches. These surface stitches can and are used in many other embroidery techniques and are not necessarily specific to whitework, but I have included them for a number of reasons. First, they have historically been combined with whitework techniques. Second, they help to neaten off certain whitework stitches and finish edges. Mainly, however, they can be used to help bring together different whitework techniques and designs, creating interest and contrast within whitework embroidery.

For me, whitework is the most beautiful form of embroidery and that is because it is all about the stitches. Because everything is white, there is no contrasting colour or shiny piece of gold to distract the eye. This means that the stitches need to be

incredibly neat, well planned and designed. Whitework is therefore a great technique for beginners and advanced stitchers alike. This is because it not only makes you think about the individual stitches themselves, but also how the stitches work as a whole when they are combined. Instead of using colour, whitework uses the combination of threads, materials and stitches to create interest, texture, depth and tone.

Trying whitework for the first time can seem a little daunting as there is so much to think about, so it is best to concentrate on the individual techniques first. This way you will learn how each technique is stitched, what preparation is needed and

Whitework moth, worked in various whitework techniques including pulled thread, satin, eyelets and cutwork. Stitched by the author.

how the stitches in each technique can all work together. As you begin to advance and practise more techniques, you will soon learn and better understand how the different techniques and stitches can complement each other when combined.

USING THIS BOOK

The aim of this book is to be a practical handbook that will guide you through your journey into whitework embroidery. Whether you are just starting out on that journey or have experimented with whitework embroidery before, I hope this book inspires and enlightens, as you learn new stitches and techniques and gain the confidence to design and produce your own whitework embroideries.

Each chapter focuses on a different area of whitework, from the materials and tools needed to create even the simplest whitework embroidery, to the chapters on specific whitework techniques or types of stitch. As you work your way through this book I also give hints and tips on best working practice, and some practices I use in my daily stitching, that I hope will help you create perfect results.

Choosing the materials and threads for a piece of whitework may seem much easier than other techniques; after all, they all need to be white! But there is a huge array of options out there to choose from. The chapter on materials and equipment is by no means exhaustive and the materials and threads noted are in keeping with the more traditional materials used, though they are the modern derivatives and alternatives. Fine muslin is just not what it used to be! In each of the chapters I have also stated what materials and thread I used to stitch the samples. Again, I have tended to keep to the more traditional threads and mate-

Eighteenth-century cap crown, worked in various whitework techniques including pulled thread, counted satin, shadow appliqué and buttonhole. Stitched by the author.

rials for my samples, but feel free to experiment when stitching your own work, especially if you find certain threads difficult to use or certain materials difficult to count.

If starting whitework for the first time I would work your way through the book in order, learning and practising each technique in turn. This way you will build up your skills, improving all the time till you are ready to tackle the more advanced stitches and learn to combine techniques towards the end of the book.

For advanced stitchers and those who have done whitework before, feel free to pick up and start learning from wherever you choose. I have tried to include a variety of stitches varying from the simple to the more complex and intricate. You may also want to try experimenting with finer materials and threads, which give much more delicate results but are more of a challenge to work with. Imagine working a pulled-thread pattern on a cotton mousse of 106 threads per inch (TPI)!

One of the last chapters in the book is on designing and planning for whitework

embroidery. On reflection, this was the most difficult chapter for me to write as design is very personal and everyone has their own style and types of images and motifs they like to stitch. I have tried to give as much information and detail as I can, but there is no one rule for designing whitework embroidery, and each design, stitch plan and order of work will be completely different. The best advice I can give is just give it a go! The more you do the more confident you will get and there is nothing quite like seeing your own design being transformed from pencil and paper into a beautiful piece of embroidery.

Most of the sample motifs and the projects have a template included at the back of the book so feel free to trace these and work the samples for yourself.

At the very end of the book there are chapters on washing your whitework and mounting. When you finish a piece of whitework embroidery, washing it then mounting it is not essential, especially if you are just sampling or practising. However, if you have worked on a piece of whitework

From the Olive Matthews Collection at Chertsey Museum. The shepherdess, items: M.2009.18 Floral silk brocade open robe dress with a closed bodice, accessorized with whitework, cuffs, kerchief and apron. (Image © The Olive Matthews Collection, Chertsey Museum. Photo: John Chase Photography)

for a long time, these steps are well worth the effort as a clean piece of whitework, mounted effectively, can really bring the embroidery to life.

A final note on stitch names. During my time as a student and in the process of writing this book, I have read much on whitework embroidery. At times I found it very confusing as different books used different names and terminology for the same things, and in other books those same names were used for something entirely different again. In this book I have used the terminology I was taught and understand. This does not however make my terminology correct and you may find that some of the stitch names, especially in the pulled-thread and drawn-thread chapters, differ from other publications or names that you already know.

Finally, I hope you enjoy this book for all the things you will learn, and that it will inspire you whatever stage you are at on your journey into whitework embroidery.

HISTORY

The history of whitework embroidery is as varied as it is long. It is an ancient technique that has no one place in history, and in one form or another has been created and produced all over the world. Whitework was, and still is, ever evolving and adapting to the new tastes and ideas of the time in which it is being worked. This is why there are so many different whitework techniques, as one technique transformed into another. The first ever use of whitework embroidery is difficult to date exactly, but primitive forms of whitework on linen have been found in the tombs of Egyptian nobility as far back as 1500BC. Over its long history, whitework embroidery has been used to embellish and create many different items, from church hangings, clothing and accessories (both men's and women's), bed linen and tablecloths to christening gowns, bonnets, caps and tea cosies.

For the purposes of this book I will mainly focus this brief history of whitework on the techniques covered. These techniques were traditionally used across European countries from as early as the medieval period, through to the late nineteenth and early twentieth centuries. Many of these techniques will have originally derived and been inspired by embroideries from places like India and China, but my focus will be on the Western European techniques and styles that inspired and informed the techniques included in this book.

OPUS TEUTONICUM

Although Opus Teutonicum is not included as a technique in this book, many of the stitches used to create a piece of Opus Teutonicum are, such as counted satin, early forms of pulled thread, buttonhole, stem and chain. I have therefore included it as part of this history as many of the stitches and techniques used in creating Opus Teutonicum clearly influenced and inspired whitework embroidery techniques in future centuries, as the stitches continue to be used in extremely similar ways.

Opus Teutonicum is the term given to a form of whitework embroidery that was widely used across Europe, notably in and around the area we now call Germany. It can be said to be the first notable whitework technique used in Europe. Being produced as early as the twelfth century, it continued to be used through the thirteenth and fourteenth centuries, and its production was often associated with convents and other religious houses of the time. It was mainly produced for items that today we would term 'church embroideries', such as altar cloths, frontals, lectern veils and hangings.

As Opus Teutonicum was almost exclusively used to create church embroideries, early examples depict biblical figures and religious imagery. However, by the fourteenth century secular motifs were being widely used, including non-religious figures alongside elements from nature such as animals, birds and foliage. Opus Teutonicum was originally created on a linen ground and stitched with linen thread, although later some light-coloured wools and silks began to be introduced.

There are two very different forms of Opus Teutonicum. The first was worked on a plain linen ground, where figures and motifs were filled with geometric patterns created using counted satin or brick stitches, along with Gobelin stitch and an early form of pulled thread. The outlines were often worked in chain or braided stitches, which we see later in Elizabethan embroidery worked in gold. The second form is where outlines are worked in buttonhole stitch. The inside of the motif is left mainly plain, with just a few stitches adding small details, while the surrounding area is made to look like net, using a simple pulled-thread technique.

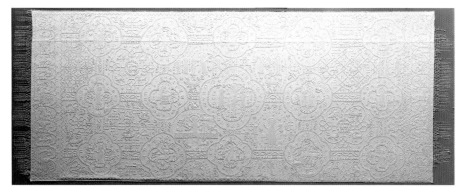

Altar cloth c.1350 Germany, Altenberg on the Lahn, Premonstratensian Convent. Size overall: 154.3 × 374.5cm (60 × 147in). (Image: The Cleveland Museum of Art)

Detail of the altar cloth showing chain stitch, pulled thread and counted satin stitches. (Image: The Cleveland Museum of Art)

DRAWN THREAD

Throughout history, drawn thread is a term that has been used to describe many different embroidery techniques, which has led to some confusion. In essence, drawn thread describes a technique where the threads of the ground fabric are withdrawn and cut away, or the ends woven in and secured. This could be as simple as a few threads being withdrawn to create a delicate hem or many more threads being withdrawn to create large bands or corners. It is impossible to give an exact date for when drawn-thread techniques were first introduced and it has been surmised that different variations of drawn-thread techniques were being created wherever cloth was being woven.

The most renowned early form of drawn-thread work is now known as reticella and was produced throughout Western Europe during the sixteenth century. This technique involved removing nearly all the warp (the vertical threads) and weft (the horizontal threads) threads from the linen, leaving only a basic grid structure. The design was pinned in place underneath the linen, so when the threads were removed the design was then revealed. Threads were then laid across the design lines and temporarily held in place with couching (*see* Chapter 9) stitches forming the foundation for the design. This foundation structure was then embellished further with button-hole bars and fillings, picots (*see* Chapter 6), wheels and spider's webs (*see* Chapter 6). Intricate and delicate curved shapes could be produced within designs; when the technique was more established, even pictorial designs showing animals and simple figures were created. When the design was complete, the couching stitches were cut and the embroidery could be lifted free from the design.

Reticella is most recognizable seen in portraits of the late sixteenth and early seventeenth centuries, where it has been depicted in spectacular detail, showing examples of ruffs, cuffs, collars and rebatos (standing collars) favoured by Elizabeth I. Reticella was also widely used in the decoration of cushion covers at this time, often having a brightly coloured fabric underneath the drawn-thread work. These cushions were not for sitting on, though; they were used as a way of presenting gifts and showing status.

Drawn-thread techniques are often associated with samplers and there must be

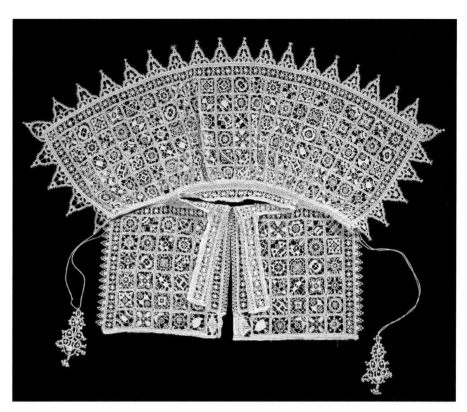

Reticella panels joined into a 'collar' with two akers. Origin: Italy. Date: c.1880–99. (Object ID: BK-14612. Rijksmuseum)

Drawn detail of a reticella rebato worn by George Villiers, Duke of Buckingham, 1592–1628. From the painting by Michiel Jansz van Miereveld 1625–26. Currently held in the Art Gallery of South Australia.

thousands of drawn-thread samplers still in existence in museums and private collections alike. This is partly because few pattern books or prints for samplers were printed and also because the design possibilities and stitch variations were endless. A sampler was basically an embroiderer's practice and developmental piece showing new and favoured stitches and designs. Embroiderers would show their samplers to each other so stitches, techniques and designs were passed around, learned and copied in this way.

Drawn thread continued to be worked in similar and various forms in the following centuries. However, not until the mid to late nineteenth century through to the twentieth century did it come back into such favour, and more like we know it today. At this point, being worked on both linen and cotton, it was used to create and decorate borders on bed linen, pillowcases, tablecloths and handkerchiefs. During the mid nineteenth century it was also used as a filling stitch for open areas within designs, as well as along the edges of under-sleeves, cuffs and collars.

PULLED THREAD

Examples of pulled-thread embroidery can be dated as far back as the twelfth, thirteenth and fourteenth centuries, as seen in the examples of the church embroideries known as Opus Teutonicum. It was from this time that pulled-thread embroidery was developed as a technique in Europe, though still in a rather primitive and simple form, most notably in Italy during the seventeenth century. Though worked in brightly coloured silk threads like deep reds and greens, the background was worked in both vertical and horizontal rows of crossed stitches, pulled tightly, leaving designs and motifs plain in the middle.

Pulled thread did not really become a technique and style in its own right till the eighteenth century. At this time, lace in any form was in high demand, very expensive to buy and slow to produce. Because of this, 'embroidered laces' were created as a less expensive imitation, though no less beautiful. These 'embroidered laces', also known as Point de Dresde, Dresden lace and Ponte de Saxe, were much quicker

to work; using a combination of intricate pulled-thread filling stitches, drawn-thread techniques, shadow work and decorative surface stitches, the intricate designs of the bobbin and needlepoint laces were easily recreated. Because of this, Dresden lace in all its forms became highly sought after and grew into a technique and skill in its own right, with pulled thread at its heart. It was worked on the finest muslin and linens, with designs varying from simple floral springs to elaborate and intricate scrolling edges to the tree of life.

Throughout the eighteenth century, Dresden lace can be seen worked on items of clothing and accessories worn by both men and women. There are many fichus, kerchiefs, aprons, caps and lappets found in museums and private collections all over the word showing beautiful pulled-thread filling stitches, worked by professionals and amateurs alike. Pulled-thread stitches can also be found on men's waistcoats, being worked in combination with other forms of embroidery like quilting and decorative surface stitches.

From the Mark Wallis Collection. An eighteenth-century fichu, showing various pulled-thread stitches, counted satin, eyelets and chain stitch.

From the RSN Collection (RSSN 635). Detail of a Dresden lace border showing a variety of pulled-thread stitches in combination with counted satin patterns. Buttonhole leaves and flowers, with eyelets and chain stitch stems.

From the Olive Matthews Collection at Chertsey Museum. Item M.1994.28 White muslin apron with scalloped edges, embroidered with floral sprigs and three rows of white silk thread swags, with upper-edge casement housing cream silk waist tapes; c. 1782–89.

From the RSN Collection (RSNL124). Panel of Venetian cutwork.

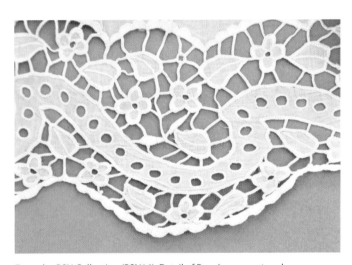

From the RSN Collection (RSN16). Detail of Renaissance cutwork on a nineteenth-century under sleeve.

Pulled-thread stitches and fillings continued to be used in the nineteenth century, though they became much less common, and a much less dominant stitch when worked in the styles of embroidery that were popular during that time, like Ayrshire and broderie anglaise.

CUTWORK

Over the centuries, the term 'cutwork' has been used to describe many different embroidery techniques and styles. What they all have in common is that part of the foundation fabric they are worked on is 'cut' away, leaving solid areas of design, and that the main stitch being used to outline the cutwork is buttonhole stitch.

The more modern cutwork styles and techniques, and the ones included in this book, get their form and inspiration from as early as the seventeenth century. They have many similarities both in style and technique to Venetian lace, which was popular at the time.

Cutwork as we know it today was introduced in the early nineteenth century and is often called Richelieu cutwork. This is thought to be because of Cardinal Richelieu, who was a prominent French politician in the early seventeenth century when Venetian lace was in fashion, especially in the French court. His name, Richelieu, seems to have been borrowed to give this style of embroidery its title, even though Cardinal Richelieu himself was known for his simple style of dress. However, there are four main types of cutwork, Richelieu being only one of them.

All four styles of cutwork look very similar at a glance but it is the details and features that define them.

Cutwork in all its forms was very popular throughout the mid to late nineteenth century and was used in many ladies' fashion garments and accessories, from collars and cuffs to dress fronts and plastrons. Items of homeware, such as table linens, bed linens and tea cloths, were also decorated with different forms of cutwork, the designs being mainly floral.

During the 1930s and 1940s, cutwork had a revival though the designs were much less intricate than those of previous years. Again being used for the cuffs and collars of dresses, cutwork was now mostly produced by machine, although patterns, kits and transfers to be worked at home were hugely popular and can still be bought today.

Broderie Anglaise

Originally known as 'eyelet work', the technique broderie anglaise became extremely popular in England around the mid 1800s, hence where it got its new name, 'English embroidery'. It is thought however that the technique was being used much earlier in Eastern Europe.

In its earliest form, broderie anglaise entirely consisted of eyelets, whether they be round, oval, teardrop or leaf shaped. These eyelets were designed in such a way to create swooping waves along borders, scalloped edges and eyelets decreasing in size to create the stalks and veins of flowers and leaves.

Broderie anglaise was the natural rival of Ayrshire needlework, which was hugely popular around the same time. It has been suggested that broderie anglaise started to introduce elements of surface stitches, such as satin stitch (*see* Chapter 10), trailing as a direct influence of the more intricate and floral designs of Ayrshire needlework.

Throughout the nineteenth century, broderie anglaise was widely used. However, it was during the 1850s and 1890s especially that it was most popular on fashion and costume accessories, such as dress sleeves, collars and cuffs, frills on petticoats, baby clothes and household linens. Though there were many professional embroiderers producing broderie anglaise, many women and girls were stitching their own pieces at home, as patterns and blocks were readily available to buy. Fabric could also be bought with the patterns already printed in washable ink to save the user the time of transferring the pattern themselves.

Because of the simple repetitive nature of broderie anglaise, towards the later part of the century machines began producing broderie anglaise by the length, as they could easily, and much more quickly, replicate the hand work of rows of eyelets, satin-stitch flowers and buttonhole edges. To an untrained eye it is very difficult to know what has been worked by hand and what by machine. The easiest way of knowing is to turn the embroidery over and look at the back. In machine embroidery, the point where the thread travels across the back from one part of the design to another is the same every time. With hand work, the threads are usually finished well hidden or invisible on the back, but if they do travel from one shape to the next, these points are more random.

Broderie anglaise is still extremely popular in fashion today, with items of clothing for both female and children's fashion being widely produced in spring and summer collections. This, however, will almost all be done exclusively by machine, excepting possible examples being produced for haute-couture fashion.

Shadow Work

The exact origins of shadow work are unknown. Some say that it was first introduced from Persia into India many centuries ago, and there are many romantic and mysterious stories of how it first flourished and became popular as a specific technique. One of those stories is that a weary traveller was passing through a village and, being thirsty, asked a peasant for a drink of water. The peasant gave the traveller a drink, who had nothing to give the peasant in return.

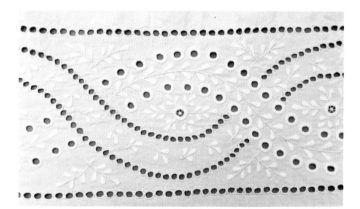

From the Mark Wallis Collection. Detail of an unfinished length of broderie anglaise, possibly for a skirt or petticoat hem.

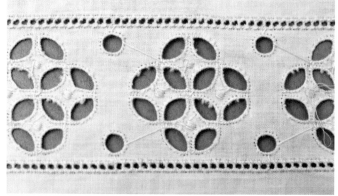

From the Mark Wallis Collection. Detail showing the reverse of a machine-made broderie anglaise border. Note that where the thread travels from one part of the design to the next is consistent on every motif.

From the RSN Collection (RSN27). Detail of a length of cloth whose possible use may have been for an overskirt or front panel. Showing multiple whitework techniques on a fine cotton lawn. See multiple areas of shadow work on the flower petals, leaves and borders.

As a way of saying thank you, the traveller taught the peasant the art of chikankari, giving the peasant a means of making money for the rest of his life. However it came in to being, it is an exquisite technique that is still a hugely popular embroidery style in India today, with chikankari meaning 'fine embroidery'.

Shadow work was first introduced in Europe during the eighteenth century and was one of the combination of techniques used in the creation of Dresden lace, as it contrasted with the more open pulled- and drawn-thread stitches and eyelets that were also being used at the time. The fact the herringbone part of the stitch is on the reverse of the fabric means that the stitches themselves looked softened and lighter and more like lace.

From this introduction, even though tastes and fashions changed throughout the eighteenth and then the nineteenth century, shadow work continued to be used widely and can been seen on many types of ladies' whitework garments and accessories, from chemisettes to cuffs and collars, all the way to 1900.

In the early twentieth century, and continuing through the 1930s, shadow work continued to be used, though at this point the fabrics and the colour changed. Having previously been worked on fine cotton muslins and linens, a stiffer crisper cotton called organdie was used, and rather than only white threads, coloured threads also began to be used. The use of coloured threads

From the RSN Collection (RSN183). Detail of a baby's bonnet crown worked in Ayrshire whitework.

gives a lovely effect as the colours look shadowy and slightly muted as the stitches are worked on the reverse. During this later period and especially with the use of colour, shadow work was often seen being used to decorate and embellish children's clothing.

AYRSHIRE WHITEWORK

Although it has not been included in this book, Ayrshire is an extremely important whitework technique and is really the last original style of whitework to be created. I have decided to include it in this brief history of whitework as many of the stitches and techniques used in Ayrshire are included in this book, and are combined in Ayrshire embroidery in their finest and most delicate form.

The style and technique Ayrshire whitework gets its name from the place it originated, the county of Ayrshire in the south west of Scotland. However, in Ayrshire the technique was known as 'sewed muslin'. It was first developed in the early 1800s and was extremely popular until the late 1860s when it fell into decline. This was due to the disruption of the cotton trade because of the American Civil War and the new machine-produced embroidery that quickly superseded the more time-consuming and expensive hand work.

Ayrshire seems to have been the perfect place for a new style of fine embroidered cotton muslin to be developed, due to the many mills that opened in the area around the late 1700s; there were many mill streams that could power the machines that spun the raw cotton into yarn and weaving machines that then wove it into fine muslins.

The introduction of Ayrshire whitework can be credited to Lady Montgomerie, who travelled through Europe with her husband, an army officer, during the Napoleonic Wars. While abroad, she gave birth to a son for whom a christening robe was made using traditional whitework tech-

From the RSN Collection (RSN1347). Detail of a baby's christening robe worked in Ayrshire whitework. Showing the bottom front panel of the skirt.

niques already in practice in England but also the fine needle-lace fillings known to French needlewomen. When her husband died, Lady Montgomerie returned to Ayrshire with her son and this christening robe.

The development of Ayrshire whitework is credited to Mrs Jamieson, who at the time was one of the key organisers of the embroidered muslin trade. Mrs Jamieson was shown this christening robe, and she then went on to teach the fine needle-lace and buttonhole fillings to muslin embroi-

ders, who developed these techniques further. These embroiderers were known as the 'flowerers'.

Ayrshire whitework designs were ornate, delicate and always floral based, with trailing and curling stems and leaves surrounding and framing the large eyelets that were filled with the delicate needle-lace fillings. The stitches used to create Ayrshire whitework were many, the most defining feature being needle-lace fillings, of which there were endless opportunities as the workers

would often invent their own. Other stitches include satin and padded satin, eyelets, trailing, stem, chain and seeding to name but a few. These fine and delicate floral designs were used to adorn babies' garments, particularly christening robes of which there are many examples still in existence today, in museums and private collections all over the world. They were also used on women's fashions accessories, from collars and cuffs to the frills on caps, to handkerchiefs and men's shirts and collars.

CHAPTER 2

MATERIALS AND EQUIPMENT

Many embroidery techniques have a wide range of materials and threads you can choose to work with; when starting out it can be a little daunting knowing what material to start off with, never mind picking what colour to choose. With whitework, however, that decision has been made for you. All you need to start is white fabric and white thread. Some of the materials and equipment you will need for whitework are specialist but are easily sourced, while others you might already have at home. This chapter will explain the different types of fabrics, threads, tools and equipment you will need to create beautiful whitework embroideries, covering a range of techniques for beginners through to advanced embroiderers.

EMBROIDERY HOOPS AND FRAMES

It is very important to work any type of embroidery in a frame but especially so for whitework. Working your embroidery in a frame will prevent the fabric from distorting, wrinkling or puckering and helps to keep the threads from tangling as you work. It also helps to keep the embroidery stitches neat and the stitch tension even.

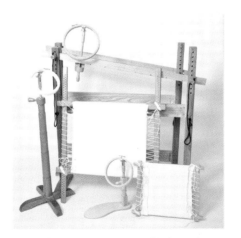

A pair of trestles and selection of different frames including a slate frame, roller frame and three ring frames. The three ring frames are attached to a floor stand, barrel clamp and seat frame.

Most importantly for whitework, it helps to keep your embroidery clean and white.

There a many different types of frames available to choose from but it is important that you use a frame you are comfortable with. However, some frames are better suited to different whitework techniques, as some of those techniques need to be worked under a very tight tension, while others require a looser tension.

RING FRAMES

Ring frames or embroidery hoops are ideal for working small embroidery projects. They come in many different sizes and are easy to transport. Ring frames also come in a range of styles from simple, plain frames that are held in the hand to supported frames that have a barrel clamp, allowing you to clamp your frame to a table. Similar supporting ring frames are seat frames that have a paddle-like attachment that you sit on or ring frames with a floor stand. The supported ring frames are preferable as they allow you to use both hands while embroidering, which helps with speed, tension and when working intricate stitches.

Binding a Ring Frame

Binding a ring frame is very important as it protects the fabric from being damaged while it is in the frame. This is especially so in whitework as the fabrics are very easily marked and often delicate. Binding the frame also helps to keep the tension on the fabric for longer. Ideally you should wrap both the inner and outer rings.

To bind a ring frame, use a very long strip of white or cream fabric such as cotton, calico or bias binding. For the outer ring, start at the screw fastening and wrap the fabric around the ring frame, overlapping the fabric slightly with each new wrap. When you have wrapped a few times, secure the start with a few stitches. Continue to wrap the frame until the whole ring frame is covered. Cut off any excess fabric and secure the end with a few stitches. For the inner ring, start anywhere and wrap the frame till you get back to where you started. Overlap the starting and finishing wraps and secure with a few stitches.

Bound ring frames attached to a seat and barrel clamp.

Bound outer ring frame showing the securing stitches.

ROLLER FRAMES

Roller frames are very similar to slate frames in that they pull the fabric evenly within the frame. Roller frames are more affordable and more lightweight than slate frames. They come in a variety of sizes and will still allow you to work larger pieces of embroidery. A roller frame will need to be tightened more often than a slate frame but they are a good first step if you do not want to purchase a slate frame straight away. Like a slate frame, roller frames also need supporting. Trestles are the best option but, as roller frames are more lightweight, floor clamps or table clamps work well too.

FABRICS AND THREADS

One of the beautiful things about whitework is that all the ground fabrics and threads are white. In the absence of colour, it is the combination of these fabrics and threads that create the textures, contrasts and depth that will bring your whitework designs to life.

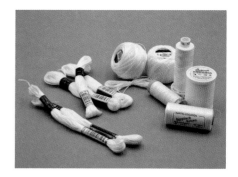

A selection of whitework embroidery threads, including stranded cotton, coton à broder, perle cotton and a selection of lace threads.

SLATE FRAMES

Slate frames are generally used for larger projects that will be worked over a longer period of time and embroideries that need to be worked under a very tight tension. Working on a slate frame does require more preparation but it is worth taking your time over. A badly framed-up slate frame means a wonky embroidery. Slate frames are made up of two rollers, which are the top and bottom of the frame, and two arms that slide through the rollers and form the sides. The two rollers have a length of webbing stapled along the middle and it is this webbing that you will sew the top and bottom edges of your fabric to. The arms have holes along both edges and when slotted through the rollers will stretch your fabric when held in place by split pins.

Using a slate frame allows the fabric to be pulled evenly in all directions and allows you to work with one hand above and one hand below the frame, which means faster stitching and an even stitch tension. Slate frames can be quite large and will need to be supported while you work. The best support for a slate frame is a pair of trestles that the slate frame can balance on. The height and angle of the trestles can be adjusted to your needs and comfort. Clamps can also be used to support a slate frame; either a sturdy floor clamp or a G-clamp can be used to clamp your frame to a table.

Whitework is traditionally worked on densely woven linen or cotton fabrics, which can be either heavy or fine in weight. Many of the techniques require an even-weave fabric. This is where the number of threads per inch (TPI) is the same for both the warp and weft of the fabric. There are many fabrics to choose from, and some are better suited to different techniques. This section will explain what fabrics and threads work well for each of the whitework techniques included in this book.

Threads Per Inch Explained

Threads per inch (TPI) is a term used to identify how many threads are in an inch of any chosen even-weave fabric. To work out the TPI, place a tape measure along the grain of the fabric. Then count the vertical threads that fit inside 1in of the tape measure. If you counted twenty-six threads, that fabric has a TPI of 26. A higher TPI means the fabric has been more densely woven; a lower TPI means the fabric has been more loosely woven. The main thing to think about when choosing fabric for counted whitework techniques is whether you can see the grain. If you cannot, it might be easier to choose a fabric with a lower TPI. This will make your embroidery easier to stitch and more enjoyable too.

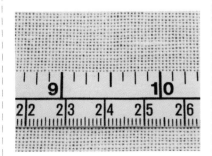

A 28TPI even-weave linen.

PULLED THREAD

Materials

Pulled thread is a counted technique so therefore needs an even-weave fabric to be worked correctly. It can be worked on either cottons or linens with a slightly open weave. A more open weave will create a lacier effect.

Linen in different varieties with different TPIs, such as Edinburgh 36, Newcastle 40 and Quaker (Bantry) 28, are generally used for pulled thread. Kingston 55 can also be used but as this has a higher thread count, it will be more difficult to see the threads in order to count them. Working pulled thread on cotton fabrics will give a more delicate effect as cotton has a finer weave than linen. Cottons such as voile, mousse and muslin work very well with pulled thread. More densely woven linen and cottons can be used, like cotton lawn or cambric, or linen and cotton batiste. These however will be more of a challenge to work.

Threads

The thread you choose to work the pulled stitches should be a similar texture and thickness to one thread of the ground fabric. Cotton or linen threads work best, such as a Tanne or Cotona, but finer lace threads may also be used if they are strong. Threads that are slightly heavier, like coton à broder 16–30 or fine cotton perle 12, also work well for pulled stitches, but create a chunkier effect.

DRAWN THREAD

Materials

Drawn thread is a counted technique, where threads are removed from the ground fabric; it is therefore easier to work on an even-weave fabric. Linens or cotton fabrics work best, especially those with a slightly open weave as the threads are easier to see and withdraw. Bear in mind that the threads of the fabric need to be strong so they will not snap when being withdrawn.

Linens like Edinburgh 36, Newcastle 40 and Quaker (Bantry) 28 are generally used for drawn thread as the threads are easier

A selection of vintage needles and threads. Producers do not make threads as fine as they used to, so if you have or can source any vintage threads by all means use them in your embroideries. Just make sure that they are clean and not rotten before using them.

to see and therefore remove. Finer linens and cottons such as Kingston 55, cotton lawn or cambric, or linen and cotton batiste can also be used but due to their higher thread count, the individual threads are much harder to see and can be trickier to withdraw. As they are finer they are also more likely to snap when being removed.

Threads

The thread you choose to embellish the drawn thread needs to be fine and strong, such as cotton and linen lace threads like Egyptian cotton, Tanne and Cotona. The weight of the thread should match the weight of the ground fabric, but finer or heavier threads can also be used. Coton à broder 16–30 or fine cotton perle 12 also work well for decorating the withdrawn area as do some novelty threads, beads and ribbons. Stranded cotton may also be used in some areas of drawn thread.

CUTWORK

Materials

The fabrics used for cutwork need to be densely woven linens or cottons. The fabric needs to be firm but can be either heavy or light in weight. It needs to be strong and dense enough to support heavier stitching and large holes. Dense, firm linens and cottons include cotton or linen batiste, Zula linen, cotton Kilberry, cotton cambric and fine embroidery linen.

Threads

The threads used to stitch cutwork need to be strong as it is supporting and keeping the shape of any cut-out areas. Threads such as stranded cotton, fine perle 12 and coton à broder 16–30 work really well for this technique.

EYELETS AND LADDERWORK

Materials

The fabric you choose for eyelets needs to be lightweight but firm, closely woven, fine cotton fabric or occasionally linen fabric. Cotton lawn, poplin, cambric or batiste fabrics are best for this technique but if you wish to use linen make sure the threads are very fine and densely woven, such as a fine embroidery linen. For ladderwork, most types of fabric would work well. Ladderwork is technically a pulled technique, but as it is not counted it also works well on finer-weave linens and cottons.

Threads

The threads used to work eyelets should be similar in texture and quality to the ground fabric. Smooth threads like stranded cotton, coton à broder 16–30 or fine perle 12 or floche create a smooth texture and clean edges. For ladderwork, a lace thread or Cotona thread work well for the initial backstitch as they are strong and fine, but you could use any type of thread for the couching; just make sure the thread you use is not too thick so that it does not fill up the holes – coton à broder 30 or 25, or even a few strands of stranded cotton as the core would work well.

SATIN

Materials

The fabrics best used for satin are densely woven linens or cottons. The fabric needs to be firm. It can be either heavy or light in weight but it needs to be strong and dense enough to support the heavy padding, and the final layer of satin on top. A more open-weave fabric can be used but when the satin is finished there tends to be larger holes around the edge of the satin stitch. Dense, firm linens and cottons include cotton or linen batiste, Zula linen, cotton Kilberry, cotton cambric and fine embroidery linen.

Threads

The threads used to stitch satin give very different effects. Stranded cotton gives a very shiny, smooth finish as all the stitches should blend into each other. Coton à broder and fine perle 12 also work really well but each stitch is more noticeable, but you should still get a smooth, shiny finish. If padding, use one of the chunkier threads like perle, coton à broder or even tapestry cotton.

A selection of whitework fabrics including cotton mousse, organza, Kingston linen, Zula linen, Newcastle linen and Edinburgh linen.

SHADOW WORK

Materials

Shadow work needs to be worked on a sheer, transparent or semi-transparent fabric that has a fairly dense weave. Organza, organdie or muslins work best. Cotton voile or fine cotton lawn work well too, though the shadow work is more subtle as the fabrics are not as transparent.

Threads

The threads you choose for shadow work should be fairly fine. Stranded cotton, perle 12 and coton à broder 25–30 work really well. Finer threads can also be used, but the shadow effect created by the stitch will be softer and more delicate.

ALTERNATIVE MATERIALS AND THREADS

Historically the whitework techniques included in this book had very specific types of materials and threads that were used to stitch and create them. Therefore, throughout this book I have tried to use these same materials and threads where possible or the modern-day equivalents. I made this choice because I felt that these traditional materials and threads would demonstrate the individual techniques at their best. As the saying goes, 'if it ain't broke, don't fix it'. That being said, there is no reason why you can't experiment and see what new textures and designs can be created. When you are confident with the basic and traditional techniques, try incorporating some alternative and unconventional materials and threads, and have fun experimenting and finding new ways to adapt these historical techniques and stitches.

There a few samples in the following pages where I have combined traditional whitework techniques with unconventional materials, such as shells, beads and even dried flowers. Always practise using the alternative threads and materials as a sample first, to see how they stitch, before working them on a final piece of embroidery. Think of a fluffy chenille running through a drawn-thread band or tiny glass beads glistening across a cut work bar.

A selection of alternative materials that could be used when experimenting with the traditional whitework techniques, including silver pearl purl, silk-wrapped purl, beads and sequins, spangles, silk ribbon, shells, dried flowers and vintage linen covered buttons.

NEEDLES

When working any type of embroidery it is important that you use the correct size and type of needle. If you use the wrong size or type it can make working the piece more difficult and can cause problems with both your thread and the ground fabric. If you use a needle where the eye is too small, this will damage the thread as you take it through the fabric. If you use a needle that is too big it will distort the ground fabric and can leave holes around your stitches. Each different type of needle has a numbering system for the different sizes available and in most cases the larger the number the smaller the needle. In whitework, a range of different needles are used across the different techniques. The following list will explain the different types of needles used in whitework embroidery and what specific techniques they are used for.

A selection of needles in various sizes including chenille, embroidery, tapestry and curved.

TAPESTRY

These needles have large eyes and blunt points. The blunt point allows the needle to pass between the threads of the ground fabric rather than piercing them, which makes them perfect for stitching counted whitework techniques such as pulled thread, drawn thread and counted satin. The size of the needle depends on the thickness of the working thread but also on the density of the even-weave ground fabric.

CREWEL/EMBROIDERY

These needles have very sharp points and a long, thin eye, which makes them easy to thread. In whitework they are predominantly used for surface stitching so can therefore be used across all the whitework techniques. Crewel/embroidery needles have a good range of sizes, which means a variety of the whitework threads can be used in these needles.

CHENILLE

Chenille needles are the same in length and diameter as tapestry needles, the difference being that they have a very sharp point. In whitework they are useful for many types of stitches, for example surface stitches with some of the thicker threads, as the larger eye makes them easier to thread. They are also useful for padding with thicker, fluffier threads and plunging trailing when there are multiple stands in the needle. The size of the needle depends on the thickness of the thread.

CURVED

These needles are not often used in whitework but they can be quite useful if you are securing plunged ends to the back of your work. They are mainly used if you are mounting your work on a board. The smaller/finer varieties are best when being used for embroidery but they are not the easiest needle to use and it will take practice.

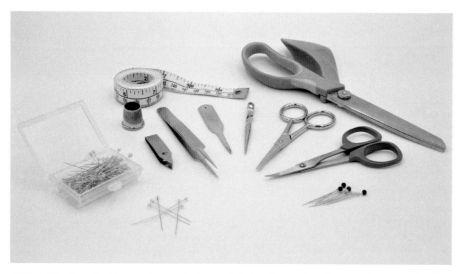

A range of basic embroidery equipment that you will find really useful and is a must for any sewing kit.

> ### Scissor Care
>
> Try not to use your fabric sheers or embroidery scissors to cut anything else other than your fabric and embroidery threads. This will keep them sharper for longer.

SEWING EQUIPMENT

Before starting any whitework embroidery project there are a few essential pieces of equipment you will need. If you have done some embroidery before you will probably already have most of them but there are a few specialist items that are really useful for certain whitework techniques.

SCISSORS

Small, sharp embroidery scissors are very important and are an essential part to any sewing kit. There are a few different varieties to choose from. Some have curved blades that allow you to cut very close. Others have angled blades that help with cutting and snipping into awkward angles. Others have straight blades. You don't need to have all three; use what you are comfortable with and do your best to keep them as sharp as possible.

Fabric sheers are best for when you are cutting out pieces of ground fabric. They allow you to make long, straight cuts so you are more likely to cut the fabric along the grain.

Lace scissors are mostly used when working on embroidery that has layers of fabric that need cutting away, especially around areas of net. They allow for precise cutting but the distinctive bump on the bottom blade prevents accidental snipping with the points of the blade.

Thimbles

Whether or not you choose to work with a thimble is up to you, especially as they can take some getting used to. They are however a great tool, especially for whitework. When using finer needles like a number 12 crewel/embroidery needle, you will find that over time you end up with holes in your finger where you are consistently pushing the needle through the fabric. This can become very painful. They can also bleed, and blood is the last thing you want anywhere near your whitework. Thimbles come in lots of different sizes but make sure you pick one that fits snugly on your finger and does not drop off when you are stitching. Traditional thimbles are made from metal but leather, plastic and silicone variations are available too.

Stiletto

In whitework, stilettos are used to create small holes in the ground fabric that are then stitched to create eyelets and other similar stitches. They have a long, very sharp tapered point that pushes open the weave of the fabric rather than cutting it. They are available in metal, wood and plastic, but remember the sharper the better.

Tape Measure

Tape measures are a vital piece of equipment for embroidery. They are used for many things, from measuring fabrics to checking the distance of your slate frame and measuring up for designs.

Pins

There are many different types of pins that can be useful for embroidery but the most commonly used are glass-headed dressmakers' pins. These are used for such tasks as securing layers of fabric together, marking out your design, creating raised stitches, preparing your frame and mounting your work. There are finer versions available, like fine patchwork pins, which work better if you are using fine or delicate fabrics.

Mellor

A mellor or laying tool is not traditionally used in whitework but I have found it quite helpful for laying and guiding threads into place, rather than using a finger, which can make the white threads dirty and fluffy.

Magnifiers

Magnifiers can be very useful if you struggle to see the weave of the fabric, especially when working counted techniques. They also help for very intricate work, which is more difficult to see when it is white on white. There are different styles of magnifier available, some having lights built in, but the best are ones that have a clamp attachment so you can clamp it to your frame or work table.

Magnifier Alternative

If a magnifier does not work for you, another way to help see the weave is to work with a dark material underneath the frame, as this shows through the weave more clearly.

FRAME EQUIPMENT

Depending on which frame you have decided to use for your embroidery, there are a few extra pieces of equipment you will need in order to get started. If using a ring frame, then a small flat-headed screwdriver will help to tighten the screw on the ring frame, which will help keep the tension in the frame tighter for longer. If you choose a slate or roller frame then you will need webbing tape, parcel string, split pins, a bracing needle and button thread.

TISSUE PAPER AND SHOWER CAPS

Protecting your embroidery is always important but even more so for whitework as the smallest piece of coloured fluff or speck of dust will show up quite visibly. Acid-free tissue paper is ideal for protecting your work, whatever frame you use. It is most efficient when the whole piece is covered with tissue paper and only the areas you are working on are revealed. If you are working in a ring frame then covering your work with tissue paper and then a shower cap is the best guard against dust when you are not stitching.

DESIGN EQUIPMENT

When designing your own embroidery projects, the basic pieces of equipment you will need to start are a sketchbook, HB pencil, ruler, eraser and a pencil sharpener. In order to move forward with your design and begin turning it into a piece of embroidery, the following list of equipment will be essential.

PENS AND PENCILS

Fineliner pens are perfect for finalizing your design. They can be worked on top of a pencil drawing to create sharp, clean design lines. They can also be used on both ordinary and tracing paper.

Coloured pencils in shades of blue or turquoise can be used to colour the design and help you to see how the design is balanced. This colour plan will in turn help you to decided what stitches to use and where.

TRACING PAPER

Tracing paper is really useful throughout the design process. If you have multiple versions of a design on different pieces of tracing paper all layered together, by removing certain layers you can change and rearrange a design as many times as you like before tracing over all the chosen layers and finalizing the design.

The equipment you need to frame up will depend on which type of frame you are using.

Light Box

Although light boxes can be expensive they are really handy while designing for embroidery, as you can easily trace round designs and motifs. They are especially useful for whitework as they are the quickest and simplest method for transferring your design onto the fabric.

Lights

Working in good light is important for all types of embroidery, but especially so for whitework. Whitework can be quite straining on your eyes as you are trying to focus on white fabric and white thread at the same time. There are lots of different bulbs and lamps available but, if you can, try to use a 'daylight' or 'natural-light' lamp. You will need to have the lamp quite close to your work so one with a clamp attachment or floor stand would be best.

Transfer Pens and Pencils

In whitework there are a few different ways of drawing the design onto your chosen fabric. Some methods work better for certain techniques but if you are using either a transfer pen or pencil there are a few things to bear in mind. Always transfer the design onto the fabric in a pen or pencil that is *blue*. If you use a different colour and the design lines are not completely covered or they do not wash off properly, they will make your whitework look dirty. If you use blue, it is not ideal if the lines are still visible but blue will make the whitework look brighter. You can use a very sharp or propelling blue pencil to trace the design onto the fabric and will achieve quite a fine line. Blue water-soluble fabric markers and pencils are another alternative. Whichever method you choose to use, it is always a good idea to check that the pen or pencil will wash out properly or that it will not bleed into the fabric when wet.

Tissue and Tacking Thread

A different way of transferring designs onto fabric in whitework is the tacking method (*see* Chapter 3). For this you will need acid-free tissue paper and a light-blue polyester thread. It is worth testing that the thread is dye-fast before using.

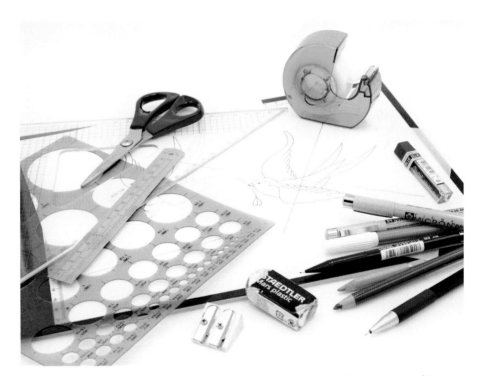

Your own style of designing will determine what equipment you need, but this is a selection of the basic design equipment I use.

CHAPTER 3

FRAMING UP AND TRANSFERRING YOUR DESIGN

The start of a new embroidery project is always exciting. There are lots of things to think about and choices to be made, but there is a tendency to jump ahead because you cannot wait to start stitching. It is important to remember that preparing your embroidery correctly is key to producing a beautiful, well-worked piece. When you prepare and frame up the fabric for your embroidery, you are in a way creating the foundations for your stitches to sit upon. If the foundations are not right, then what you work on top will not be right either. So take your time when preparing your embroidery; it will be easier and more enjoyable to work and you will achieve better results in the end.

GETTING STARTED

Once you have chosen the fabric you are going to use, there are a few basic steps to follow that will help you achieve the best results when you begin to frame up. The first of these steps is checking your chosen fabric for marks, stains and large uneven slubs. This is especially important for white-work as even the tiniest mark or trapped piece of fluff will show very clearly against the white fabric. If there is a mark or stain on the fabric, see if you can cut out the piece you need, avoiding that area. If you are unable to do this, wash the fabric to see if you can remove the mark. With white-work linens and cottons this is usually easily and successfully done. If, however, the mark or stain cannot be removed with washing and you cannot position the mark or stain away from the embroidery then *do not* use that piece of fabric. There is nothing more disappointing than dedicating your time and effort to completing a beautiful piece of whitework only to have the eye drawn away from the stitching to focus on a mark or discoloured area. Just get a new piece of fabric and save the marked piece for another project where it can be used.

Large and very uneven slubs do not occur often in whitework fabrics. If you do see a noticeably large or uneven slub, however, try to avoid it when cutting out your fabric. If you cannot, then see if you can hide the slub somewhere in your embroidery design. The whitework technique you are using will make a difference to what solution you use but working satin stitch over the top, or cutting the slub out completely using cutwork, works best. If working a pulled or drawn technique, try to place your design so that a worked area incorporates the slub. In the end, you just need to try to make the slub blend in with the embroidery as much as possible.

The second step in getting started is ironing your fabric. Due to storage or postage, most fabrics will have some folds or wrinkles, and you need to make sure these can be removed before you go any further. If the folds or wrinkles disappear with ironing, you are good to go. If ironing does not work initially then submerge the whole piece of fabric in water and iron it again until it is dry. This method should remove even stubborn folds and creases.

Test the Iron

Check the iron is clean before using and check the temperature settings too. Although irons are usually used on the highest setting for linens and cottons, test on a small or spare piece first. If the iron is too hot it will burn/singe the white fabric, which will give it a yellowish tinge.

The final step is cutting out the fabric along the grain. To do this, as you cut the fabric out, the blade of the scissors needs to follow the straight grain/line on which the fabric has been woven. This is more easily done for some fabrics than others.

If you struggle to see the grain or are not confident using scissors, there is another method for making sure the fabric is on the grain. For this method, cut out the fabric slightly larger than you need, but still try to cut the edges as straight as possible. Once the fabric has been cut, from one edge pull a single thread away from the fabric and it will slide off the cut edge. Keep pulling a single thread away at a time until one thread can be pulled off from one edge to the other, continuously and in one piece. Your fabric will now be on the grain. When you have completed all four sides, if you have long fluffy edges it is best to cut these off as close to the newly straight edge as possible so they do not get in the way.

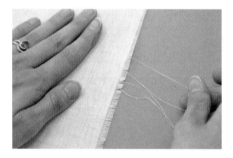

Pulling the threads out individually so the edge of the fabric is on the grain.

will depend on the following factors: what whitework technique you are stitching; how much tension is needed on the fabric and whether it will vary; whether you are working with multiple layers; the size of your embroidery. Most importantly, choose a frame you are comfortable with.

RING FRAMES

Ring frames are usually used for smaller embroidery projects or for techniques that do not need to be worked under an extremely tight tension. It is possible to get a tight tension on the fabric in a ring frame but as you work it will slacken off, so you need to make sure that you re-tighten the fabric as you work. Binding the ring frame will help to keep the tension longer and will also help to protect your fabric from marking and bruising while it is in the frame. The whitework techniques that can be worked in a ring frame are pulled and drawn thread, broderie anglaise and cutwork. If working drawn thread, broderie anglaise or cutwork in a ring frame, you need to be aware that as you withdraw more threads, create voids and cut away holes, you compromise the tension of the fabric. Therefore only small and basic embroidery designs for these techniques should be worked in a ring frame.

SLATE FRAME

Using a slate frame is the surest way to keep the tension on your fabric tight, even and under your control. Slate frames are usually used for larger-scale embroidery projects that will be kept in the frame for longer periods of time, or densely stitched projects that require extremely tight tension in order to be worked correctly. Any of the whitework techniques included in this book can be worked on a slate frame, but projects that include lots of cutwork areas, large drawn-thread areas or broderie anglaise voids, will need to be worked in a slate frame in order to achieve the best results.

ROLLER FRAMES

Roller frames are very similar to slate frames and are a good alternative if you want to work a smaller embroidery project but still need the tension of a slate frame. Like with slate frames, any whitework technique can be worked on a roller frame. However, roller frames tend to lose tension quicker than slate frames so you will need to check and re-tighten a roller frame more often.

FRAMING UP

Choosing the right frame to work your embroidery on is really important, as keeping the fabric taut will prevent all sorts of problems from occurring as you work. It will also help to keep an even tension on your stitches, which is crucial with all whitework techniques. Which frame you choose

Best Practice

Cutting your fabric on the grain is essential if you are going to work on a slate or roller frame. It does not really matter too much if you are going to work on a ring frame but, for any embroiderer, preparing your fabric in this way is good working practice.

Regularly Re-Tighten Your Fabric

If you choose to work on a slate frame you need to remember that the tension on the fabric will still slacken off over time. Every time you sit down to work you should re-tighten the strings of your slate frame.

Ring Frame Set-Up

Depending on how you plan to transfer the design onto the fabric, you may need to do this before you start to frame up your ring frame. Also make sure you have cut your fabric big enough to fit into the ring frame. As a guide, if you are working in a 20cm (8in) ring frame, the fabric should be cut to about 30 × 30cm (12 × 12in).

A piece of linen with the design drawn on, framed in a ring frame with tissue trapped in to protect the work.

Before starting you need to bind your ring frame (*see* Chapter 2). Once this is done make sure the two rings of the ring frame fit snuggly together and adjust if needed by tightening or loosening the screw at the top of the outer ring. Lay the outer ring down on a clean, flat surface, with the screw at the top, placing a piece of acid-free tissue paper over the top.

Place the fabric over the top of the outer ring and the tissue paper. If you have already transferred the design onto the fabric, then make sure you place the fabric with the design face-down onto the ring. Try to place the fabric down so that the design will sit in the centre of the ring.

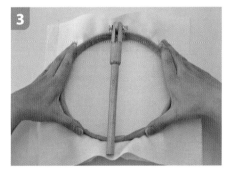

Place the inner ring inside the outer ring and, if you can, try to align the screw of the outer ring with the stalk of the inner ring. With the inner ring in place, push down into the outer ring, trapping the fabric and the tissue in between the two rings. Turn the ring frame over and see how the design is positioned on the front. If you are not happy, remove the inner ring and try again.

When you are happy with the placement of the design, ease the fabric around the edge by pulling the edges of your fabric outwards. This will pull out any wrinkles of fullness left in the fabric, and ensure the tension on the fabric is even all the way around the frame. Try to keep the grain of the fabric as straight as possible.

Once the wrinkles have been pulled out, the grain has been pulled straight and the fabric is as tight as you can get it, use a screwdriver to tighten the screw at the top of the outer ring. You can then tear away just enough of the tissue paper to reveal the area of the design that is going to be stitched.

Shower Caps

If you are working on a ring frame, showers caps (in addition to tissue) are a great way to cover and protect your work when you are not stitching.

Ring frame covered with tissue and a shower cap to protect the work.

Slate Frame Traditional Method

There is a lot more preparation to frame up a slate frame but the extra time and effort is really worth it in the end. Take your time and get it right; it will make stitching a lot easier. If you choose to use a slate frame to work on, the design is usually transferred once the fabric is tight in the frame. The following instructions are for the traditional method of framing up a slate frame.

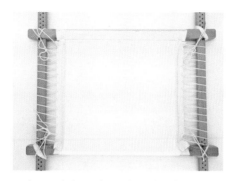

A whitework design framed in a slate frame and protected with tissue paper.

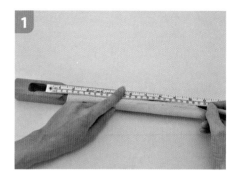

Start by measuring the centre point between the two holes at either end of each roller. To do this, place a tape measure on the inside edge of one hole, then measure along the length of the roller to the inside edge of the opposite hole. Divide this measurement by two and you will find the centre point. With a pencil, mark this centre point on both the roller and the webbing.

Fold the top and bottom edges of your fabric under by 1–1.5cm (½in). It is important that you fold the fabric along the grain. Use your fingers to finger-press this fold and keep it in place. At this point make sure that the top and bottom edges of your fabric are not longer than the webbing that is attached to your rollers. Otherwise you cannot frame up correctly. The fabric needs to be the same length or shorter than the webbing on the roller.

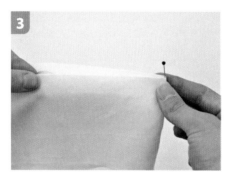

Now fold the top and bottom edges of your fabric in half to find the centre point, press with your fingers to make a crease and then mark with a pin. Be sure to mark these centre points accurately.

Match the pin that marks the centre point of your fabric to the pencil mark on your webbing, which marks the centre point of your roller. Pin these two centre points together, making sure the 1–1.5cm (½in) folded edge is facing the webbing. The top of the folded edge of the fabric needs to be at the same level as the webbing.

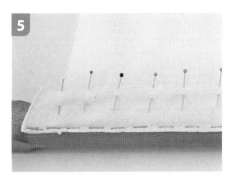

From this centre point, continue to pin the folded edge and the webbing together. Work towards one edge of the webbing first, before returning to the centre point and pinning towards to opposite edge. It is important to insert the pins at right angles to the fabric and webbing. As you pin outwards, make sure to pull the fabric tight so it sits flat against the webbing with no fullness. The pins should be about 2.5cm (1in) apart. Repeat these steps until both the rollers are pinned in place at the bottom and top of your fabric.

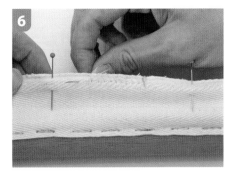

Thread up a length of buttonhole thread in an embroidery needle and make a knot in the end of the thread. Starting at the centre point, take the needle through both the fabric and the webbing, from back to front. Oversew in the same place a few times to secure the end of the thread. Then work oversew stitches from back to front, encasing the webbing and the folded edge of the fabric. These stitches should be about 3mm (⅛in) apart. Continue in this way till you reach the end of the fabric. Remove the pins as you go.

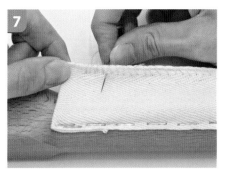

When you have stitched to the end of the fabric, stitch back on yourself for about 2cm (¾in). Then work a few oversew stitches in the same place to secure the end of the thread. Come back to the centre point and repeat these steps, oversewing the other half of the fabric and webbing together. With one roller attached to your fabric, repeat this process for the second roller.

These oversew stitches are functional not decorative, so it does not matter too much if they are not all the same length and distance apart. They do however need to be strong and tight, especially if you are working with a more open-weave fabric. Pull the fabric away from the webbing where you have stitched to see if any gaps appear. If they do, then your stitches need to be tighter, smaller or closer together.

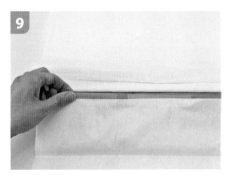

Before you slide the arms through the rollers you need to attach some acid-free tissue paper, which will help to protect the fabric should you need to roll the rollers in. Turn the rollers and the fabric over onto a clean surface, so the right side of the fabric is facing down. Use Scotch Tape to tape a sheet of acid-free tissue paper along the length of each roller.

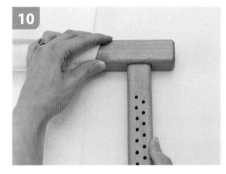

Turn the rollers and fabric back over so the right side is facing up. Slide the arms through the holes in the rollers, making sure that on each side the holes drilled in the arms are mirrored. You may need to roll in the rollers a few times before inserting the arms to reduce the size of the frame and to have the correct amount of fabric visible. Try to roll the rollers with equal turns.

continued on the following page…

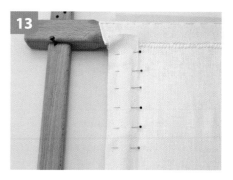

At this point your fabric does not need to be stretched too tightly. Insert split pins into the holes of the arms – two split pins for each arm, one being at the top and the other at the bottom. The split pins should sit just inside each of the rollers to help keep them in place. It is very important that you count the holes and that the same hole is used on either side. This will ensure that when pulled tight the tension is even throughout the frame.

Cut two pieces of webbing that are slightly longer than the sides of the fabric in your frame. Place these lengths of webbing along each side of the framed fabric. When placed in the right position, three quarters of the webbing should sit on top of the fabric, with one quarter hanging over the edge.

If placed correctly, the lengths of webbing should be in line with the grain of the fabric. Pin both lengths of webbing in place, making sure to insert the pins horizontally and without disturbing the position of the webbing. The pins should be inserted roughly 2.5cm (1in) apart. When pinning, make sure the webbing is flat against the fabric.

Thread an embroidery needle with a long length of buttonhole thread, making a knot in the end. Start at the top of the webbing, working a few oversew stitches in the same place to secure the thread. Make sure the stitches go through both the webbing and the fabric. Work a horizontal stitch about 2.5cm (1in) in length, with the needle about 2.5cm (1in) below your starting stitches. When pulled tight the thread sits diagonally between the stitches. This is called basting.

Continue basting down the length of the webbing, with stitches that are about 2.5cm (1in) apart and 2.5cm (1in) in length. You need to pull these stitches very tightly. As you work down the webbing, a bump will start to appear underneath the stitches. This is a good thing and means your stitches are being pulled to the right tension. When you reach the bottom of the web-bing, work a few oversew stitches in the same place to secure the end of the thread. Repeat these steps for the second length of webbing.

With the webbing attached, stretch out the rollers as far apart as you can, adjusting the split pins to keep the rollers in place. This will stretch the fabric as tightly as you can get it. Thread the bracing needle with some parcel string, leaving it on the ball rather than cutting a length. Start at the top of the webbing and take the needle down into the webbing that is hanging over the edge of the fabric. Pull a length of string through.

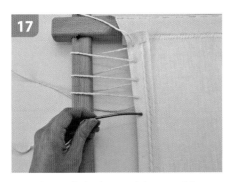

17

Bring the needle back around the arm of the frame and make another stitch into the webbing, about 3cm (1¼in) away from the previous stitch. Continue working in this way down the length of the webbing, making sure to bring the needle up over the arm of the frame before every new stitch. The needle should enter the webbing in a straight line, as this will ensure the tension is pulled evenly across the fabric.

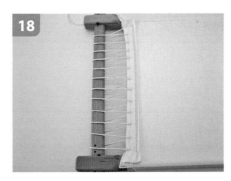

18

As you work you will need to stop and start so you can pull enough string through the webbing, allowing you to continue. When you reach the end of the webbing, pull through an extra length of string so you have around 50cm (20in) excess string. Cut the other end off the ball, leaving the same amount. This will allow string for if you need to roll the rollers back out in the future. With one side complete, repeat the string steps for the webbing on the other side.

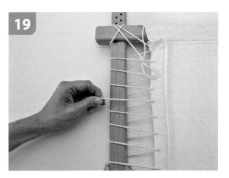

19

On one side of your frame, wind the excess string around the join of the arm and the roller, securing the last length with a slip knot to the string that has been stitched through the webbing. Starting from this secured end, pull the string against the arm of the frame, gradually tightening the fabric. When you reach the other end, loosely wrap the excess string round the arm to hold it in place. Repeat this process on the opposite side.

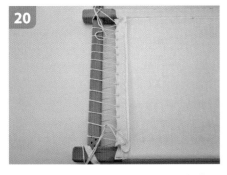

20

It works best if the fabric is tightened gradually, so you will need to repeat this process a few times, tightening one side of the fabric first, then the other. Make sure that the fabric is pulled evenly; if it is then the webbing will sit parallel with the arms of the frame. You will know when the fabric has been pulled tight enough because the string will be too tight to pull any more. At this point you can secure the ends of the string with a slip knot.

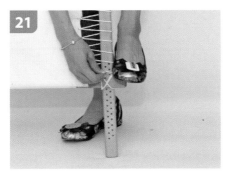

21

The fabric can now be tightened again, but in the opposite direction. Place the frame on the floor with a roller along the bottom. Stand on the end of the roller, pushing it further down the arm, and adjust the split pin to keep it in place. Repeat at the other end of the roller. Make sure that the roller has been moved down by the same number of holes. For a final check, measure the distance between the two arms. If they are the same you are good to go. If not, then the frame is uneven and the rollers need to be adjusted again.

Getting Ready to Stitch

Over time the frame will relax and the fabric will loosen. It is a good habit to make sure that every time you want to start stitching you tighten the frame before sitting down. This is especially important if the frame has been left for a while. The best support for a slate frame is a pair of trestles that the frame can balance on. The height and angle of the trestles can be adjusted, so it may take a bit of manoeuvring to find the best height and angle for you.

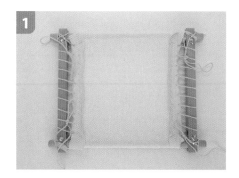

Roller frames work in the same way as slate frames. The difference being that the arms are slotted into place and tightened with bolts and wing nuts. Also, roller frames are tightened or loosened by rolling the rollers round, rather than stretching the rollers further down the arms, like you would with a slate frame. There are usually more sizes available in roller frames. Just like slate frames, the design is usually transferred once the fabric is tight in the frame.

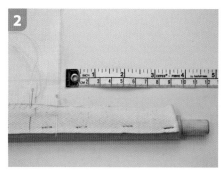

To frame up a roller frame, you need to follow the same steps as for a slate frame. However, for a roller frame you need to make sure that the length of your fabric is shorter than the length of the webbing attached to the roller. Leave at least 5cm (2in) of empty webbing at each end. If you do not leave this gap at either side of the webbing then there will not be enough space to attach the side webbing and tighten with string.

When you have stitched the fabric to the rollers, they can be slotted into place at the end of the arms. At this point you need to roll the rollers outwards, round and round till the fabric has been pulled taught. Secure the rollers in place by tightening up the wing nuts or bolts at the end of the arms.

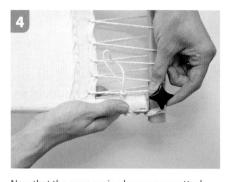

Now that the arms are in place you can attach the webbing to the fabric and tighten with the parcel string, following the same steps as for a slate frame. When the fabric has been tightened using the string, the rollers can then be rolled outwards again, tightening the fabric in the opposite direction. Secure the rollers in place using the wing nuts or bolts at the end of the arms. If using a roller frame, remember to re-tighten the frame every now and then as you work, since roller frames do not hold tension as well as slate frames.

TRANSFERRING YOUR DESIGN

In whitework there are a number of different ways you can transfer your design onto the fabric. The method you choose will depend on a number of different factors, as some whitework techniques are better suited to certain transfer methods. In some cases it may be that you use a number of different transfer methods to transfer a single design onto fabric.

TRACING

For whitework, the tracing method is the easiest and quickest way of transferring a design onto fabric. This is because the fabrics that are used in whitework are white and generally lightweight, so it is easier to see the design clearly through the fabric. Using a light box or a window will help the image to be more visible through the fabric, but if the design has been drawn on white paper with a fine black marker it should be clear enough. The tracing method can be used when the fabric is in the frame or before you have framed up.

If using the tracing method to transfer the design there are a few options available. The first is to use a blue pencil. This can done with an ordinary blue colouring pencil, a propelling pencil with a blue lead, or a blue quilter's chalk. Any of these pencils will make clean, fine lines when transferring the design. Before starting, make sure

Keep Your Work Surfaces Clean

Once the whitework fabric has been cut and is ready to use, it is really important to keep it clean and white. Therefore make sure all surfaces are clean before putting your fabric down or working on them.

the lead has a sharp point for more accurate lines. It is important to remember if using a pencil to transfer the design, the lines will be permanent, and so when stitching you will need to make sure the lines are completely covered.

Another option is to use a blue water-soluble fabric marker. The lines made with a water-soluble fabric marker tend to be thicker, as even the fine tips bleed a little, so the design can look a little chunky once it has been transferred. However, they will wash out once the piece has been finished so it doe not matter if the blue lines are visible once they have been stitched. If using a water-soluble pen, make sure to test it on the fabric first to see if it does wash out properly.

Outline drawn in blue pencil.

Outline in water-soluble pen.

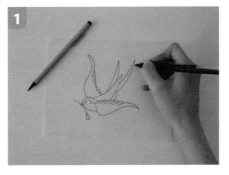

The first step is to draw a neat and clear outline of the design onto white paper. If you used a HB pencil to draw the design originally, you need to go over the design again with a fine black marker. Then rub out all the pencil lines. This is an important step as the HB pencil could be transferred to the fabric when the lines are traced over, which will make the clean white fabric dirty and greying.

Straight Lines

If there are straight vertical or horizontal lines in your design and you decide to trace the design onto an even-weave fabric, *do not* transfer the straight lines. These can be added afterwards with a blue tacking thread. This ensures that the straight lines in the design will definitely match up with the straight grain of the fabric.

With the design drawn, the next step is to draw the central vertical and horizontal lines through the design, which will mark the centre point. Again, these lines need to be drawn in fine black marker so no pencil marks can be transferred onto the fabric. These lines will be used as a guide, to match up with the vertical and horizontal grains of the fabric, and are *not* transferred.

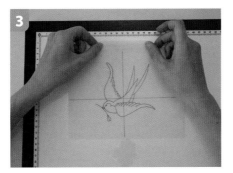

The next step is to tape the design down ready to lay the fabric on top. If the design is clear enough, tape it to a clean, flat surface or for clearer, sharper visibility, tape the design to a light box or window. Then lay the fabric on top, making sure the central lines drawn on the design match up with the grain lines of the fabric. The design should be transferred centrally onto the fabric.

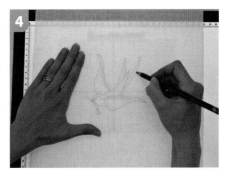

The final step is trace over all the design lines with the pen or pencil of your choice. But remember that for whitework it must always be in blue. Take your time and get it right. The aim is to transfer clear, clean and fine design lines onto the fabric, ready for stitching.

TACKING

For whitework, the tacking method is best used when transferring straight vertical or horizontal lines from a design, as you can ensure they follow the grain of the fabric exactly. As the tacking is removable, it is also used to mark out areas of a design that will not be covered with stitch, such as marking out where pulled or drawn stitches will be placed.

The tacking method does not work so well on intricate details. So in some cases you can transfer the basic straight and angular outlines with the tacking method, and smaller intricate details with the tracing method. If using the tacking method, you need to have the fabric already stretched in the frame.

In whitework, a light-blue machine thread is used to make the tacking stitches. The reason being that the light blue thread is clearly visible against the white as you work, and although the tacking threads are removed, sometimes traces of the tacking thread can get caught within the whitework stitches. If the finished piece is then washed, a light blue thread will not bleed on the white fabric or thread, and is generally not as noticeable against the white as other colours would be.

Tacked outline also showing straight tacked lines following the grain of the fabric.

The first step is to draw the design onto a piece of acid-free tissue paper. For whitework you need to use a blue pencil to do this – either an ordinary blue colouring pencil or a propelling pencil with a blue lead. This is because a HB pencil will transfer through the tissue as you work the tacking stitches, dirtying the thread and the fabric at the same time. If you have straight lines within your design, make sure to use a ruler when drawing these.

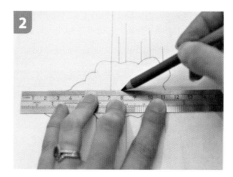

With the design drawn, the next step is to draw the central vertical and horizontal lines through the design, which will mark the centre point. Again, these lines need to be drawn in blue pencil. These lines will be used as a guide, to match up with the vertical and horizontal grains of the fabric.

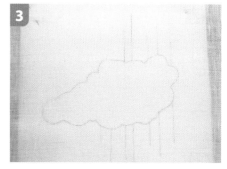

If you have any straight lines or borders within your design, it is important to tack these lines first. Doing this ensures that the straight lines in the design follow the straight grain of the fabric exactly. The rest of the design is then placed and tacked, using these tacked straight lines as a guide. With your fabric already stretched in the frame, place the design underneath the fabric, trying to match up the straight lines of the design to the straight grain of the fabric. When happy with the position, pin the corners and edges of the design to hold it in place.

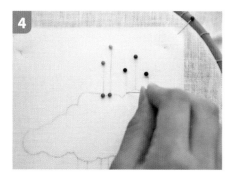

Then push pins down through the holes of the fabric, going through the start and finish points of the straight lines on the design. This will temporarily mark out where all the straight lines of the design need to be tacked. When all the straight design lines are pinned, carefully remove the design from underneath.

5

With the design removed, the remaining pins will show you where the tacking lines need to go. Thread up a small tapestry needle with a length of light-blue machine thread and tie a knot in the end. Take the needle down into the fabric, leaving the knot on the surface next to one of these pins. Then bring the needle back up through the same hole as the pin. Stitch along this grain line with a running stitch (long stitches on the surface and small stitches on the back), till you reach the corresponding pin at the opposite end of the design line.

To secure the thread, simply do a small backstitch over the last stitch, leaving a small tail of thread on the surface. Remove the other pins as you go. Repeat till all the straight design lines have been tacked.

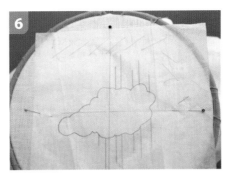

6

With the straight lines now tacked, the next step is to tack the remainder of the design. Place the tissue paper on the surface of the fabric, matching up the straight lines of the design to the newly tacked straight lines or to the grain of the fabric. Pin the four sides of the tissue in place. Thread up a small sharp needle with a length of light-blue machine thread and tie a knot in the end. Make large basting stitches round the edge of the tissue paper to hold it temporarily in place.

Grain Lines

It does not matter if, when you are tacking the straight lines, the pins are not running along the same grain line. What does matter is that once you have started tacking, you need to continue to tack along the same grain line. The pins will indicate where the line starts and finishes. This will ensure all the straight tacking lines are actually straight.

Even-Weave Fabric

As most whitework techniques need an even-weave fabric, it is important to remember that when tacking your design, unless the lines are straight, the needle does not have to go down through the holes in the fabric. Where it needs to, the needle can pierce the grains of the fabric in order to follow the design line accurately.

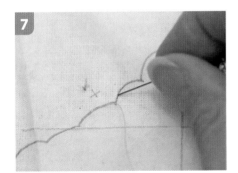

7

With the tissue held in place you can now tack the rest of the design. Thread a length of light-blue machine thread into a sharp needle, tying a knot in the end. Take the needle down outside the design and work a small cross stitch. Bring the needle back up to the surface through a design line. It is best to start the tacking in the centre of the design and work outwards.

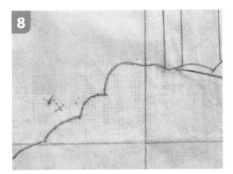

8

Work small running stitches (long stitches on the surface and small stitches on the back), no longer than 5mm (¼in) in length, along all the design lines. If the spaces between your stitches are too big, the tacked design lines become disjointed and are less easy to follow. You need to pull the stitches quite tight so they will not become distorted when the tissue is removed. To secure the ends of the thread make a small backstitch and leave a small tail of thread on the surface.

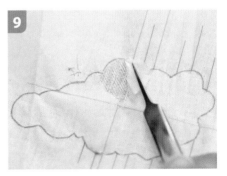

9

When all the design lines have been tacked it is time to remove the tissue paper. Start by removing the long basting stitches from the edge of the tissue. Then gently pull away at the tissue paper, one bit at a time, leaving the small tacking stitches in place. Using a pair of tweezers can help to remove small pieces of tissue, and helps to focus on removing small areas at a time. When removing the tissue, take care not to distort or pull the tacking stitches.

KEEPING YOUR WORK CLEAN

It is important to keep any piece of embroidery clean but especially so for whitework. In the absence of colour the tiniest bit of dust or stray fibre can draw the eye away from your beautiful stitching, and the smallest mark can be glaringly obvious. It is best to keep your embroidery covered as much as possible, even while you are working.

The framing-up instructions explain how to prepare the tissue paper during the framing up process, but this is not enough. This next section will go into further detail of how to keep you whitework clean and dirt free.

COVERING YOUR WORK

When you are not working on your embroidery, you need to make sure that it is always covered and protected with at least tissue paper. Even if you are only going to make a cup of tea, always cover your frame!

Ring Frames

If you followed the instructions for framing up a ring frame, then you should already have a piece of tissue covering the fabric trapped between the two rings. To start embroidering you need to tear away a small section of this tissue paper to reveal the design underneath. If you tear away small sections at a time, only revealing the areas as they need to be worked, the remaining areas will continue to be protected until they need to be revealed. When not working on your embroidery, use another piece of tissue to cover the whole of the ring frame. Shower caps are great for covering and protecting ring frames when not in use, but you could also use a clean white cloth or pillowcase to wrap around the ring frame.

Slate and Roller Frames

If you followed the instructions for framing up a slate or roller frame, then you should have two pieces of tissue taped in place along each roller. These pieces of tissue can now be drawn to the front of the frame and folded to reveal an area of the fabric on which you plan to work. Pin the tissue in place through the webbing. Fold two more sheets of tissue into strips and tuck them underneath the tissue that is pinned in place, leaving only a small area of the design exposed. All these pieces of tissue can be moved and re-folded as you work, to reveal different areas of the design as you need to work them. When you are not working on your embroidery the tissue can be unpinned and wrapped around the front and back of the frame, protecting both sides. As an extra precaution the whole frame can then be wrapped in a clean white sheet or pillowcase.

KEEPING EVERYTHING ELSE CLEAN

Washing your hands before you sit down to start embroidering is good working practice for any embroiderer, professional or otherwise. With whitework, however, it is also good working practice to wash your hands more often, to keep the threads that you

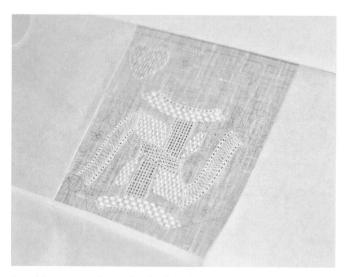

A work-in-progress picture showing how the tissue paper is pinned in position, only revealing the area of the design that is currently being worked on. The rest of the design and fabric is covered and protected by the tissue.

Ring frame protected with extra tissue and a shower cap.

are handling clean and white. So if you are sitting down for a long stint, every time you stop to stretch, wash your hands.

If you wear make-up try not to touch your face as you work. Make-up will easily transfer from your face to your fingers and then to your threads and work. Whitework pieces are generally washed when complete anyway, but even washing will not remove all stains, so it is best to try to prevent stains or marks altogether.

When sharp needles and finger tips are in close proximity to each other it is almost guaranteed that at some point there will be blood. If you do prick your finger, move away from the frame; most of the time blood will not be drawn but if it is, wash your hands and do not start work again till the wound has stopped bleeding completely. If blood has been transferred onto the thread, cut off the bloodied section, secure the end and start again with a new thread. If blood has been transferred onto the fabric there is a method to minimize the damage but you must work quickly. As soon as you see blood on the fabric, stop working and put a piece of white cotton thread in your mouth until it is soaked with your saliva. Take the piece of soaked white cotton thread into a ball and dab the blood stain with it. Do not rub the stain, only dab. This must be done before the blood has dried onto the fabric. I am no scientist so I am not sure how it works but in most cases the blood is successfully removed.

In whitework, even the tiniest bit of coloured fluff and fibre can show up quite visibly, especially if it has been trapped within part of the stitching. So when sitting down to work, think about what you are wearing. I am not saying you have to wear white in order to stitch whitework but wearing a bright red fluffy jumper probably is not the best idea!

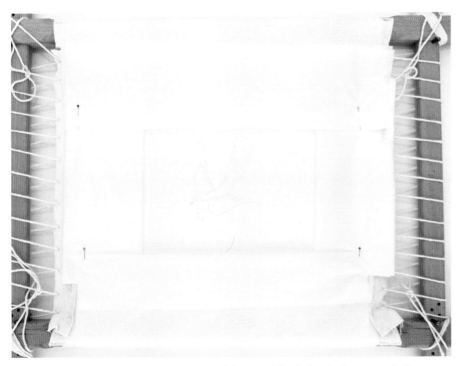

Slate frame with tissue folded and pinned to reveal the area of the design that is to be worked.

CHAPTER 4

PULLED THREAD

Pulled thread is a really beautiful technique that creates exquisite lacy patterns and textures. A misconception is that pulled thread is difficult. This is because when worked on very fine fabrics it can be extremely intricate and delicate. However, if you start with simple fabrics it is surprisingly easy once you understand how it works and you will be surprised at how quickly you can stitch an area. After all, once you have started to stitch you just repeat the same pattern of stitches.

The technique 'pulled thread' does exactly what the title suggests. The stitches pull the weave (threads) of the ground fabric together in order to create more open or dense spaces. The many different stitch patterns pull and manipulate the weave differently and in different directions, creating holes and stitch patterns in different ways, thus creating many varied lace-like effects and textures.

The following pages show how to prepare an area before pulled thread is worked and a number of pulled-thread stitch patterns and their variations. Within the instructions, when the word *pull* is used, you need to give a sharp *pull* on the thread in the direction of the stitch. It is this *pull* that opens up the holes in the weave, which creates the lacy patterns. It is important that the tension of the *pull* is consistent, otherwise the pattern may not look even.

All pulled-thread stitches here have been worked on a 35TPI Edinburgh linen, and stitched with a lace thread. I have also used a blue machine thread to make some of the stitching more visible.

PREPARATION

Areas of pulled thread that will be encased in a decorative outline stitch should first be outlined with a double running stitch. This acts as a barrier and stops the weave of the fabric outside the shape from becoming distorted. Regardless of the thread you choose to work, for the pulled-thread stitch I would always use a lace thread (or similar) to work the double running stitch as you want it to be strong yet discreet and easy to cover over with the decorative outline later on.

Pulled Thread Tips

When working an area, try to start stitching so the pulled-thread pattern will start across the widest point. This will make it easier for you to continue stitching the pattern across the shape as you have a solid line of stitches to follow. Depending on the shape you are stitching, you will need to break up the pattern when you reach the edges as none of the stitches should reach over the outline. At times you may need to work fake or half stitches next to the outlines to complete the look of the pattern.

DOUBLE RUNNING STITCH

A complete double-running-stitch outline.

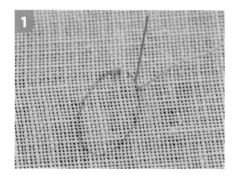

1 Using an embroidery needle, start the thread by tying a knot in the end and taking the needle down on the design line. Work two tiny back (stab) stitches along the design line, piercing the threads of the linen.

2 Work running stitches around the shape, following the design line. These stitches should be about 2mm (1⁄16in) long, with gaps of the same length. These stitches need to be worked well and neatly as they will act as a barrier against the pulled-thread stitches. When you can, try to pierce the threads of the linen rather than going through the holes as this will make the stitches stronger.

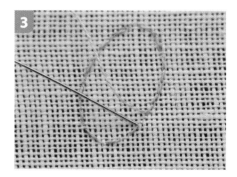

3 When you reach the starting point, work round the shape again but this time filling in the gaps on the surface to create a double-running-stitch outline. Make sure that the stitches are sharing the same holes.

HONEYCOMB

Honeycomb is a simple pulled-thread stitch that is worked in horizontal rows. I have worked the pattern over four threads of the linen but it can be worked over any number of threads to create the desired effect.

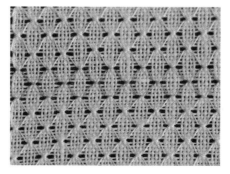

An example of honeycomb.

Lengths of Thread

When working pulled-thread patterns, make sure that you have enough thread in the needle to complete a full row of stitching as you can't finish and secure threads in the middle of a row. If a thread snaps mid-row, unpick that row, secure the end and start again.

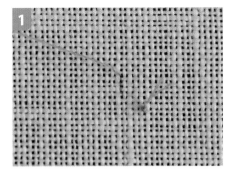

Start the thread by tying a knot in the end and taking the needle down close to where you want to start stitching. Work three backstitches in a vertical row, each stitch being worked over a single thread of the linen.

The first stitch of the honeycomb is a vertical stitch over four threads of the linen, worked from top to bottom. This hides the starting stitches.

From where the needle has just been taken down, count four threads to the left and bring the needle back up.

Make a horizontal stitch back over the same four threads, taking the needle down through the same hole as the first vertical stitch.

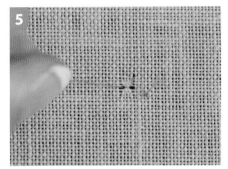

Bring the needle back up through the same hole and *pull* this stitch tight! This will form a hole at each end of the horizontal stitch.

Then make a vertical stitch upwards over four threads.

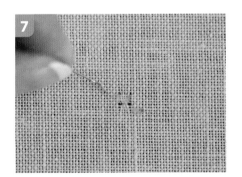

From here count four threads to the left and bring the needle back up.

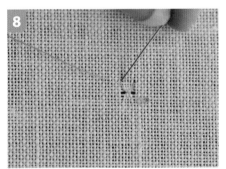

Make a horizontal stitch back over the same four threads and take the needle down.

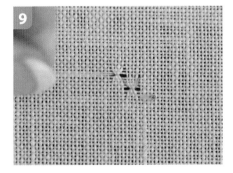

Bring the needle back up through the same hole and *pull* this stitch tight. Again, this forms a hole at each end of the horizontal stitch.

continued on the following page…

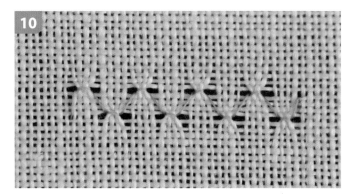

These steps are then repeated till you reach the end of your first row of stitches.

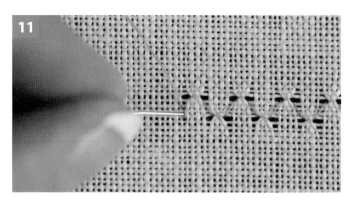

At the end of each row, a small locking stitch is worked over a single thread of the linen in order to secure the tension of that row. This stitch is hidden behind the last stitch worked before moving on to the next row.

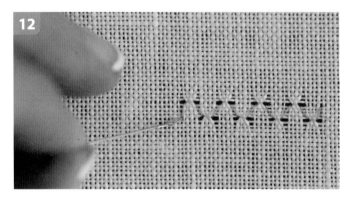

The second row is then worked in the same way but the stitches travel across the area in the opposite direction, thus forming a mirror image. Start by bringing the needle up in the same place the first row ended.

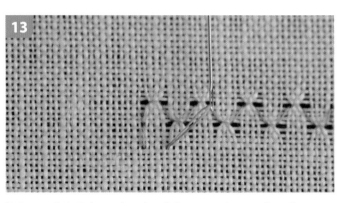

Make a vertical stitch over four threads from top to bottom. Count four threads to the right and bring the needle back up.

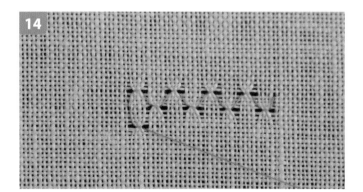

Make the horizontal stitch back over these same four threads, bring the needle back up and *pull* the stitch tight.

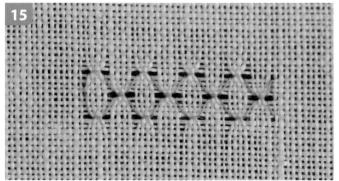

Continue the pattern, travelling back across the first row, and notice where the two rows join the horizontal stitches become double as they share the same holes. When you have completed all rows secure the thread with three backstitches in a vertical row underneath the last stitch.

HONEYCOMB DARNING

Honeycomb darning is a variation of honeycomb and is worked in the same way. The difference being that there is no horizontal backstitch. Here I have worked the threads over three threads of the linen but it can be worked over any number of threads.

An example of honeycomb darning.

Fix Mistakes Early

If you make a mistake in a row, the only way to fix it is to unpick and start that row again! If you leave the mistake and carry on stitching, the pattern on all the subsequent rows will be offset. In pulled-thread, mistakes can be glaringly obvious if left, so it is best just to get the unpicking over and done with so you can crack on with stitching.

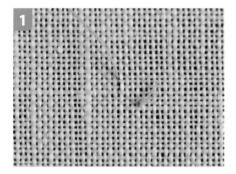

Start the thread by tying a knot in the end and taking the needle down close to where you want to start stitching. Work two backstitches in a vertical row, each stitch being worked over a single thread of the linen.

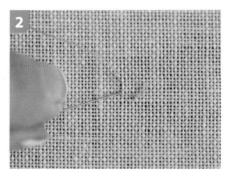

Make a vertical stitch over three threads of the linen, worked from top to bottom. This hides the starting stitches.

From where the needle has just been taken down, count three threads to the left and bring the needle back up.

Pull this stitch tightly to the left.

Make a vertical stitch upwards over three threads.

From here count three threads to the left, bring the needle back up and *pull* the thread tightly.

continued on the following page…

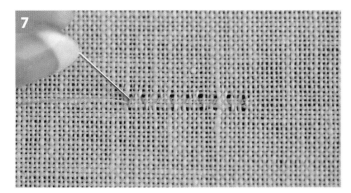

Repeat these steps to complete your first row. A small locking stitch is now worked over a single thread of the linen in order to secure the tension in that row. This stitch is hidden behind the last stitch worked, before moving on to the next row.

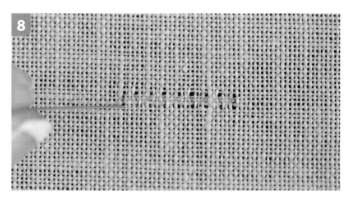

The second row is then worked in the same way but the stitches travel across the area in the opposite direction, thus forming a mirror image. Start by bringing the needle up in the same place the first row ended.

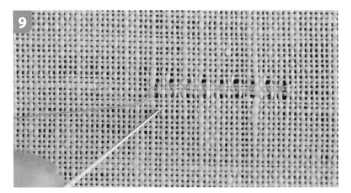

Make a vertical stitch over three threads from top to bottom.

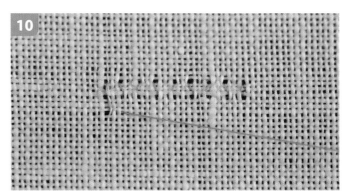

Count three threads to the right and bring the needle back up. *Pull* this stitch tightly to the right.

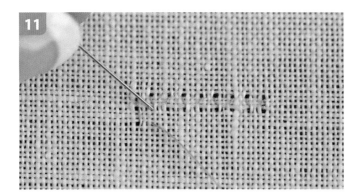

Then make a vertical stitch over three threads from bottom to top.

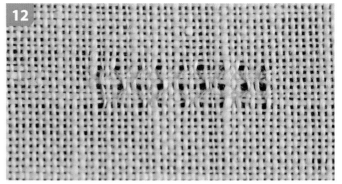

Continue the pattern, travelling back across the first row, and notice where the two rows join, the horizontal stitches share holes where they enter and exit the fabric. When you have completed all rows, secure the thread with three backstitches in a vertical row underneath the last stitch.

WAVE STITCH

Wave stitch is also worked in horizontal rows and makes quite open holes. For this example I have worked the stitch over four threads of the linen but it can be worked over any number of threads.

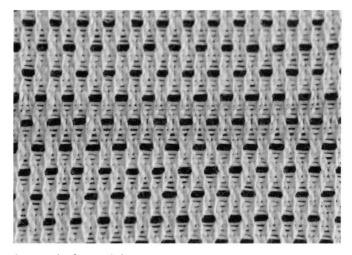

An example of wave stitch.

Start the thread by tying a knot in the end and taking the needle down close to where you want to start stitching. Work two backstitches, one vertical and one diagonal, each stitch being worked over a single thread of the linen.

Bring the needle up just slightly above these holding stitches. Count four threads of the linen down and two threads to the right and take the needle down. This will create a diagonal stitch.

Count four threads of the linen to the left, bring the needle back up and *pull* this stitch tight.

Now count four threads of the linen up and two threads to the right and take the needle down. This stitch should share the same hole with the previous stitch; if it doesn't, something is not quite right.

Now count four threads of the linen to the left, bring the needle up and *pull* this stitch tight.

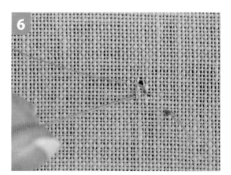

From here count four threads down and two threads to the right and take the needle down. This stitch should share the same hole as the previous stitch.

continued on the following page…

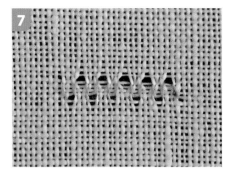

Continue this pattern to complete the first row.

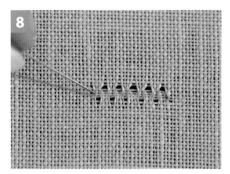

At the end of each row a small locking stitch is worked over a single thread of the linen in order to secure the tension of that row. This stitch is hidden behind the last stitch worked, before moving on to the next row.

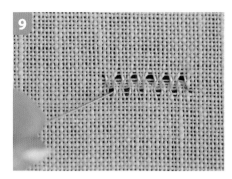

To start the second row, bring the needle up through the same hole created by the last stitch of the previous row.

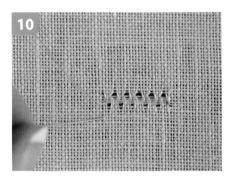

Then count four threads down and two to the left and take the needle down. This creates a diagonal stitch.

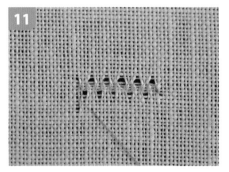

From there count four threads of the linen to the right and bring the needle back up. *Pull* this stitch tight.

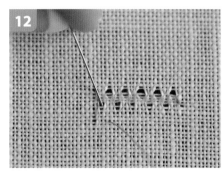

Now count four threads of the linen up and two to the left and take the needle down. This stitch should share the same hole as the previous stitch and the previous row.

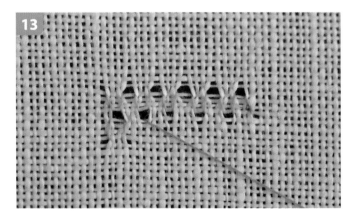

Count four threads of the linen to the right and bring the needle back up. The needle should be coming up in the same hole as the previous row.

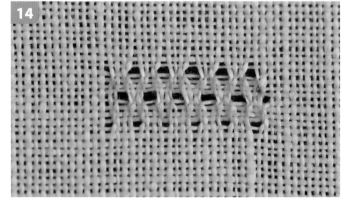

Continue the pattern, travelling back across the first row, and notice where the two rows join, the horizontal stitches share holes where they enter and exit the fabric. When you have completed all rows secure the thread with two backstitches hidden underneath the last stitch.

SINGLE-FAGGOT

Single-faggot stitch is a simple stitch worked in diagonal rows. The half squares worked in rows create a simple pattern of large regular holes. I have worked this stitch over three threads of the linen but it can be worked over any number of threads.

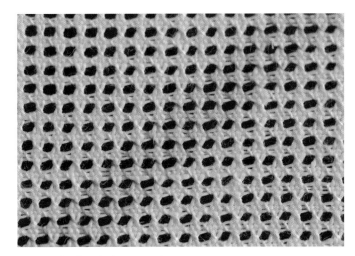

An example of single-faggot stitch.

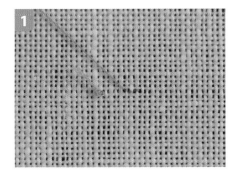

Start the thread by tying a knot in the end and taking the needle down close to where you want to start stitching. Work three backstitches in a horizontal row, each stitch being worked over a single thread of the linen.

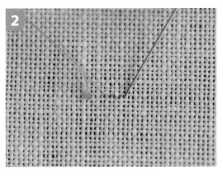

The first stitch is a horizontal stitch counted over three threads of the linen and worked from left to right. This first stitch should cover the backstitches.

Then count three threads of the linen down and three to the left and bring the needle back up. The thread has travelled diagonally across the back.

Pull this stitch tight. You will see holes appear at either side of the first stitch.

Make a vertical stitch worked bottom to top counted over three threads. This stitch should share the hole with the first stitch. If it doesn't, something has gone wrong.

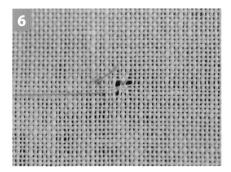

From here count three threads to the left and three threads down and bring the needle back up. *Pull* the stitch tight.

continued on the following page…

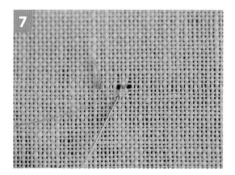

Now make a horizontal stitch from left to right over three threads of the linen. This stitch should share the hole with the previous vertical stitch.

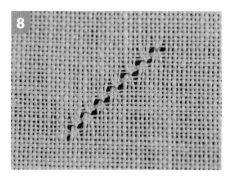

Continue working this pattern until you reach the end of the row. *Pull* every stitch tight.

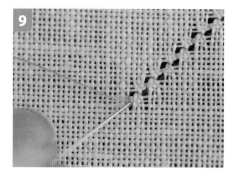

At the end of each row a small locking stitch is worked over a single thread of the linen in order to secure the tension of that row. This stitch is hidden behind the last stitch worked, before moving on to the next row.

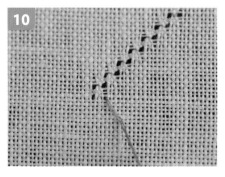

To start the second row, count three threads to the right from the last hole created by the first row, and bring the needle up.

The first stitch of the second row is horizontal from right to left counted over three threads. This stitch should share the same hole as the last hole from the first row. If it does not, something is not right.

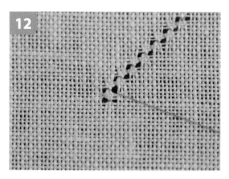

To bring the needle up, count three threads of the linen to the right and three up. The needle should be coming up through the same hole as the first row. *Pull* the stitch tight.

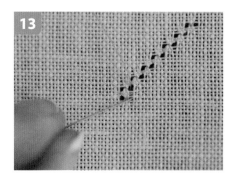

Then make a vertical stitch worked from top to bottom over three threads of the linen. This should share the hole with the previous stitch.

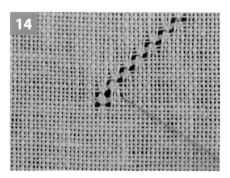

From here count three threads of the linen to the right and three up. Bring the needle back up ready for the next horizontal stitch. *Pull* tight.

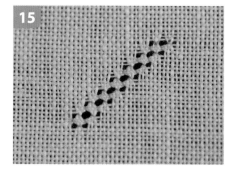

Continue the pattern, travelling back across the first row, and notice where the two rows join, the stitches share holes. When you have completed all rows secure the thread with two backstitches hidden underneath the last stitch.

SPACED SINGLE-FAGGOT

Spaced single-faggot is worked in the same way as single-faggot but with the rows separated. A crossed window effect appears between the rows rather than a hole. I have worked this stitch over four threads of the linen but it can be worked over any number of threads.

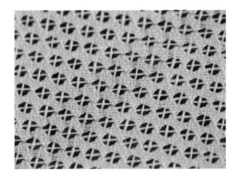

An example of spaced single-faggot stitch.

Work the first row of single-faggot stitch remembering to *pull* every stitch tight. At the end of the first row work a locking stitch to secure the tension of that row.

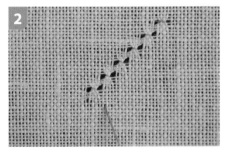

To start the second row, count one thread of the linen down and five to the right from the last hole created by the first row. Bring the needle up.

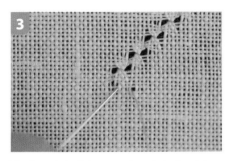

The first stitch of the second row is horizontal from right to left counting over four threads of the linen.

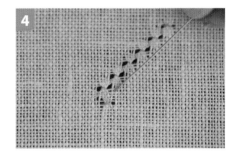

To bring the needle up, count four threads of the linen to the right and four up. *Pull* the stitch tight.

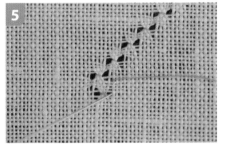

Then make a vertical stitch worked from top to bottom over four threads of the linen. This should share the hole with the previous stitch but *not* the previous row. Notice the cross appearing between the two rows.

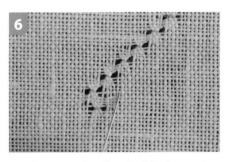

From here count four threads of the linen to the right and four up. Bring the needle back up ready for the next horizontal stitch. *Pull* tight.

Second Row Threads

The amount of linen threads you choose to work the stitch over will determine how many threads of the linen you will need to count in order to start the second row. Here I have worked over four threads of the linen, so to move on to the second row I counted one thread down and five across. If I had worked over three threads of the linen, to start the second row I would count one thread down and four across. If I had worked over five threads of the linen, to start the second row I would count one thread down and six across. This ensures that the cross always separates the rows.

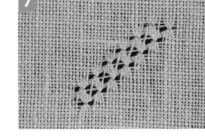

Continue the pattern, travelling back across the first row, and notice the crossed hole that separates the two rows. When you have completed all rows secure the thread with two backstitches hidden underneath the last stitch.

FOUR-SIDED

Four-sided stitch is another simple stitch that creates a simple pattern of large regular holes, and is worked in vertical rows. I have worked this stitch over four threads of the linen but it can be worked over any number over threads.

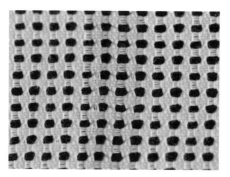

An example of four-sided stitch.

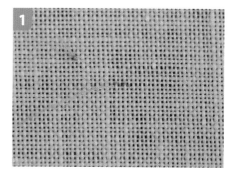

Start the thread by tying a knot in the end and taking the needle down close to where you want to start stitching. Work three backstitches in a horizontal row, each stitch being worked over a single thread of the linen.

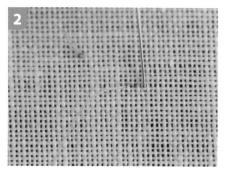

The first stitch is a horizontal stitch over four threads of the linen worked from left to right. This hides the starting stitches.

From here count four threads of the linen down and four to the left and bring the needle up. *Pull* this stitch tight. This makes a diagonal stitch underneath.

Then make a vertical stitch by counting four threads of the linen up. This stitch should share the same hole as the first stitch.

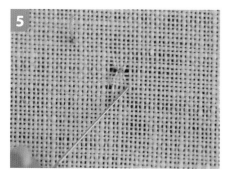

From here count four threads of the linen to the right and four down. Bring the needle up and *pull* tight. This makes a diagonal stitch underneath.

Then make a vertical stitch by counting four threads of the linen up. This should share the same hole as the first stitch.

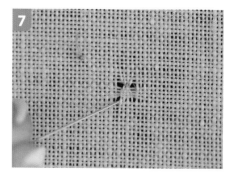

From here count four threads of the linen to the left and four down. Bring the needle up and *pull* tight. This makes a diagonal stitch underneath.

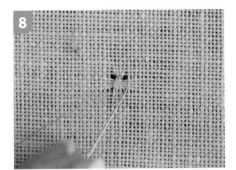

Make a horizontal stitch over four threads of the linen from left to right. This stitch should share holes with previous stitches. This stitch is the first stitch of a new square but it also completes the previous square.

From here count four threads of the linen down and four to the left and bring the needle up. *Pull* this stitch tight. This makes a diagonal stitch underneath.

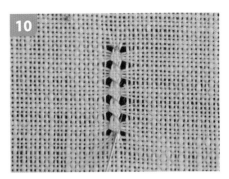

Continue working this pattern until you reach the end of the row. *Pull* every stitch tight. At the end of each row a small locking stitch is worked over a single thread of the linen in order to secure the tension of that row. This stitch is hidden behind the last stitch worked, before moving on to the next row.

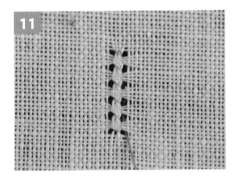

To start the second row bring the needle up through the same hole made by the last stitch of the first row.

The first stitch of the second row is a horizontal stitch over four threads of the linen worked from left to right.

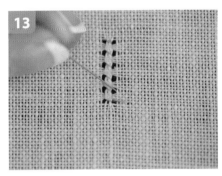

From here count four threads of the linen up and four to the left and bring the needle up. This makes a diagonal stitch underneath. This stitch should share a hole with the previous row.

Make a vertical stitch over four threads of the linen worked from top to bottom. This stitch should share holes with the previous stitch and the previous row. Notice how the two vertical stitches are doubled up.

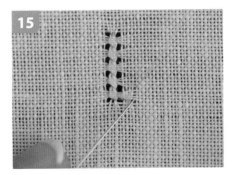

Now count four threads of the linen up and four to the right. Bring the needle up and *pull* tight. This makes a diagonal stitch underneath. Make another vertical stitch over four threads of the linen worked from top to bottom.

Continue this pattern, travelling back across the first row, and notice how the vertical stitches are doubled up. Also see how the horizontal stitches almost look like diagonal stitches because of the direction in which they are being pulled. When you have completed all rows secure the thread with two backstitches hidden underneath the last stitch.

CROSSED STITCH

Crossed stitch is worked in vertical rows and creates a pattern that almost looks like cable knit. I have worked this over six threads of the linen but it can be worked over any even number of threads.

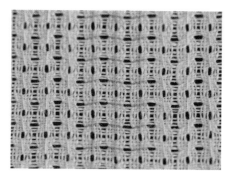

A sample of crossed stitch.

Start the thread by tying a knot in the end and taking the needle down close to where you want to start stitching. Work three backstitches in a horizontal row, each stitch being worked over a single thread of the linen.

The first stitch is horizontal and is worked left to right over six threads of the linen.

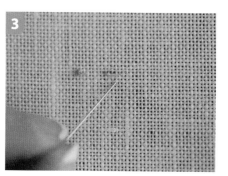

From there count three threads of the linen down and three to the left, bring the needle up and *pull* tight.

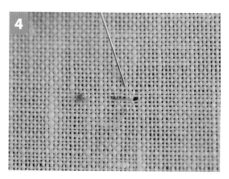

Now make a vertical stitch from bottom to top, counting over six threads of the linen. This vertical stitch sits over the top of the horizontal stitch, forming the cross.

To start the next cross, come back to the hole where the first horizontal stitch starts and count six threads of the linen down. Bring the needle up and *pull* tight!

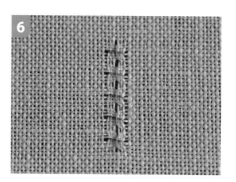

Repeat these steps until the first row is complete. Notice how the vertical stitches of the crosses share holes and that the horizontal stitches are pulled down slightly on the right.

Before starting the next row a holding stitch is worked over two threads of this linen. This holding stitch secures the tension of each row.

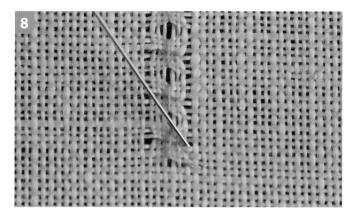

To start the next row, bring the needle up in the hole made by the last horizontal stitch of the previous row.

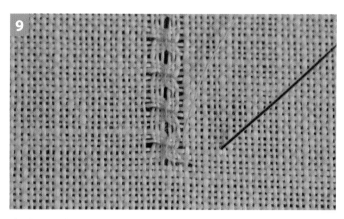

The first stitch of the second row is horizontal and is worked left to right over six threads of the linen.

From there count three threads of the linen up and three to the left, bring the needle up and *pull* tight.

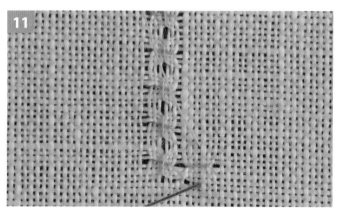

Then make a vertical stitch from top to bottom, counting over six threads of the linen. This vertical stitch sits over the top of the horizontal stitch, forming the cross.

To start the next cross, come back to the hole where the first horizontal stitch of that row starts and count six threads of the linen up. Bring the needle up and *pull* tight. This should share a hole with the cross from the previous row also.

Repeat these steps until the second row is complete. Notice how the horizontal stitches share holes with the previous row and that the horizontal stitches in the second row are pulled up slightly on the right.

Open Trellis

Open-trellis filling is a pretty stitch that gives quite a lacy effect when worked over large areas. It looks complicated but it is not, as it is just rows and crosses worked in diagonal rows. I have worked this pattern over six threads of the linen.

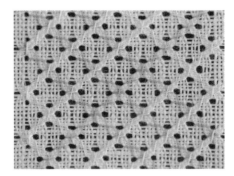

An example of open trellis.

Start the thread by tying a knot in the end and taking the needle down close to where you want to start stitching. Work two backstitches in a vertical row, each stitch being worked over a single thread of the linen.

Make a vertical stitch from top to bottom counting over six threads of the linen. This stitch should hide the two backstitches.

From here count three threads of the linen to the right and three up. Bring the needle up and *pull* the stitch tight.

Now make another vertical stitch from top to bottom counting over six threads of the linen.

Continue working this pattern till you have reached the end of the first row. *Pull* every stitch tight.

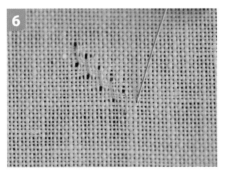

Then count three threads of the linen to the right and three up.

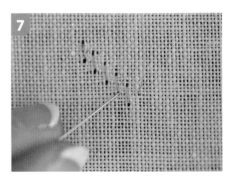

Then make a horizontal stitch from right to left counting over six threads of the linen. This stitch sits on top of the vertical stitch to form a cross.

8

From there count three threads of the linen up and three to the right. Bring the needle up and *pull* the stitch tight.

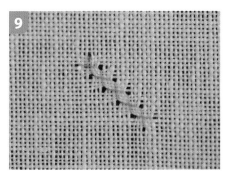

9

Repeat this, completing the crosses as you travel back over the row. *Pull* every stitch tight. The stitches should be sharing holes. If they are not then something is not right. This is the first complete row.

10

For the second and each subsequent row, follow the above steps, but leave a space between each of the rows. To leave the space, from the first hole created by the first stitch of the previous row, count across twelve threads of the linen to the right.

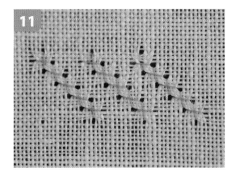

11

Fill the shape with these evenly spaced rows. Notice how the rows have been stitched from top left to bottom right.

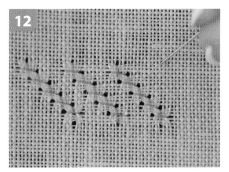

12

The next step is to fill the shape with rows travelling in the opposite direction. These will be stitched starting top right to bottom left. These need to be spaced the same as the other rows. To start in the correct place count across twelve threads of the linen from the first stitch of the last row.

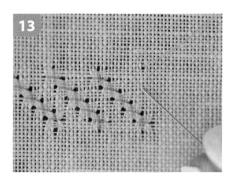

13

Make the first vertical stitch from top to bottom counting over six threads of the linen.

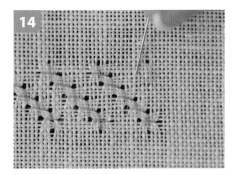

14

Then count three threads of the linen to the left and three up. Bring the needle up and *pull* the stitch tight.

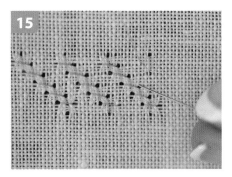

15

Make the next vertical stitch counting over six threads of the linen. Notice how this stitch shares a hole with the previous row. If it doesn't then something is not right.

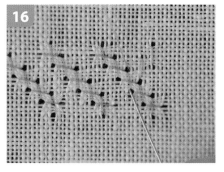

16

Continue this pattern till you reach the end of the row. *Pull* every stitch tight. Notice that this new row is worked straight over the top of the previous rows and that the stitches share holes.

continued on the following page…

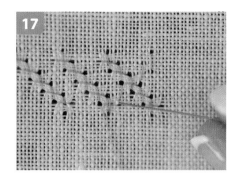

Then count three threads of the linen to the left and three up. Make the first horizontal stitch from left to right, travelling back along the row. Again, notice how the stitches are sharing holes and that where rows cross over each other, the new crossed stitch sits on top of the previous one.

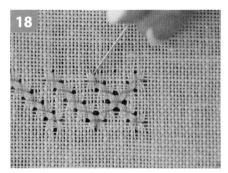

Repeat this, completing the crosses as you travel back over the row. *Pull* every stitch tight. As before, to start a new row leaving the space, count twelve threads of the linen but this time to the left.

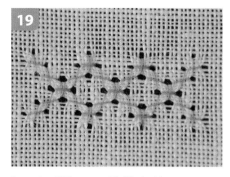

Repeat until the spaced is filled with rows travelling from top right to bottom left.

CHEQUER FILLING

Chequer filling is a really beautiful stitch that creates a lacy effect and, if stitched with a thicker thread, creates a starry pattern in stitch. It is one of the more complicated pulled patterns but is well worth the effort.

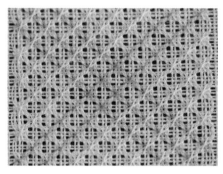

An example of chequer filling.

Start the thread by tying a knot in the end and taking the needle down close to where you want to start stitching. Work two backstitches in a cross, each stitch being worked over a single thread of the linen. Bring the needle up.

From here make the first stitch from left to right, counting six threads of the linen to the right and two down. This stitch should hide the crossed backstitches.

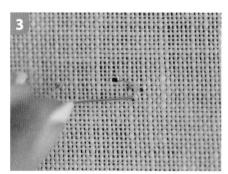

Then count two threads of the linen down and two left, bring the needle up and *pull* the stitch tight.

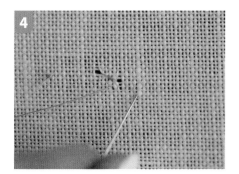

Make the next stitch from left to right, counting six threads of the linen to the right and two down.

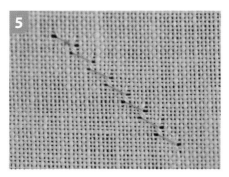

Continue working this pattern till you reach the end of the row. *Pull* every stitch tight.

To start stitching back over the row, count two threads of the linen down and two left, bring the needle up and *pull* the stitch tight.

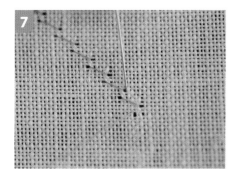

This stitch is worked bottom to top and is counted over six threads of the linen up and two left. When working back over a row, the steps are the same just in reverse. The stitches should share holes. If they don't then something has gone wrong.

To move on to each new row, count across eight threads of the linen from the first stitch of the last row.

Repeat these steps until the shape has been filled with rows worked from top left to bottom right. Make sure to *pull* every stitch tight.

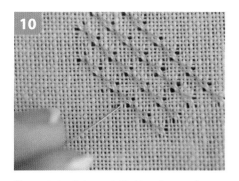

The next step is to start stitching the rows in the opposite direction, starting from bottom left to top right. To do this count two threads of the linen to the left from one of the lower holes formed by a row. Here I have started in the middle to show the pattern more clearly.

Make the first stitch from bottom to top counting over two strands of the linen to the right and six up.

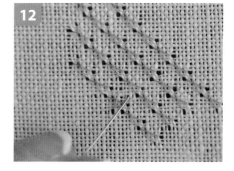

From there count two threads of the linen to the right and two down. Bring the needle up and *pull* the stitch tight.

continued on the following page…

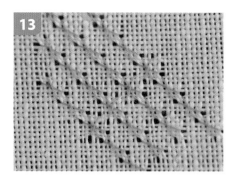

13

Continue this pattern till the end of the row. Notice how the stitches worked in this direction sit on top of those stitches worked previously.

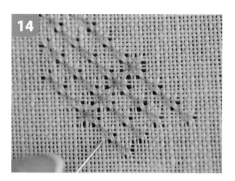

14

Stitch back over that row in the same way as before, but this time the stitches are worked from top to bottom. The stitches should share holes. If they don't, something has gone wrong. When that row is complete, move on to the next row.

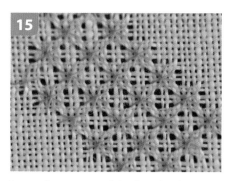

15

Repeat these steps until the shape has been filled with rows worked from bottom left to top right. Make sure to *pull* every stitch tight. Notice that where all the stitches cross each other a star shape is formed. In between each star two horizontal and two vertical threads of linen are left un-pulled.

Eyelets

Pulled-thread eyelets are a kind of satin stitch, with all the stitches converging in a central hole. They can be worked individually or combined to create different patterns and textures. There are many different-shaped eyelets; you can even create your own but the method of working a pulled-thread eyelet is the same for all.

The most important thing to remember is to bring the needle up on the outer edge and take the needle down through the central hole. Your choice of thread and the size of the eyelet will create different textures and densities.

All pulled-thread eyelets have been worked on a 35TPI Edinburgh linen and stitched with a single strand of stranded cotton.

> ## Try Different Sizes
>
> Eyelets can be worked over any number of threads so when you get the hang of them, why not try experimenting with different sizes

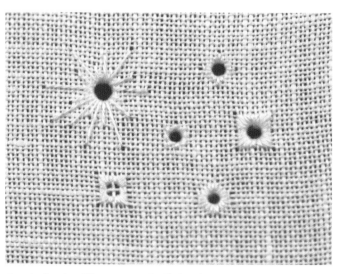

Sample showing different types of pulled eyelets.

Full Eyelet

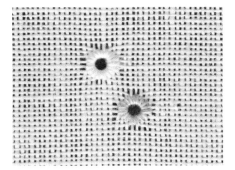

A complete full eyelet.

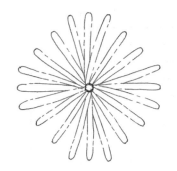

Diagram for a full eyelet.

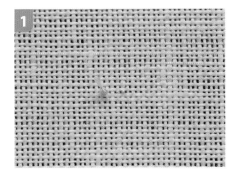

1 Start the thread by tying a knot in the end and taking the needle down close to where you want the eyelet. Work two backstitches in a horizontal row, each stitch being worked over a single thread of the linen.

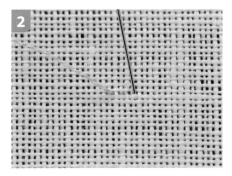

2 Bring the needle up and make the first horizontal stitch, from left to right counting over four threads of the linen. Where you take the needle down becomes the central hole of the eyelet.

3 Bring the needle up one thread of the linen above the starting point. *Pull* the stitch tight. Pulling every stitch tight is what will open up the central hole of the eyelet.

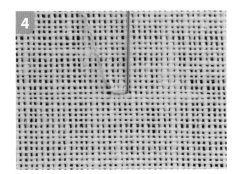

4 Make the next stitch by taking the needle back down through the central hole.

5 Continue to stitch round the eyelet, bringing the needle up on the outside edge of the eyelet and taking it down through the central hole. Follow the diagram for the placement of the stitches.

6 Make sure to *pull* every stitch tight. When the eyelet is complete, secure the thread by working two backstitches close together. Hide these stitches underneath the stitches of the eyelet.

Small Round Eyelet

Small round eyelet.

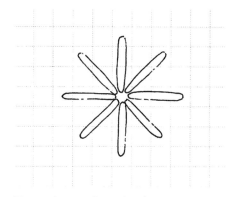

Diagram for a small round eyelet.

Diamond Eyelet

Diamond eyelet.

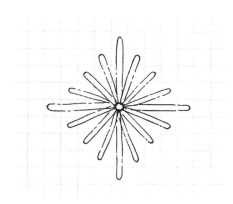

Diagram for a diamond eyelet.

Square Eyelet

Square eyelet.

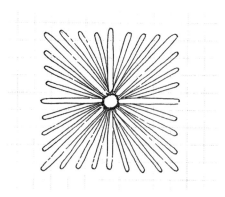

Diagram for a square eyelet.

Free Eyelet

Free eyelet.

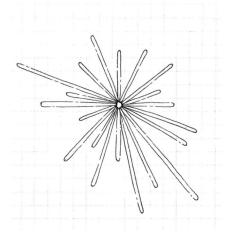

Diagram for a free eyelet.

Crossed Eyelet

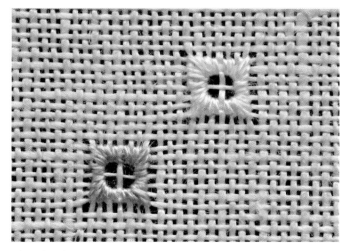

Crossed eyelet.

Diagram for a crossed eyelet.

Combining Pulled-Thread Stitches

When you are confident working pulled-thread stitches, try experimenting with the patterns, working two different patterns together. Beautiful new textures can be created if you get the combination just right.

All the combined pulled-thread stitches have been worked on a 35TPI Edinburgh linen and stitched with a lace thread.

Choosing Patterns to Combine

It helps if the patterns you are combining are worked in the same direction, either horizontally, vertically or diagonally.

When working out if two patterns will merge well together, think about the count of each of the patterns. Does the count need to be changed for them to work together? It is okay to do this as all of the pulled patterns can be worked over any number of threads.

The best thing to do is just have a go on a spare piece of cloth before you work the stitches on your finished piece.

Chequer Filling and Single-Faggot

This pattern is a single row of chequer filling, a space of four threads, then a single row of single-faggot stitch, then a space of four threads and so on.

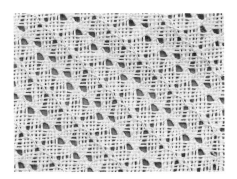

Chequer filling and single-faggot.

Honeycomb Darning and Four-Sided

This pattern is worked vertically, stitching honeycomb darning and four-sided stitch simultaneously in vertical rows. Notice the two-thread gap in the middle of the honeycomb darning. Each of these patterns is counted over four threads.

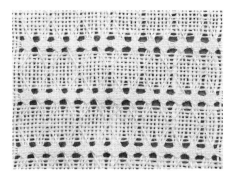

Honeycomb darning and four-sided.

Wave and Diamond Eyelets

This pattern is worked horizontally: two rows of wave stitch counted over four threads, then a row of diamond eyelets counted over four threads and so on. Notice how the eyelets are offset in alternating rows.

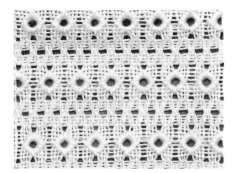

Wave and diamond eyelets.

WORKING PULLED STITCHES

WORKING PULLED STITCHES WITHIN AN OUTLINE

Pulled-thread stitches can be worked within an outlined shape or can be free flowing with no hard outline to follow, meaning that you decide where and when you want the pattern to begin and end in a more natural/spontaneous way.

The examples below show you how to work pulled-thread stitches in both ways and explain how the patterns need to be counted when meeting a defined outline.

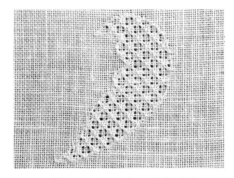

Chequer filling worked within a defined shape.

Work the double-running-stitch outline as described at the beginning of the chapter.

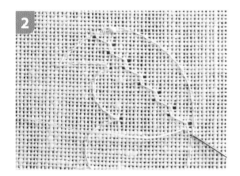

Begin working the chosen pattern with two stab stitches hidden in the double running outline. Aim to start the pattern so it cuts across the widest part of the shape. Work the pattern across the shape. When you reach the other side you may find that the outline cuts through the middle of the final stitch. This is fine. Count the stitch as normal, and find the point where the stitch crosses the outline. This is where you need to take the needle down through the outline. This counts as a half or broken stitch.

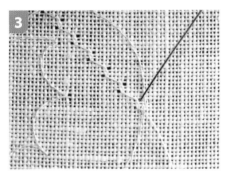

Work two stab stitches, again hiding them within the outline. These stitches will secure the row, in case you need to do some unpicking later or the thread snaps. As you return and work in the opposite direction, the first stitch you do will need to be a half or broken stitch, starting from within the outline. You can use your first row of stitches to count and find where this stitch needs to start.

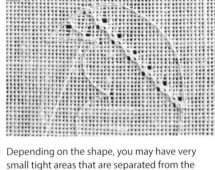

Depending on the shape, you may have very small tight areas that are separated from the main shape. In these places the pulled pattern should still be worked, even if they are just half or broken stitches. Again, use the first row of stitching to help count where the new stitches need to be.

If you need to, work a few small stab stitches around the outline to reach a new starting point, rather than trailing the thread across the back of the work, which can be visible. You are then ready to continue the pattern as before.

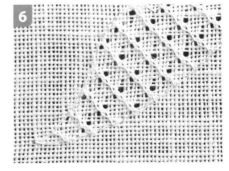

Continue to work the rows of pattern across the shape. Work half or broken stitches along the outline as required until the whole shape is complete.

Working Pulled Stitches Freely

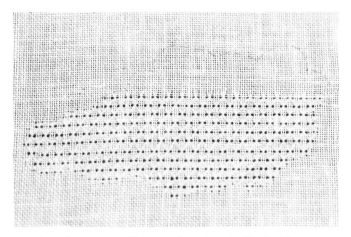

A partly worked example of honeycomb stitch worked freely with no stitched outline.

Using a blue tacking thread, tack the outline of the shape you wish to fill with a pulled-thread stitch.

Begin working the chosen pattern with two stab stitches that will be hidden underneath the first pulled stitch. Aim to start the pattern so it cuts across the widest part of the shape.

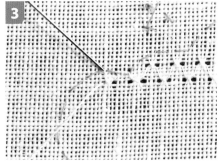

When you reach the opposite side of the shape, if you need to, work half or broken stitches to follow the tacking-thread outline.

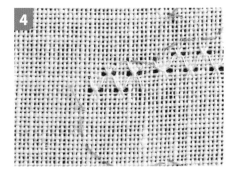

If the tacking thread is in the way you can cut it and remove the area you no longer need. Start the second row working back on yourself, again, working half or broken stitches as needed.

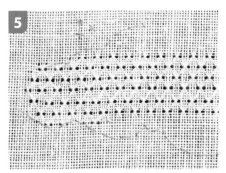

Continue working the rows of pattern across the shape. At the end of each row, work two stab stitches hidden underneath the final stitch in that row to secure it. Along the edges, work half or broken stitches as needed.

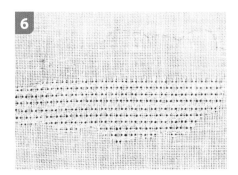

You can either remove the tacking thread as you go or unpick it all when the shape is complete. Just try not to catch any of the tacking thread in the stitches of the pulled-thread pattern.

PULLED SATIN

Pulled-satin stitch patterns are worked in the same way as the other pulled-thread stitches, the difference being that the pulled-satin patterns are based on satin stitch. The stitches are worked like normal stain stitch and are worked in uniform blocks. However, the tension of each stitch is pulled tight in order to create the open, lacy effect. Like pulled-thread patterns, there are many traditional patterns but you can easily make up your own. Here are a few examples to show you the different effects that can be created. The thread used should be slightly heavier than a single thread of the ground fabric.

All pulled satin stitches have been worked on a 35TPI Edinburgh linen, and stitched with a coton à broder 20 thread.

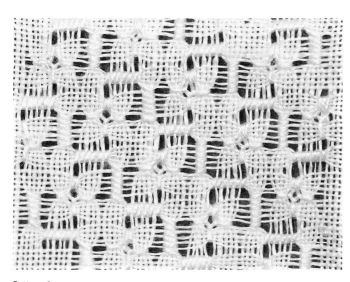

Pattern 1.

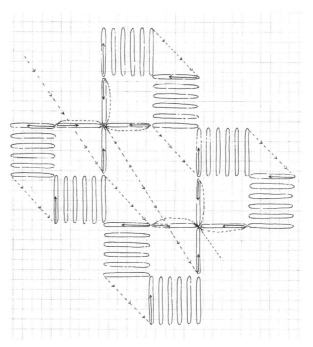

Pattern 1 diagram.

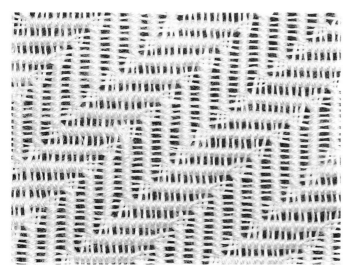

Pattern 2.

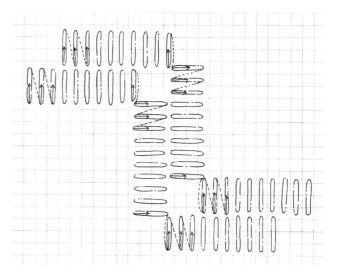

Pattern 2 diagram.

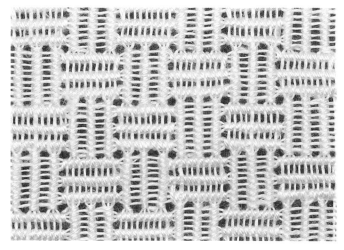

Pattern 3.

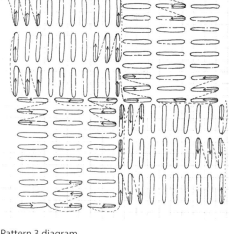

Pattern 3 diagram.

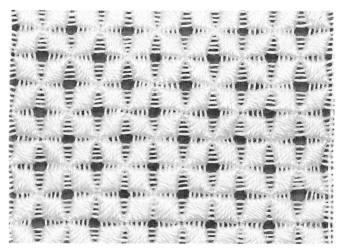

Pattern 4.

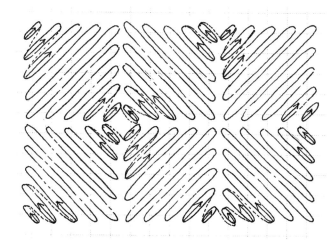

Pattern 4 diagram.

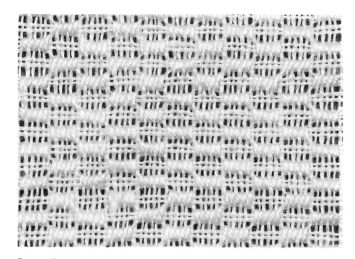

Pattern 5.

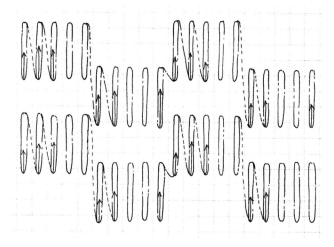

Pattern 5 diagram.

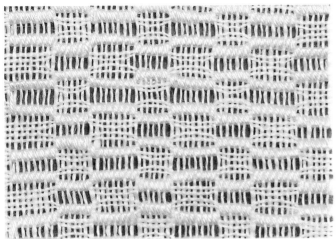

Pattern 6.

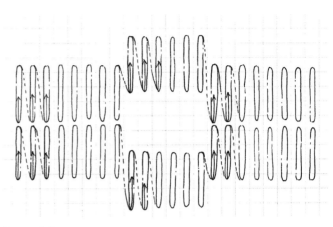

Pattern 6 diagram.

Counted Satin

Counted-satin stitch is not a pulled-thread technique but I have included it in this chapter as it is often worked in conjunction with pulled-thread patterns to create density, in contrast to the pulled stitches' lightness. It is worked in a very similar way to the pulled satin patterns only now the stitches *are not* pulled tight. Counted-satin patterns are composed of blocks of straight stitches and can be worked horizontally, vertically or diagonally. There are numerous patterns to try and you can easily create your own. You can experiment with different threads but usually the thread should be slightly thicker than a single thread of the ground fabric.

All counted stitches have been worked on a 35TPI Edinburgh linen, and stitched with a coton à broder 20 thread.

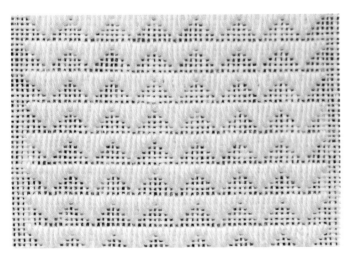

Pattern 1.

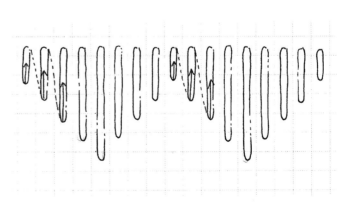

Pattern 1 diagram.

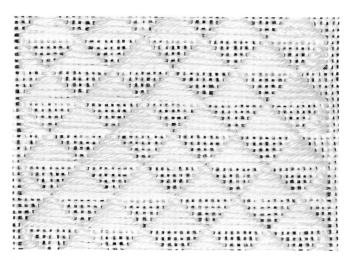

Pattern 2.

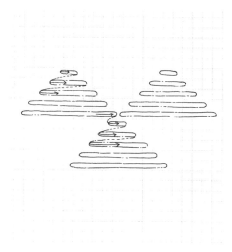

Pattern 2 diagram.

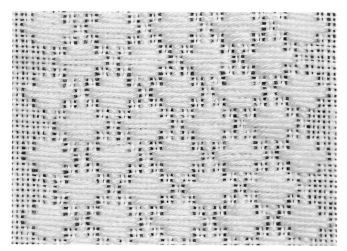

Pattern 3.

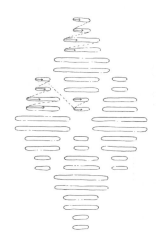

Pattern 3 diagram.

Pattern 4.

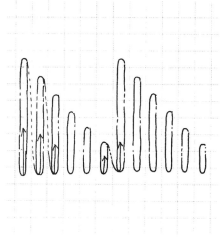

Pattern 4 diagram.

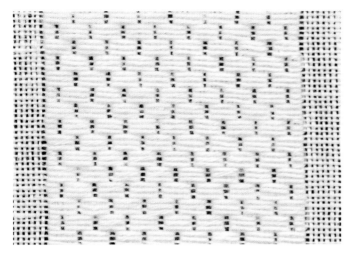

Pattern 5.

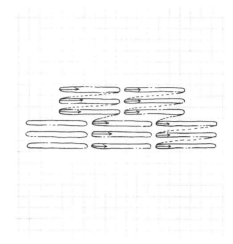

Pattern 5 diagram.

Pattern 6.

Pattern 6 diagram.

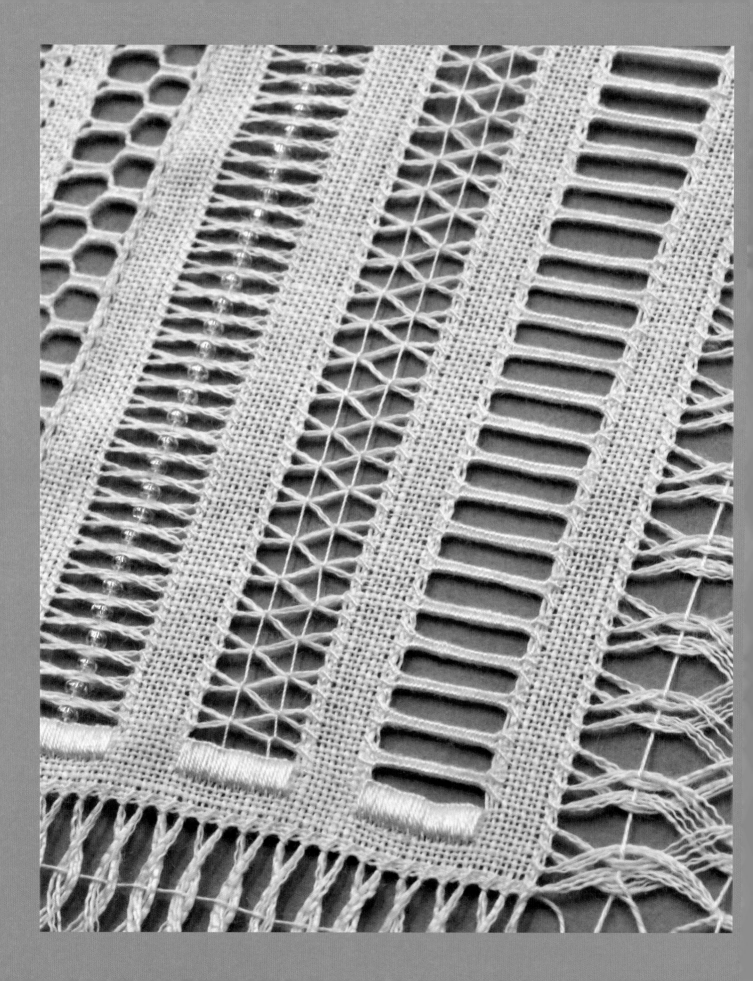

CHAPTER 5

DRAWN THREAD

Drawn-thread work is extremely versatile and is most commonly used to create borders, but it can also be used to fill shapes in a number of different ways as it creates lovely lace-like effects. The withdrawal of the fabric's warp or weft threads, and sometimes both, creates bold open areas; the remaining threads are then pulled, stitched and manipulated into patterns that delicately fill the voided areas.

The following pages show how to prepare an area by withdrawing the threads of the fabric. Then a number of different hem stitches that group the reaming threads create a foundation for the delicate pattern stitches to follow. There are hundreds of different drawn-thread stitches and fillings – many of them have numerous variations,

too – so I have included what I think are the principal drawn stitches that are perfect for beginners just starting out, but also for more advanced stitchers to build upon, experiment with and develop.

PREPARATION

In order to work drawn-thread stitches you first need to withdraw the threads. For the most part, the following examples show how to remove the weft threads (the horizontal threads), therefore creating horizontal bands. If you want to make vertical bands, the steps are the same to remove the warp threads (the vertical threads).

When creating drawn-thread embroidery it is best to have your design and stitches planned out in advance. As you are removing threads from the fabric, you need to make sure you are removing the right amount of thread for the patterns you want to create. For example, if your chosen drawn-thread stitch groups two threads in the hem stitch and two groups in the decorative drawn stitch, the total number of threads grouped in a drawn-thread stitch is four. This means that the number of threads that need to be exposed must be divisible by four, for example, sixty-four or ninety-two. The total number of exposed threads left remaining needs to be divisible by the number of threads grouped in the drawn-stitch pattern.

REMOVING THE THREADS TO RE-WEAVE

An example of a band with six threads removed and woven in at the end.

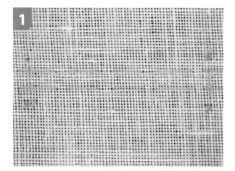

1 With the fabric framed up and pulled to a tight tension, use a blue machine thread to tack out the box from which you will withdraw the threads. This is the simplest way of ensuring the right amount of threads are withdrawn. Once all the threads have been withdrawn, the blue tacking thread can then be removed.

2 Before you begin to remove the threads, it helps if you slacken off the tension on the fabric in the frame. This makes it much easier to remove the threads. Use a tapestry needle to slip underneath one of the threads of the fabric. It is best if this is done in the middle of the area where the threads are to be removed.

3 With a pair of sharp embroidery scissors, slide the tip of the blade underneath this same thread and cut. Take care not to cut any of the vertical threads.

4 Then using the tapestry needle, carefully pick, tease and pull the thread back, little by little, until you reach the line of tacking. Do the same for the other half of the cut thread in the opposite direction.

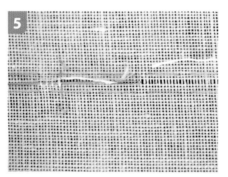

5 This thread has now been withdrawn but it needs securing. To do this, thread the needle with the withdrawn thread and re-weave it back into the fabric by four or five threads. Repeat on the opposite side so both ends of the cut thread are secure.

Tacking Not Essential

Tacking the area to be withdrawn is not essential; it is just a helpful step if you find it difficult to see the threads of the fabric. So, if you feel like you do not need to tack, skip this step and save some time!

6 Then repeat these steps for every thread that needs to be withdrawn. Only when all the threads have been withdrawn and re-woven should you trim away the excess thread. Do this carefully and one at a time.

This method of securing the threads will leave a shadow at either end of the worked band but is quite subtle.

Other Methods of Preparation

These methods of preparing for drawn thread are much more decorative than the re-weaving method and make quite a nice feature at either end of drawn-thread bands. Here I show buttonhole and straight satin-stitch examples, but any solidly worked stitch could work, so it is worth experimenting. The buttonhole technique given here is adapted from an original idea developed by Jenny Adin-Christie.

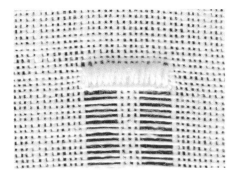

An example of the finished preparation using buttonhole stitch, worked in coton à broder 25.

An example of the finished preparation using satin stitch, worked in stranded cotton. The satin method is worked in the same way as the buttonhole, only you need to make sure that you pierce the threads of the linen as you work the satin as well as coming up through holes.

Buttonhole

Decide on the width of the withdrawn band, and work three rows of double running stitch across the width of the band. If you can, try to pierce the threads of the fabric. These stitches now form one end of the withdrawn band.

With your chosen thread, secure the thread within the rows of double running stitch. Then bring the needle up at the very end of the double running stitch and in the row of holes on the inside edge of the double running stitch.

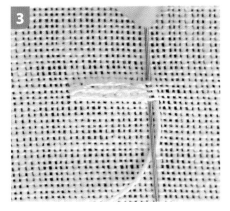

Take the needle down in the hole on the outer edge of the double running stitch and bring the needle back out in the same hole as before. Make sure that when you bring the needle back up it is sitting on top of the working thread.

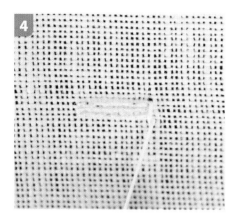

Pull the thread tight. This forms the first buttonhole stitch that encases the double running stitches.

Continue to work the buttonhole stitch, encasing the double running stitches. Make sure the stitches drop down and come up in every hole of the fabric as you work across. (If you are using a particularly fine thread you will also need to work buttonhole stitches that split the threads of the fabric.)

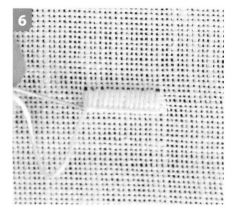

When you have covered the double running stitch completely and have worked the last buttonhole stitch, take the needle back down through the same hole but stitching over the last buttonhole stitch. This finishes off the buttonhole neatly. To secure the thread, turn the frame over and slide the needle through the buttonhole stitches on the back.

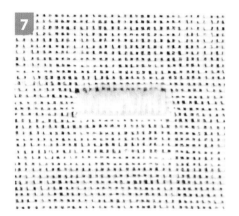

Now repeat the above steps for the other end of the withdrawn band. Make sure that buttonhole-stitch edges are stitched on the inside of the band and are therefore facing towards each other. If you have not tacked out the band in advance, make sure that the two ends of the withdrawn band correspond.

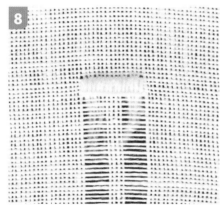

Slacken off the fabric in the frame and follow steps 2, 3 and 4 for the usual preparation. This time the threads are withdrawn till you reach the buttonhole edge. Make sure all the withdrawn threads are pulled to the back.

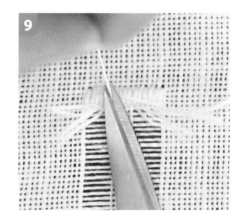

Turn the frame over and cut each of the withdrawn threads one at a time. Use very sharp scissors to do this. It also helps if you pull gently on each of the threads as you cut.

HEM STITCH

Most drawn-thread bands are hem-stitched along both edges. There a many different hem stitches and they are all quite decorative but they have a more important purpose. First, any hem stitch is the foundation for the decorative drawn-thread stitches. Its function is to secure and strengthen the edges where threads have been withdrawn, to stop the remaining threads from sliding. Hem stitches also gather together the exposed threads in groups on which the drawn-thread stitches are made.

The completed samples are worked in a strong lace thread but I have used a blue cotton thread to stitch the working samples for clarity.

Slanted Hem Stitch

This is the most basic form of hem stitch and should be worked from left to right along the edge of the withdrawn band. Make sure to pull these stitches tight in order to create clear groupings. In this sample I have stitched two threads of the linen below the band and grouped two threads of the linen within the band. However, this stitch works for any number of combinations with different effects being created.

Slanted hem stitch.

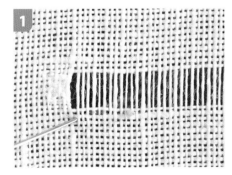

Using a tapestry needle, start the thread by tying a knot in the end and taking the needle down close to where you want to start stitching. Work two backstitches, each stitch being worked over a single thread of the linen. Bring the needle up at the start of the withdrawn band and two threads down from the edge.

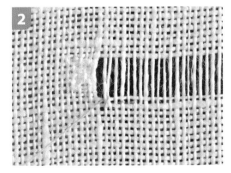

Make a diagonal stitch, passing the needle from right to left underneath two threads of the exposed fabric threads.

Take the needle back down in the same place, thereby looping over the same two exposed threads.

continued on the following page…

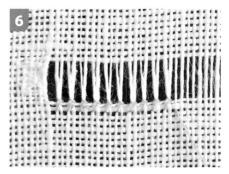

Bring the needle back up two threads directly below and *pull* the stitch tight. See how the exposed threads are gathered together.

Continue with the next diagonal stitch, passing the needle underneath the following two exposed threads.

Repeat these steps along the length of the withdrawn band, gathering two exposed fabric threads together. Make sure to *pull* each stitch tight in order to create clear groupings. When you reach the end, make two small backstitches hidden in the hem stitch to secure the thread.

Work the opposite edge in exactly the same way. It may be easier to turn the work around so you can work from left to right again.

Ladder Hem and Serpentine Hem

A ladder hem is created when the hem stitch on either side of the withdrawn band clusters together the same threads, thus forming ladder rungs. This means that an odd or even number of exposed threads can be grouped together.

A serpentine hem is created when the hem stitch on either side of the withdrawn band is offset. Therefore this only works when you group an even number of exposed threads together. In this example the bottom edge of the band gathers four exposed threads. When working the opposite edge, the first hem stitch only gathers two threads from the first cluster of four. The second stitch then takes the remaining two threads from the first cluster and two more from the second. This splits the groupings in half, creating a zigzag.

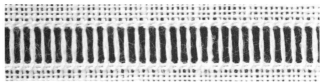

Ladder hem created with slanted hem stitch.

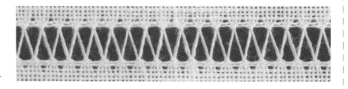

Serpentine hem created with slanted hem stitch.

Four-Sided Hem

This is another fairly basic hem stitch that creates quite a distinct edging. Although this is called four-sided hem, it only consists of three stitches – the side, the bottom and the top, worked in that order. It can therefore be worked either left to right or right to left. If you look on the reverse side, the stitches should form a cross. Make sure to pull these stitches tight in order to create clear groupings. In this sample I have stitched three threads of the linen below the band and grouped three threads of the linen within the band.

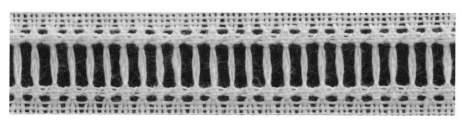

Four-sided hem stitch.

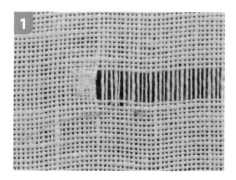

Using a tapestry needle, start the thread by tying a knot in the end and taking the needle down close to where you want to start stitching. Work two backstitches, each stitch being worked over a single thread of the linen. Bring the needle up at the start of the withdrawn band and three threads down from the edge.

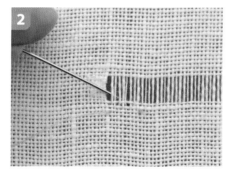

Make the first stitch vertically upwards, taking the needle down into the edge of the withdrawn band. This is the side stitch.

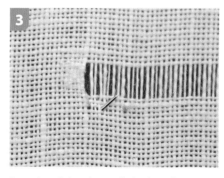

From there, bring the needle back up three threads of the linen to the right from where you first brought the needle up.

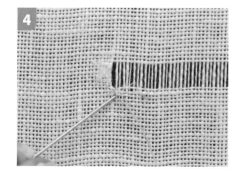

Make a horizontal stitch to the left, taking the needle back down over three threads of the linen and into the hole where you first brought the needle up. This is the bottom stitch.

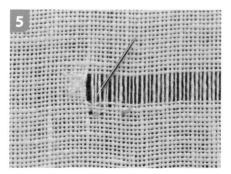

From here count three threads of the exposed fabric to the right and bring the needle up inside the band.

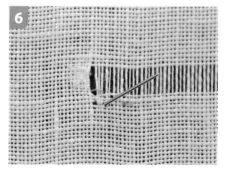

Make a second horizontal stitch to the left, over these three exposed threads and bring the needle back up three threads below where this horizontal stitch starts.

continued on the following page…

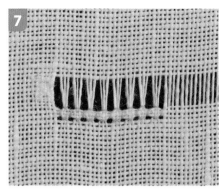

7

Make sure to *pull* every stitch tight. From this point, repeat these steps along the length of the band. When you reach the end, make two small backstitches hidden in the hem stitch to secure the thread.

Work the opposite edge in exactly the same way. It may be easier to turn the work around so you can work from left to right again.

Working in Reverse
You could also try working this stitch in reverse so that the cross sits on the front.

Chevron Hem

Chevron hem stitch is one of the most decorative hem stitches and it creates quite a deep border along the withdrawn band. For it to work effectively, you need to gather an even number of exposed threads, at least four, and also stitch at least three threads deep. This stitch is worked from left to right. In this example I have gathered four threads and worked three threads deep.

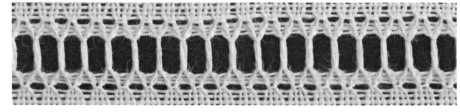

Chevron hem stitch.

Using a tapestry needle, start the thread by tying a knot in the end and taking the needle down close to where you want to start stitching. Work two backstitches, each stitch being worked over a single thread of the linen. Bring the needle up at the start of the withdrawn band and three threads down from the edge.

Make a diagonal stitch, passing the needle from right to left underneath two threads of the exposed fabric threads.

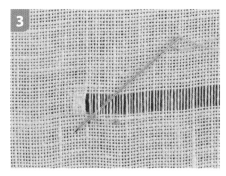

Then pass the needle from right to left underneath the next two threads of the exposed fabric threads.

Pull this stitch tight. When doing so make sure that the loop is sitting on top of the working thread.

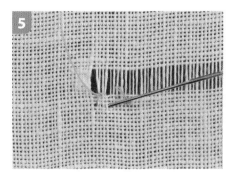

At this point your thread should be coming through the middle of this group of four threads. From here count three threads of the linen down and two to the right. Take the needle down at this point.

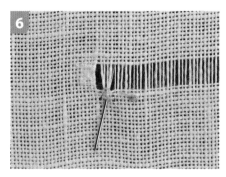

From here count two threads of the linen to the left and bring the needle up.

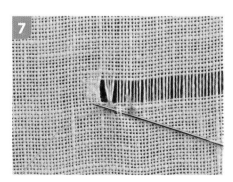

Then count four threads of the linen to the right, take the needle down and bring it back up, passing underneath two threads of the linen from right to left.

Pull this stitch tight. When doing so make sure that the loop is sitting on top of the working thread.

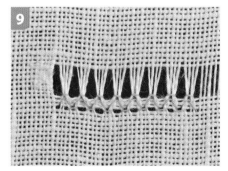

Make sure to *pull* every stitch tight. Repeat these steps along the length of the band. When you reach the end, make two small backstitches hidden in the hem stitch to secure the thread. Work the opposite edge in exactly the same way. It may be easier to turn the work around so you can work from left to right again.

Stem-Stitch Hem

Stem-stitch hem creates a very fine and delicate edge to a withdrawn band and is very quick to work. It will work for any combination of groupings but in this example I have made groups of three threads and stitched one thread into the edge. It can be worked from either left to right or right to left.

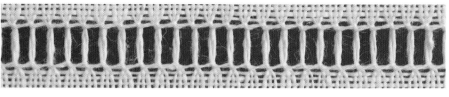

Stem-stitch hem.

Using a tapestry needle, start the thread by tying a knot in the end and taking the needle down close to where you want to start stitching. Work two backstitches, each stitch being worked over a single thread of the linen. Bring the needle up at the start of the withdrawn band and one thread down from the edge.

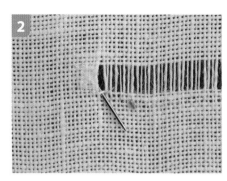

Make a diagonal stitch counting over three of the exposed fabric threads. Pass the needle underneath these three threads and bring the needle back up through the same hole as where you started. This is the first group of three.

Then make another long diagonal stitch counting over the next three of the exposed fabric threads.

Pass underneath these three threads and bring the needle back up one thread down from the edge. This is the second group of three. Make sure to *pull* each stitch tight.

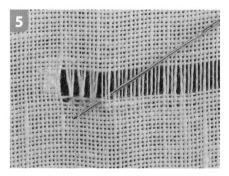

Continue to work in this way, with long stitches on the front and short stitches on the back.

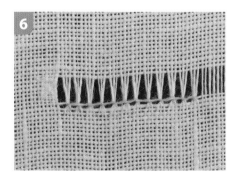

When you reach the end, make two small backstitches hidden in the hem stitch to secure the thread. Work the opposite edge in exactly the same way. It may be easier to turn the work around so you can work from left to right again.

OVERCASTING

Overcasting is another delicate and quick way to secure withdrawn edges and if worked in a fine thread can be barely visible, so it is great if you are working on very fine fabrics or delicate designs.

Overcast hem stitch.

Using a tapestry needle, start the thread by tying a knot in the end and taking the needle down close to where you want to start stitching. Work two backstitches, each stitch being worked over a single thread of the linen. Bring the needle up at the start of the withdrawn band and two threads down from the edge.

Make a diagonal stitch counting over two threads of the exposed fabric threads, taking the needle down into the edge of the withdrawn band.

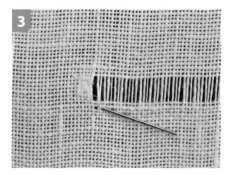

From here count two threads of the linen down into the edge of the withdrawn band and bring the needle back up.

This can be worked in movement, which makes this stitch very quick to work. Continue to work these stitches across the length of the withdrawn band.

When you reach the end, work two backstitches within the hen to secure the thread. Work the opposite edge in exactly the same way. It may be easier to turn the work around so you can work from left to right again.

DRAWN-THREAD STITCHES

KNOTTED BAND

Knotted band is one of the more simple drawn-thread stitches, but it can be highly decorative. It can be worked on a band with either an odd or an even number of exposed threads. This is also a good stitch for any size of band. In this sample ten threads have been withdrawn, the hem stitch gathers threads into groups of two and the knotting gathers two groups. Try experimenting with a larger band and having more than one row of knotting stitches for a more intricate effect. This stitch can be worked either left to right or right to left.

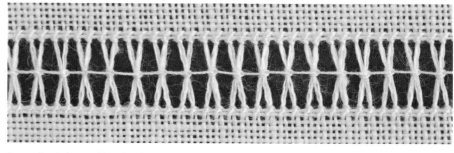

A sample of a knotted band with a slanted hem stitch.

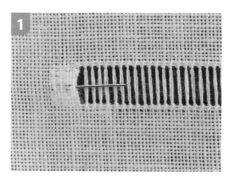

Start with two backstitches in the end of the band to secure the thread. Then bring the needle up in the centre of the band and just inside the edge.

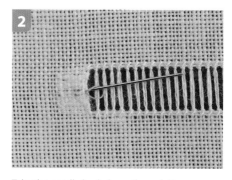

Take the needle back down through the same point and leave a small loop on the surface. Bring the needle up through the first gap and through this loop and pull tight.

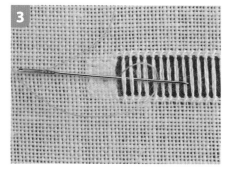

Then pass the needle underneath the first two groups. Loop the thread clockwise, making sure that the needle sits on top of the working thread.

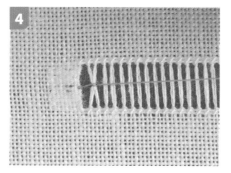

Pull the thread tight. You may need to pull the thread upwards or back on itself first to make sure it is at the right tension before pulling in the direction of the stitch.

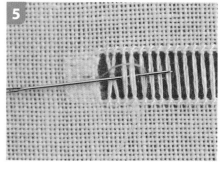

Then move on to stitch the next set of two groups and repeat till you reach the end of the band. Secure the threads with two stab stitches hidden in the end of the band. You need to make sure that the thread is pulled tight in between each stitch along the length of the band.

CHAIN BAND

Chain band is another simple drawn-thread stitch and is based on the original chain stitch. It can be worked on a band with either an odd or an even number of exposed threads. This is also a good stitch for any size of band. In this sample ten threads have been withdrawn, the hem stitch gathers threads into groups of two and the chain gathers two groups. Try experimenting with a larger band and having more than one row of chain stitches worked in opposite directions.

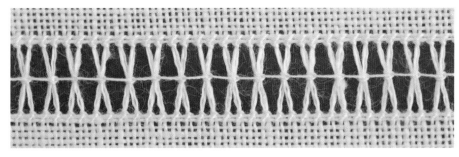

A sample of a chain band with a slanted-hem stitch.

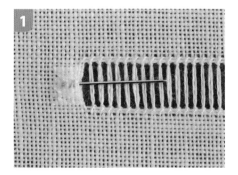

Start with two backstitches in the end of the band to secure the thread. Then bring the needle up in the centre of the band and just inside the edge.

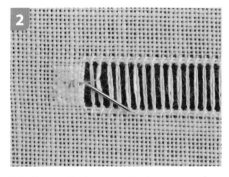

Take the needle down over the two groups of threads. Bring the needle back up in the first gap and below the working thread.

Take the needle back down through the first gap but above the working thread, and leave a small loop on the surface.

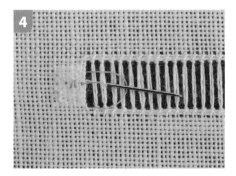

Pass the needle underneath the first two groups of thread and bring the needle back up inside the loop.

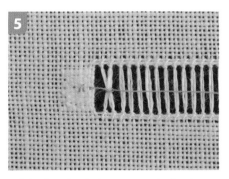

Pull the thread tight, but not so tight that the form of the stitch disappears. You still want to be able to see that it is a chain stitch.

Then move on to stitch the next set of two groups and repeat till you reach the end of the band. Secure the threads with two stab stitches hidden in the end of the band. You need to make sure that the thread is pulled tight in between each stitch along the length of the band.

TWISTED BAND

Twisted bands are really beautiful even in their simplest form. However, they can look really elaborate if worked on a wide band with multiple rows being worked. This sample has fourteen threads withdrawn. The hem stitch gathers threads into groups of two and the twist, twists two groups of two. It sounds confusing but it will work! You can then try experimenting with a larger band and having more than one row of twists and different types of thread or ribbon for different effects. This stitch can be worked from either left to right or right to left.

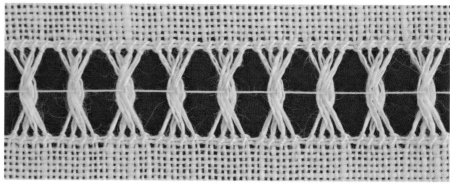

A sample of a twisted band with a slanted hem stitch.

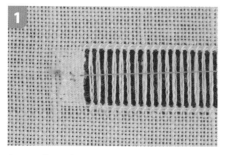

Start with two backstitches in the end of the band to secure the thread. Then bring the needle up in the centre of the band and just inside the edge.

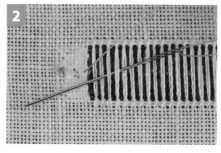

Pass the needle over four groups of threads and then underneath the last two. The needle should be pointing in the opposite direction to the way you are stitching.

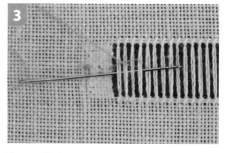

The needle then passes over the first two groups and is taken down into the first gap. Pass the needle underneath all four groups and bring the needle back up. The needle should now be pointing in the direction you are stitching.

Then *pull* the stitch tight. This pulls the groups in opposite directions so they twist over and under each other.

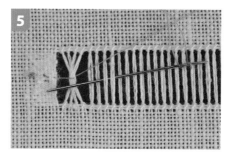

Then move on to the next set of four groups and repeat.

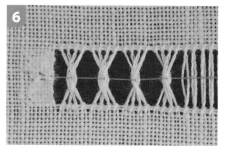

This stitch can be worked in one motion; when the needle is pointing in the opposite direction, flip it over to point it in the right direction (the way the stitch is travelling). You will know if you have done it right because the threads will twist into position round the needle. When you reach the end of the band, secure the thread with two stab stitches hidden in the end of the band. You need to make sure that the thread is pulled tight along the length of the band.

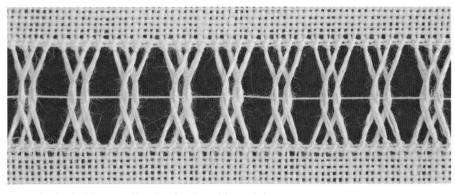

A sample of a double-twisted band with a slanted-hem stitch.

Double-twist bands sound complicated but they are not. They are worked in the same way as a basic twisted band. This time, however, you treat each group individually, rather than two sets of two groups. First twist group three over group one, then twist group four over group two. Simple!

Two-way twist bands are best worked on a larger band. Bring the needle up about one third up from the bottom edge of the band and follow the above steps. When you reach the end, secure the thread and bring the needle back up one third down from the top edge of the band. Repeat the steps but in the opposite direction.

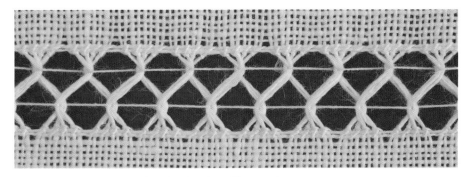

A sample of a two-way twisted band with a slanted-hem stitch.

OVERCAST BARS

Overcast bars are really simple to work and make a bold ladder-like effect across the withdrawn band. In this sample ten threads have been withdrawn, the hem stitch gathers two threads in a group and three groups are stitched into one overcast bar. This stitch is best worked on a narrow band and can be worked from either left to right or right to left. Try experimenting with a zigzag-like effect that can also be created by grouping two bars together alternately at the top and bottom edges of the band.

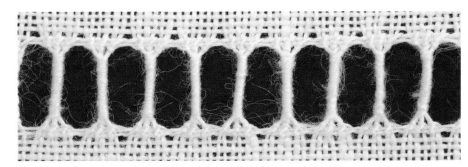

A sample of overcast bars with a slanted-hem stitch.

continued on the following page…

Start with two backstitches in the end of the band to secure the thread. Then work a few backstitches over one thread of the linen along the bottom edge of the hem. Bring the needle up in the first gap.

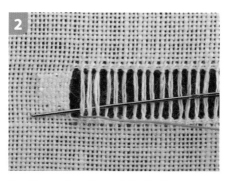

Pass the needle underneath the first three groups from right to left. *Pull* this stitch tight.

Continue wrapping over the three groups from right to left until you reach the opposite side of the band to complete one overcast bar. *Pull* every stitch tight.

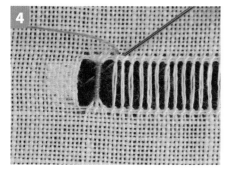

When you reach the top of the bar, make a small backstitch hidden in the hem stitch above the completed bar. To move on to the next bar, make another backstitch hidden in the hem above where the new bar starts. Repeat this, working across the band and stitching the bars from top to bottom then bottom to top. When you reach the end of the band, secure the thread with two stab stitches hidden in the end of the band. You need to make sure to *pull* all the stitches to the same tension to get even-looking bars.

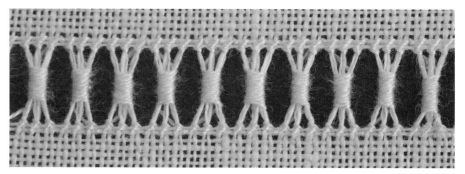

This sample shows overcast bars stitched with a looser tension on the thread and the stitching concentrated to the middle of the band. Experiment to see what other effects can be created by overcasting different groupings with different tensions.

NEEDLE WEAVING

Needle-woven blocks and bars are really simple to work and can make simple or extremely complicated patterns across a withdrawn band. In this sample a double row of needle-woven blocks are created. Ten threads have been withdrawn, the hem stitch gathers two threads in a group and two groups are stitched into each needle-woven block. This stitch can be worked from either left to right or right to left. Try experimenting with wide bands to create highly patterned needle-woven bands.

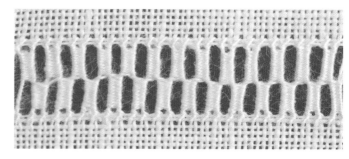

A sample of overcast bars with a slanted hem stitch.

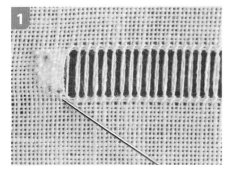

Start with two backstitches in the end of the band to secure the thread. Then work a few backstitches over one thread of the linen and bring the needle up at the bottom edge of the withdrawn band just inside the hem.

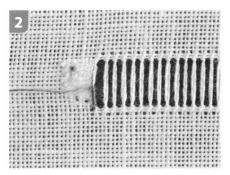

Overcast-stitch the first group from right to left until you reach the middle of the withdrawn band.

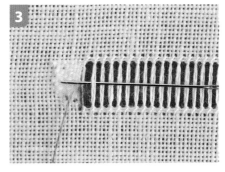

Then introduce the next group and begin to needle-weave. Pass the needle over then underneath the new group and up through the middle of the two groups.

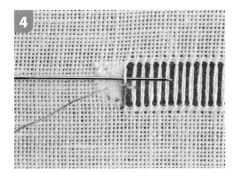

Then pass the needle over and underneath the first group, bringing the needle up in between the two groups.

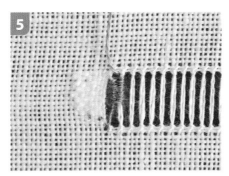

Continue to needle-weave over and under each group till you reach the top of the band. This is the first needle-woven block. Try not to pull the needle-weaving too tight as it will distort the threads too much and give an uneven finish.

To start the next needle-woven block, slide the needle through the back of the needle-woven block and out into the centre of the withdrawn band. The thread is now in the correct position to start the second woven block.

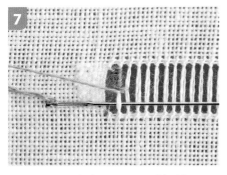

Continue to stitch the next woven block by introducing a new group. When each new block is complete, always slide the needle through the back and out into the centre of the band in order to start the next block. Try to keep an even tension on the thread across the whole band so all the woven blocks look the same. When you reach the end of the band you will need to overcast-stitch a group like you did to start the band. Secure the thread with two backstitches hidden in the end of the band.

Ladder Needle-Woven Bars

Simple ladder needle-woven bars can be created by weaving from one edge of the withdrawn band to the other, just like working the overcast bars but weaving instead.

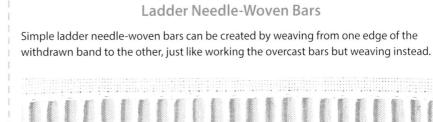

ALTERNATIVE BANDS

There are hundreds of drawn-thread stitches, fillings and hem stitches, too many to include in one chapter, so once you understand how basic drawn-thread bands work, experiment with the different hem and decorative stitches to see the different effects you can create. Also experiment with different threads and materials to embellish your drawn bands. Here are some samples to give you a few ideas.

Instead of thread, use a fine silk ribbon to decorate withdrawn bands. Ribbon can be used in many of the drawn-thread stitches and looks great in twisted bands or simply woven through the exposed threads like in this sample.

Try adding beads in between each stitch or twist. In this sample a single clear glass bead is added in between each chain stitch. You could use white beads or pearls too.

Depending on the scale of the withdrawn band, larger objects can be added for statement embellishments, such as small shells or tiny buttons, sequins or spangles.

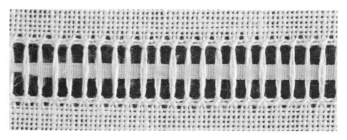

A sample of 2mm (1⁄16in) silk ribbon woven in between simple ladder bars with slanted hem stitch.

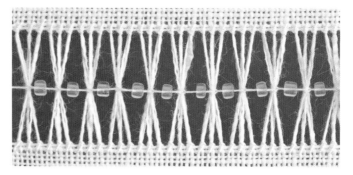

A sample of a chain band with a tiny glass bead threaded in between each chain stitch with slanted hem.

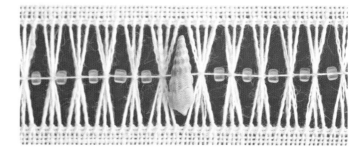

A sample of a chain band with a tiny glass bead threaded in between each chain stitch; in the centre a tiny auger shell is used instead of a bead.

Re-Weaving Broken Threads

If the worst happens and a thread of the ground fabric snaps or you cut too many threads by mistake, this is a quick and simple way of re-weaving it, in the most inconspicuous way. This technique does not just work for drawn thread, but within many techniques and different types of fabric, where the grains of the fabric play an important role in how the stitches are supported or counted.

I have chosen to demonstrate the method within a drawn band but it could easily be worked in the same way on fabric where no threads have been withdrawn.

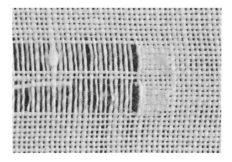

You can see how the thread has been cut by mistake, and too close to where the withdrawn threads are being woven in.

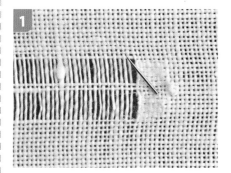

Take a thread of the ground fabric from the edge of a spare piece of fabric, making sure that it is at least 20cm (8in) longer than the area that needs to be re-woven. Tie a knot in one end and thread the other into an embroidery needle. Take the needle down into the grain of fabric that has been cut/snapped, about 5–10mm (¼in) away from where the thread has been broken. Start the re-weaving process by bringing the needle back up to the surface, piercing the broken thread.

Begin re-weaving the thread so it follows the original weave. Make sure to pierce the broken thread as you do so till you reach the point where the thread is broken.

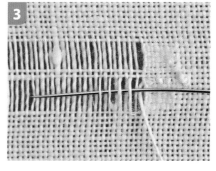

Continue to re-weave the thread, now going under and over the original grains of fabric that are running in the opposite direction. Make sure that you replicate the original weave of the fabric.

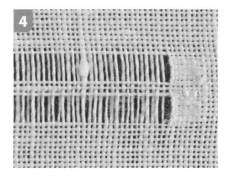

When you have re-woven the thread and reach the other side of the gap, secure the thread in the same way that you started by continuing to re-weave, but piercing the original grain for about 5–10mm (¼in). You can then bring the needle up to the surface and trim away. The re-weave is now secure at both ends as discreetly as possible so you can continue with your planned stitching.

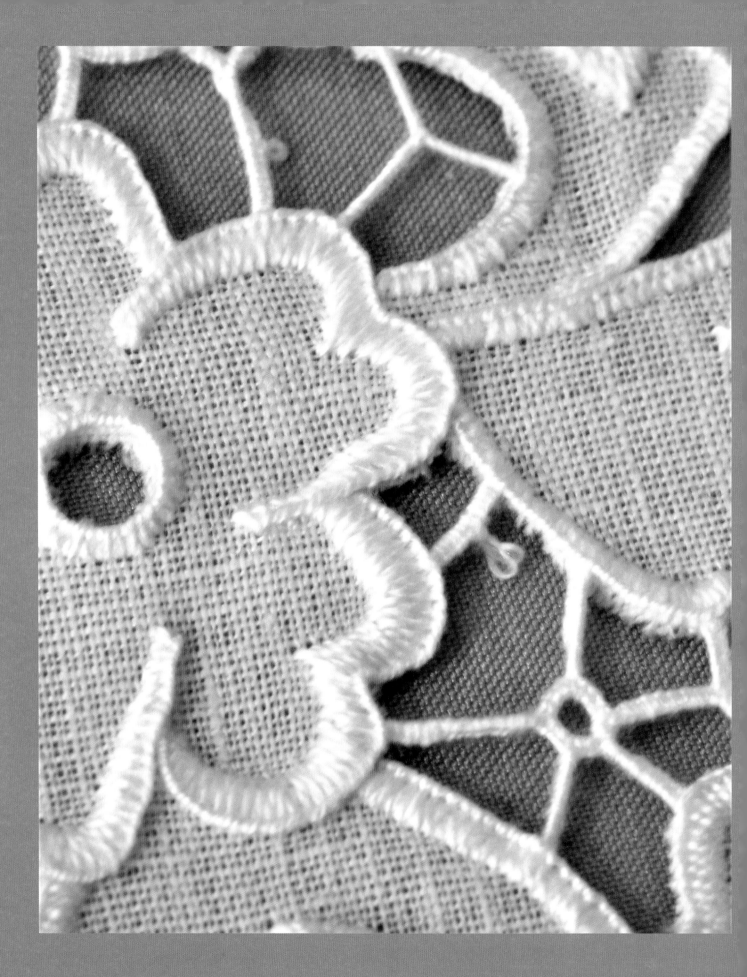

CHAPTER 6

CUTWORK

Cutwork is a bold whitework embroidery technique where parts of the background fabric are cut away leaving the design in solid areas, held in place with bars and buttonhole stitch. Cutwork designs can be very simple to extremely intricate and detailed.

There are four main modern forms of cutwork. These are Simple cutwork, Renaissance cutwork, Richelieu cutwork and Venetian cutwork. For each of these forms of cutwork the method of stitching and the stitches used are basically the same; it is the style and intricacy of the design that identifies each form.

In Simple cutwork, the areas that are cut out are quite small, and the cut-out spaces are designed in such a way that no shape within the design is completely detached in any way. This gives Simple cutwork designs a layering-type effect, as if each part of the design sits on top of one another.

Renaissance cutwork is slightly more decorative. The cut-out areas are slightly larger and therefore need to be strengthened and supported with bars or brides, and these bars are what gives Renaissance cutwork a more lace-like feel. The placement of the bars is fundamental, not only to the design

A sample showing Simple cutwork.

A sample showing Renaissance cutwork.

A sample showing Richelieu cutwork.

A sample showing Venetian cutwork.

of Renaissance cutwork embroidery but also structurally. In Renaissance cutwork the bars may be buttonholed, needle-woven or wrapped. When the spaces are too large for a single bar, bars can be branched or spider's web fillings can be used to join different edges.

Richelieu cutwork is very similar to Renaissance cutwork, and the two are often confused. In Richelieu cutwork the cut-out areas become even larger and the bars create an even lacier feel with the addition of decorative picots.

Venetian cutwork is also known as Padded cutwork and is almost a combination of the other forms of cutwork. It can be designed with or without bars, but Venetian cutwork's main feature is that it is enhanced by padding. The outlines are bolder, and vary in shape and size according to the design; they are also padded, creating a raised effect. Any surface embroidery is also padded.

Traditionally, all forms and styles of cutwork are worked with two rows of single running stitch around the outlines. If bars are needed and when bars are reached, they are worked in full and then the running-stitch outline is continued. When the running-stitch outlines and the bars are complete, the outline is then overworked with buttonhole stitch.

I however work in a slightly different way, which I find easier because there is less stopping and starting, and the threads do not become as worn and fluffy when I create the bars. The overall look is no different, but there is less thread waste. I find it much quicker to work, but most importantly the edges and bars look much neater and cleaner.

Stitch all the outlines first, using a double running stitch. This requires twice as much stitching, so it does take slightly longer, but I find it gives a much cleaner, firmer outline, which makes the buttonhole stitching neater and much faster to stitch. When the outlines are complete, then work your bars. You will find that your bars look much finer and cleaner and are more secure when they are stitched with new thread. If the bars are close together you can travel from one to the next with tiny stab stitches in between the rows of double running stitches. For bars that are further away, it is better to start and finish each bar separately.

All the cutwork samples have been worked on a 55TPI Kingston linen.

PREPARATION

Draw the design on to your chosen fabric in blue pencil. For cutwork, a closely woven fabric works best. The outlines are then stitched in double running stitch. A second row of double running stitch is then worked on the inside of the first. Depending on the design, this second row should be very close to the first unless you are working a design that is more like Venetian cutwork, in which case the second outline is included

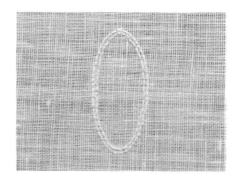

Cutwork shape outlined with two rows of double running stitch.

in the design. If you need to, draw this second line in blue pencil too. Use a single strand of stranded cotton to stitch the double running outlines, as it creates a firm and strong foundation but is not too bulky.

PLAIN BARS

Plain bars are what would be used if creating Renaissance cutwork embroidery. Although plain in themselves, the bars are used to add decoration. They are also used for structural support.

BUTTONHOLE BARS

Buttonhole bars are the strongest and most widely used bar in cutwork. In this sample, the three buttonhole bars have been worked in different threads. The top is worked in coton à broder 30, the middle in a single strand of stranded cotton and the bottom in perle 12. The buttonhole outline is worked in coton à broder 30.

Cutwork shape with three buttonhole bars.

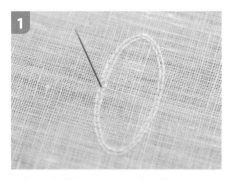

With the double-running-stitch outlines complete, anchor the new thread in between the outlines and bring the needle up in between the two rows of double running stitch, where you want the first bar to sit.

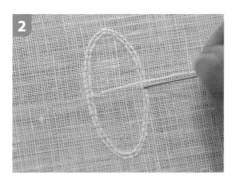

Take the needle down on the opposite side of the shape, in between the two rows of double running stitch. This will create a long stitch that sits across the width of the shape. This is the foundation for your bar.

Working Direction

Bars can be worked either right to left, or left to right. It will depend on the design and where you choose to start working the bars. These samples show bars being started from left to right, but if you chose to work from right to left the method is the same.

Bring the needle back up just next to this first long stitch, and make a second long stitch, taking the needle back down on the opposite side.

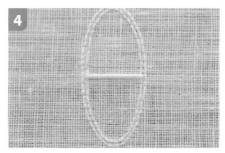

Repeat this to make a third long stitch. The foundation for the bar is now complete. The three bars should be sitting on top of each other and should be taut across the surface of the fabric. For extra security, make a small stab stitch in between the double running outlines. The needle should be on the opposite side from where you started.

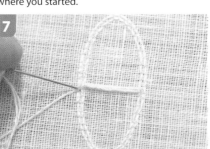

Bring the needle back up, just next to where the third bar ends. Begin to work an even buttonhole stitch, encasing the three foundation stitches. Make sure not to catch the ground fabric or pierce the foundation bars. Use the eye of the needle to help with this or change to a tapestry needle.

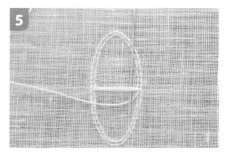

Make sure the buttonhole is pulled tight and even. There should be no gaps in between the buttonhole stitches.

When you have buttonhole-stitched over the bar and reached the opposite side, take the needle down in between the double running outlines and secure the thread. Make sure that the very ends of the foundation bars are still visible in the double-running-stitch outline. The buttonhole stitch should not encroach into the double running outline. Make as many bars as are needed.

When all the bars are complete, cut a new length of thread and secure as before in between the double running outline. Work the buttonhole outline so it completely covers both rows of double running stitch. Make sure to work the buttonhole so that the looped edge sits along the side of the outline that will later be cut away. When you reach the bars, bring the needle up where you need to, piercing the very ends of the bars to get a smooth, neat outline.

continued on the following page…

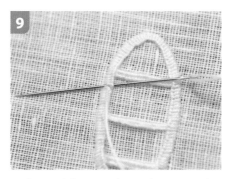

Work around the entire shape. When you reach where you started and have made the last buttonhole stitch, thread the needle through the first loop formed by the first buttonhole stitch, then take the needle down and secure. Doing this will give the effect of an unbroken line of buttonhole stitch. Then finish the thread with stab stitches hidden in the buttonhole.

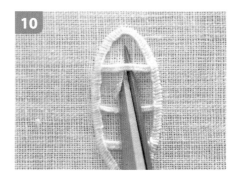

With the bars and buttonhole outline now complete, the fabric can be cut away. The first step is so make a small hole with a stiletto in the middle of the shape. Then make a cut running through the middle of the shape. Make sure you *do not* cut through any bars or the buttonhole outline.

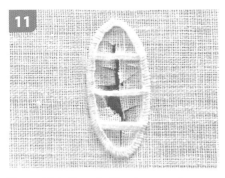

Then cut into the rest of the shape, creating small flaps, cutting right up to the buttonhole edge. Take care not to cut the bars or the buttonhole edge.

You now need to loosen the embroidery in the frame, so the fabric is no longer under tension but is still supported. Then turn the frame over. You will now work on the back of the frame.

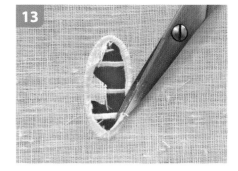

Very carefully trim away these flaps. I find it helpful to hold the flap in my free hand when I make the cut. Try to cut as close to the buttonhole edge as you can.

At this point, tidy the buttonhole by running a pair of tweezers or a finger nail along the cut edge. This will expose any fibres that have been missed.

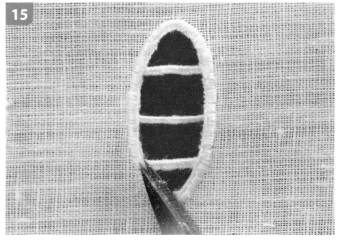

Very carefully re-trim the edge, cutting as close to the buttonhole as you possibly can. Do this as many times as it takes till you are happy with the finished edge. It can help to turn the frame over again, and check from the front if the cut edge is visible or the buttonhole is hiding it successfully.

OVERCAST BARS

Overcast bars look slightly more delicate than other forms of bars, as they are less bulky. Overcast bars work best for smaller, narrower spaces. In this sample, the three overcast bars have been worked in different threads. The top is worked in coton à broder 30, the middle in a single strand of stranded cotton and the bottom in perle 12. The buttonhole outline is worked in perle 12. For this sample I also show the traditional method of using two rows of single-running-stitch outlines.

Cutwork shape with three overcast bars.

With the running-stitch outlines complete, anchor the new thread in between the outlines and bring the needle up in between the two rows of running stitch, where you want the first bar to sit. Create the three foundation bars as before, travelling back and forth, from one side of the shape to the other.

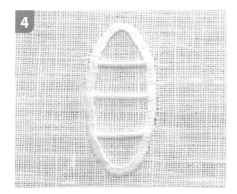

Bring the needle up, just next to where the third bar ends. Overcast the foundation bars by wrapping the bar tightly. Each new wrap should sit right up the last, and there should be no gaps in between the wraps. Make sure not to catch the ground fabric or the foundation bars.

When you have overcast the bar and reached the opposite side, take the needle down in between the running-stitch outlines and secure the thread. Make sure that the very ends of the foundation bars are still visible in the running-stitch outlines. The overcast bar should sit taut and flat across the shape. Make as many bars as are needed.

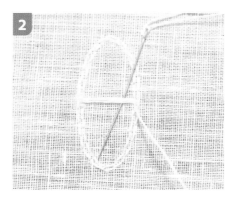

When all the overcast bars are complete, cut a new length of thread and work the buttonhole-stitch outline as previously described. With the buttonhole outline complete, you can then cut away the fabric as previously described.

Needle-Woven Bars

Woven bars are the widest and flattest form of bars and are best used for wider, more open areas of cutwork. In this sample, the three woven bars have been worked in different threads. The top is worked in coton à broder 30, the middle in a single strand of stranded cotton and the bottom in perle 12. The buttonhole outline is worked in a single strand of stranded cotton.

Cutwork shape with three woven bars.

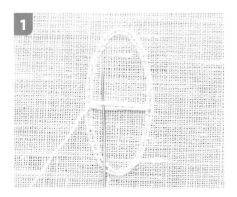

With the double-running-stitch outlines complete, anchor the new thread in between the outlines and bring the needle up in between the two rows of double running stitch, where you want the first bar to sit. This time create *four* foundation threads as before, travelling back and forth, from one side of the shape to the other. Bring the needle up, just next to where the fourth bar ends, ready to start needle-weaving.

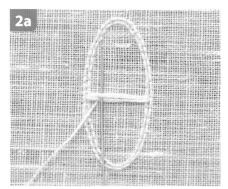
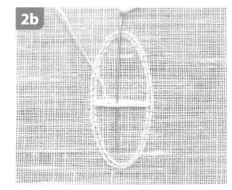

Carefully separate the four foundation bars into two sets of two. Begin to needle-weave over then under the two sets of two foundation bars. Take care not to catch the ground fabric or the foundation bars when doing this. The needle-weaving should be neat and firm, encasing and pulling together the separated foundation bars.

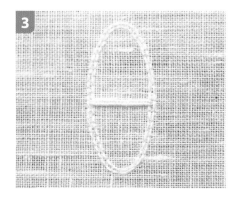

When the needle-woven bar is complete, take the needle down in between the double-running-stitch outlines and secure the thread. Make sure that the very ends of the foundation bars are still visible in the running-stitch outlines. Make as many bars as are needed.

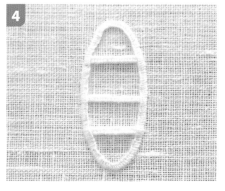

When all the needle-woven bars are complete, cut a new length of thread and work the buttonhole-stitch outline as previously described. With the buttonhole outline complete, you can then cut away the fabric as previously described.

BRANCHED BARS

For larger areas of cutwork, a single straight bar is not enough to act as a support. Rather than having lots of individual straight bars, a long bar may be branched, supporting multiple edges and being more decorative at the same time.

SIMPLE-BRANCHED BAR

A simple-branched bar is where a long single bar has one branch extending from it in a different direction. This sample has been worked in buttonhole stitch but branched bars can also be overcast. The thread used is coton à broder 30.

Cutwork shape with a simple-branched bar worked in buttonhole stitch.

As before, work the double-running-stitch outline and create the three foundation bars. Begin to buttonhole-stitch back across the bar and stop where the branch will extend.

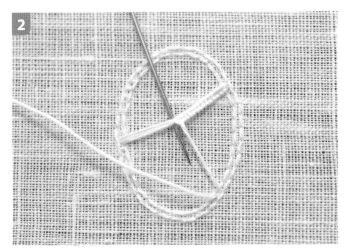

Make three new branched foundation bars in the same way as before, taking the needle down in between the double-running-stitch outlines and wrapping round the original foundation bars.

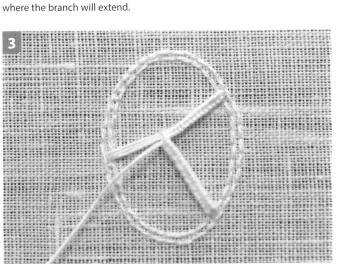

Work the buttonhole stitch back across the branched foundation bars until the original bar is reached.

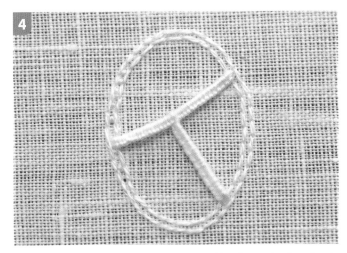

Then continue buttonhole-stitching the original bar. Secure the thread and complete the shape as previously described.

Multiple-Branched Bar

A multiple-branched bar is much like the simple-branched bar only it has more branches extending from the long single bar. These extra branches can go in any direction. This sample has been worked in buttonhole stitch but branched bars can also be overcast. The thread used is coton à broder 30.

Cutwork shape with buttonhole multiple-branched bar.

Work the double-running-stitch outline as before and create the three foundation bars. Begin to buttonhole-stitch back across the foundation bars and stop where the first branch will extend.

Make three new branched foundation bars as previously described. Buttonhole-stitch over the branched foundation bars then continue buttonhole-stitching the original bar as before. Stop where the second branch will extend.

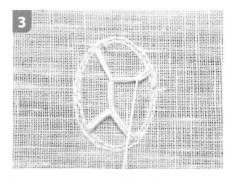

Create three new branched foundation bars for the second branch as before and buttonhole-stitch back to the original bar.

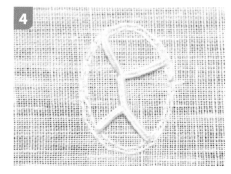

Continue like this till all the branched bars have been completed. Then, like before, buttonhole-stitch the final length of the original bar. Secure the thread and complete the shape as previously described.

Spider's Webs

Spider's webs are another way of supporting multiple edges across larger cutwork areas. These spider's webs are still strong enough to support large cutwork areas but are a more delicate and decorative alternative to branched bars.

Woven Spider's Web

The main thing to remember when creating a woven spider's web is that there will always be an odd number of spokes in order for the woven centre to work correctly. As the spider's webs are more delicate, a stronger, thicker thread needs to be used to stitch them, such as coton à broder or perle threads. This sample has been worked in coton à broder 30.

Cutwork shape with woven spider's web.

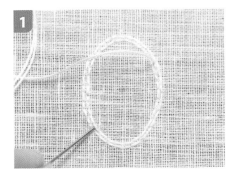

Prepare the outlines as previously described. Mark on the fabric where you want the centre of the spider's web to be; this is fine to do as the fabric will be cut away later. With a new thread, make the first long stitch across the shape, taking the needle down in between the double-running-stitch outlines.

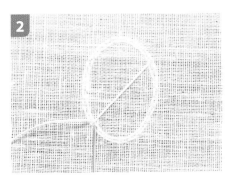

Bring the needle back up and make a tiny stab stitch, again in between the outlines. This secures the long stitch.

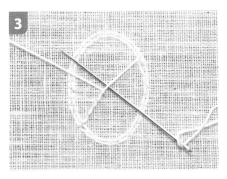

Then bring the needle back up just next to the long stitch and loosely wrap back up the long stitch to the centre.

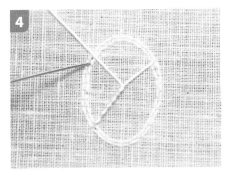

From there, create another stitch to the outlines and secure a with a stab stitch.

Then loosely wrap back up along the stitch to the centre and throw another stitch out to the outlines. Continue to create new spokes in this way, making sure that in the end there will be an odd number of spokes.

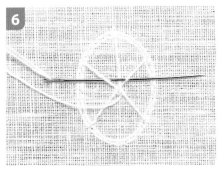

When the last spoke is made and has been loosely wrapped to the centre point, all the spokes are then secured by weaving under and over each spoke around the centre point.

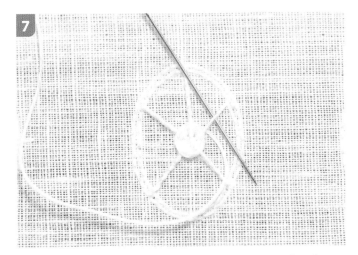

Work round and round the centre, weaving over then under each spoke as many times as you like. The weaving always needs to finish at the original spoke, which is then loosely wrapped back to the outlines, where the thread can then be secured.

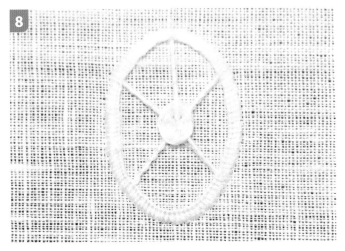

The outline can then be worked in buttonhole stitch and the fabric cut away as previously described.

Detached Spider's Web

Detached spider's web rings can be quite fiddly to work, especially if you make the detached buttonhole ring very small, but they look beautiful when finished so are well worth the effort. The size of the detached buttonhole ring will depend on what you use to wrap the thread around.

For this sample I used the tip of a number 5 knitting needle, so the buttonhole ring is quite large. For really tiny detached buttonhole rings, use a very large tapestry needle or the tip of a fine paintbrush to wrap the threads around. Whatever you use, make sure it is clean before using it. This sample has been stitched with coton à broder 30.

Cutwork shape with detached spider's web.

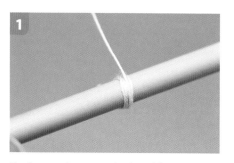

The first step is to wrap the thread five or six times around the knitting needle/paintbrush/pencil/large needle. Then, keeping the wraps together, carefully slide them off the end.

With the same length of thread, carefully work buttonhole stitch all the way around the wraps, making sure the looped edge of the buttonhole is on the outside of the ring. To secure the end of the buttonhole stitch, carefully slide the needle through a few of the buttonhole stitches and cut away excess thread. The detached buttonhole ring should look like this.

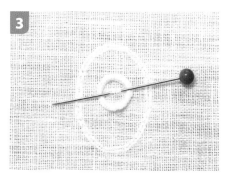

Prepare the outlines as previously described, then pin the detached ring into position on the fabric.

Then start a new thread and secure as before. Make a stitch from the outline into the centre and take the needle through, just catching the looped edge of the detached buttonhole ring. This creates the first spoke.

Loosely wrap this spoke back to the outline and secure with a tiny stab stitch. Then work around the shape to make the next spoke with tiny stab stitches.

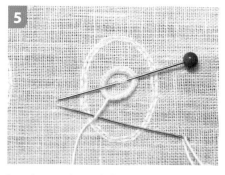

Work all the spokes in this way. Depending on the size and shape of the cutwork area, five or six spokes should be enough to hold the detached buttonhole ring in place. When all the spokes have been worked, the pin can be removed, the buttonhole-stitch outline can be worked and the fabric can then be cut away as previously described.

Keep Practice Rings

I always make two or three detached rings, one after another, then pick the best one to use. As they say, practice makes perfect, but keep the ones you do not use this time, as you might use them at a later date.

DECORATIVE BARS

Decorative bars are basically the same as plain bars with the addition of picots. They are traditionally what would be used if creating Richelieu or Venetian cutwork embroidery. The bars are formed in the same way but the addition of picots makes the bars much more decorative, and gives cutwork embroidery a more lacy and intricate quality.

LOOPED PICOT

Looped picots are the simplest and easiest to work. The bars themselves can be buttonholed, overcast or woven, and any thread can be used to make them. This sample has been stitched in coton à broder 30. This sample also shows the buttonhole bar being worked from right to left but it can also be worked from left to right.

Prepare the outlines and stitch the bar as previously explained, until you reach the point where you want the looped picot to sit.

Cutwork shape with buttonhole bar and looped picot.

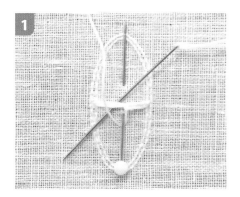

Insert a pin into the fabric where the looped picot will sit. Where the pin is inserted in relation to the bar will determine the length of the picot. Then slip the working thread underneath the pin. Pass the needle underneath the bar on the other side of the pin and pull tight so the loop sits around the pin. Make sure *not* to catch the fabric or the bar as you do this.

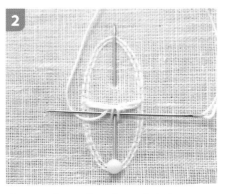

Then pass the needle underneath the loop formed around the pin from right to left. The needle then passes underneath, then over the working thread in order to create another buttonhole stitch that will secure the looped picot in place.

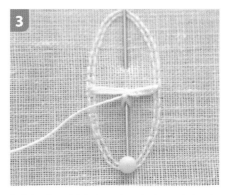

Pull the thread tightly, so that the looped picot is secure, and remove the pin.

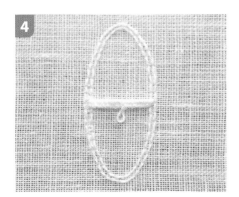

The rest of the bar is then worked in buttonhole stitch as before. The rest of the cutwork shape can then be completed as previously described.

BULLION PICOT

Bullion picots, are a little more fiddly to work, and are worked much like usual bullion knots. Bullion knots are also a little more bulky even when worked in finer threads so they make quite a statement. For bullion picots, the bars are best worked in buttonhole. This sample has been stitched in coton à broder 30. This sample also shows the buttonhole bar being worked from right to left but it can also be worked from left to right.

Prepare the outlines and stitch the bar as previously explained, until you reach the point where you want the bullion picot to sit.

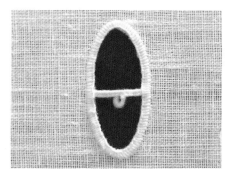

Cutwork shape with buttonhole bar and bullion picot.

When the last buttonhole stitch has been made, insert the needle through the loop of this last buttonhole stitch.

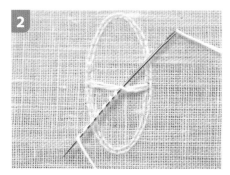

Then wrap the working thread five or six times around the needle. With your finger and thumb, push the wraps down the needle so they sit against the edge of the buttonhole bar, then pull the needle through.

Continue working the buttonhole bar as before, making sure that there is no gap in between the buttonhole stitches where the bullion picot sits. The rest of the cutwork shape can then be completed as previously described.

BUTTONHOLE PICOT

Buttonhole picots are the most decorative out of all the picots. The bars themselves can be buttonholed, overcast or woven, but I find that buttonholed looks the best. Again, any thread can be used to make them and this sample has been stitched in coton à broder 30. This sample also shows the buttonhole bar being worked from right to left but it can also be worked from left to right.

Prepare the outlines and stitch the bar as previously explained, until you reach the point where you want the buttonhole picot to sit.

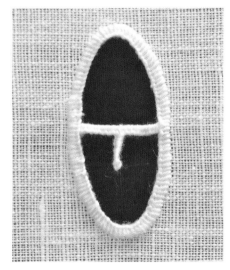

Cutwork shape with buttonhole bar and buttonhole picot.

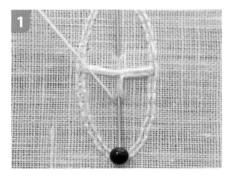

Insert a pin into the fabric where the buttonhole picot will sit. Where the pin is inserted in relation to the bar will determine the length of the picot. Buttonhole picots can be made slightly longer than looped picots. Then slip the working thread underneath the pin.

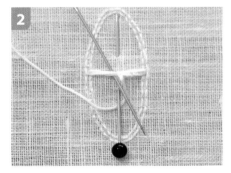

Pass the needle underneath the bar on the other side of the pin and back over the working thread. Pull tight so the loop sits around the pin. Make sure *not* to catch the fabric or the bar as you do this.

Now slip the thread underneath the pin once more, making a second loop. The needle is then passed from right to left into the two loops.

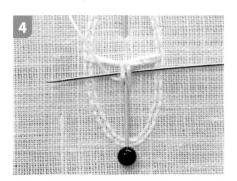

Pull tight and a knot is formed at the tip of the bar.

Then work buttonhole stitch down the rest of the picot, making sure that all the picot is encased in buttonhole stitch.

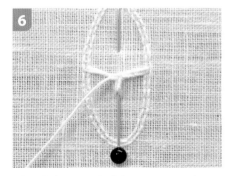

When the bar is reached, the picot is complete, and you can continue working the buttonhole bar as before. The rest of the cutwork shape can then be completed as previously described.

ISOLATED SHAPES

Isolated shapes can be created using cutwork techniques. This is where a smaller design shape is suspended within a large area of cutwork. In this example it is just a simple circle, suspended but supported by bars within a larger cutwork shape. However, any shape can be worked as long its outline can be worked in buttonhole stitch. The number of bars used to support the isolated shape will depend on the design as whole. Any thread can be used to work isolated shapes and this sample has been stitched in coton à broder 30.

Isolated circle within an area of cutwork supported with buttonhole bars.

1 Prepare the outlines as before, with double running stitch. Do this for both the cutwork outline and the isolated shape outline.

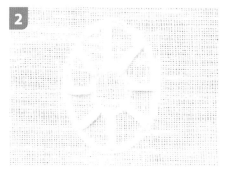

2 Work the bars as previously described. Any type of bar can be used, be it buttonhole, wrapped or woven. Picot bars can also be used. Just make sure you have enough bars to fully support the isolated shape.

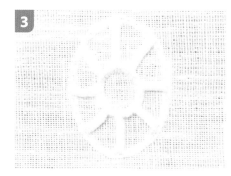

3 The isolated shape is then outlined in buttonhole stitch. Remember that when you work this buttonhole stitch, the looped edge of the buttonhole needs to be worked to the outside of the isolated shape.

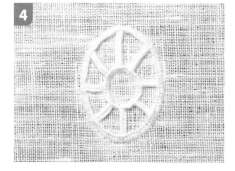

4 The outline for the cutwork area can then be stitched in buttonhole stitch. When this is done the rest of the cutwork shape can then be completed as previously described.

OVERCAST CUTWORK

Another method for working cutwork shapes is the overcast method. This creates a more delicate outline and is less structured than the traditional buttonhole stitch, so it should only be used for smaller cutwork shapes. This sample has been worked in coton à broder 30, but any thread can be used.

Prepare the outlines and stitch the bars as previously explained.

Overcast cutwork shape with buttonhole bars and a looped picot.

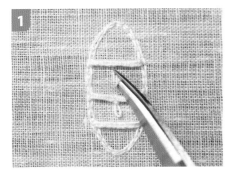

With tip of your sharp embroidery scissors or a stiletto, make a small hole in the centre of the shape that is to be cut away.

Carefully cut through the centre of the shape, taking care not to cut the bars. From this central cut, snip out in sections all the way around the shape. Snip right up to the double-running-stitch outline.

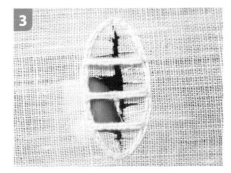

From underneath the frame, use a finger to fold back the flaps, finger pressing along the fold right on the edge to keep them in position.

Introduce the working thread as previously described, and begin to overcast the cut edge. Bring the needle up on the outside of the rows of double running stitch and take the needle down into the newly cut shape.

Work around the whole shape in this way, making sure that the overcast stitches lay neatly next to each other and they are all evenly pulled. As you work round you may need to re-fold and finger-press the flaps. When you reach the end, secure the thread as before.

When the shape has been stitched, turn the frame over. On the back you will see where the flaps have been folded back. Using sharp embroidery scissors, carefully cut away the excess flaps around the shape. Take your time, and cut as close to the edge of the stitching as you can. If you don't cut close enough to the stitching on the front you will see a halo of shadow around the overcast cutwork shape.

VENETIAN CUTWORK SHAPE

Venetian cutwork shapes are worked slightly differently as the outlines vary in size throughout the shape, creating bolder and denser outlines. They are also padded, which creates height and dimension. This technique is also used for cutwork edges for things like collars and cuffs, where the whole outline is cut away. This sample has been worked in coton à broder 30, but any thread can be used.

Venetian cutwork shape with a buttonhole bar with a looped picot.

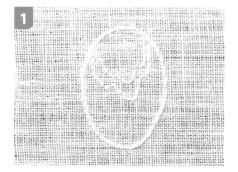

Following the design lines, outline the Venetian cutwork shape with a double-running-stitch outline.

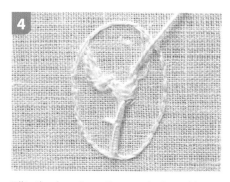

Work the bars as previously described. Any type of bar can be used, be it buttonhole, wrapped, woven and even picot. Make sure the foundation bars sit just inside the Venetian cutwork shape or they will interfere with the buttonhole later.

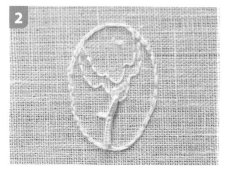

Then fill the double-running-stitch outlines in with long running stitches. Try to work in rows and keep the stitches long on the surface and short on the back. This will help to concentrate the padding to the surface.

Fill in the shape in sections, gradually working your way around. Make sure the running stitches follow through the shape and that the surface is completely covered in long running stitches.

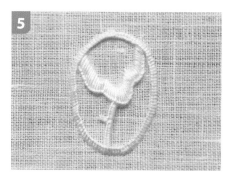

The buttonhole is then worked over the top and completely covers the outlines and the padding. Bring the needle up on the outside of the shape and take it down on the inside of the shape, so that the buttonhole edge forms along the edge that is to be cut away. Depending on the shape, the angle of the buttonhole may change subtly throughout the shape. When all the buttonhole is complete, fabric can then be cut away as previously described.

EXPERIMENTAL CUTWORK DECORATION

When you are confident with all the traditional cutwork techniques, have a go at experimenting with different ways to decorate your bars, be it venetian, renaissance or richelieu. Here I've simply used different types of beads to add a bit of interest and sparkle to the bars, which could work well on a contemporary piece of whitework.

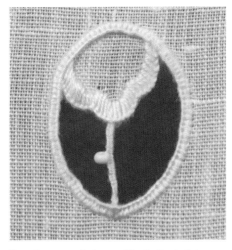

Venetian cutwork shape with a buttonhole bar decorated with a tiny white seed bead.

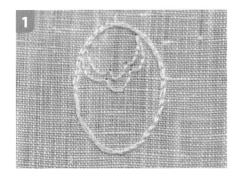

Outline the shape as previously described with a double running stitch outline.

Work the bars as previously described. Start the buttonhole stitch encasing the bars and when you reach where you want the bead to sit, stop stitching. Thread the bead and push it all the way down until it sits against the buttonhole stitch. Then continue with the buttonhole to complete the bar.

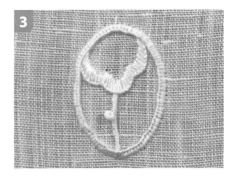

When the bar is complete, work all other stitching as required (like buttonhole edging), then cut away the fabric as previously described, taking care not to cut the bar. If needed, use a pair of tweezers or a mellor to arrange the bead.

Another sample showing an overcast bar being decorated with a transparent bugle bead. This time you need to add the bead when you make your first bar, and make sure the 2nd and 3rd bars also pass through the bead. You can then overcast the bar as previously described moving the bead out of the way as needed.

CHAPTER 7

EYELETS AND LADDERWORK

Broderie anglaise is a versatile and exquisite whitework embroidery technique and its most recognizable feature is the eyelet, in varying shapes and sizes. Other voided stitches such as ladder stitch are also worked alongside the eyelets. Satin stitch, trailing stem and many other surface stitches are also worked into broderie anglaise designs to enhance and create contrast with the voided shapes. In this chapter I will focus only on eyelets and ladderwork as the other stitches are covered in other chapters of this book.

EYELETS

Eyelets are a really simple way of creating depth and interest in a piece of embroidery. Whether they are worked singly, in groups or in rows, they are like little windows that draw and focus the eye. Eyelets can come in many different shapes and sizes but the principal elements of stitching eyelets are nearly always the same. The following section will show you how to create basic eyelets, then a few different variations on the eyelet.

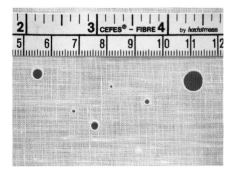

A series of eyelets worked in various sizes.

All the following samples have been worked in stranded cotton on a Kingston 55, unless stated otherwise.

Practice Eyelets

Eyelets are notoriously hard to unpick so when making eyelets you need to get them right first time round. Before starting on my finished designs I always do at least three practice eyelets to get my rhythm and tension right.

SMALL ROUND EYELET

In broderie anglaise, small round eyelets are most commonly used, and are made by first creating an outline/barrier. The ground fabric threads within this barrier are then pushed apart and then bound to the edge with stitches, which create the eyelet.

When stitching single eyelets, it does not matter if you stitch in an anticlockwise or clockwise direction. When your eyelet is complete, push the stiletto back into the eyelet as this will neaten it up, ensuring the eyelet stays round. For each new eyelet, start with a new length of thread.

A small round eyelet worked in a single strand of stranded cotton.

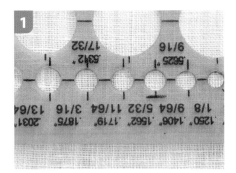

Start by drawing a circle using a circle template and a blue pencil. These types of eyelet are limited in size to about 5–6mm (⅛in).

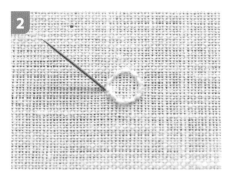

Work a row of evenly stitched double running stitches around the edge of the eyelet. The size of these stitches will depend on the size of the eyelet but they should be about 1mm in length. When complete, bring the needle back up to the surface right at the edge of the double-running-stitch outline.

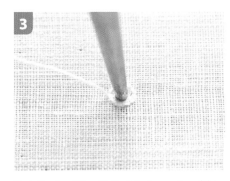

Push the tip of the stiletto into the centre of the circle formed by the running stitches. Give the stiletto a twist until the fabric has been pushed out and reaches the double running stitches.

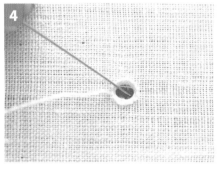

Then take the needle down into the hole of the eyelet. This stitch binds the edge of the hole. Pull the thread gently against the edge of the eyelet hole as this will stop the hole from closing.

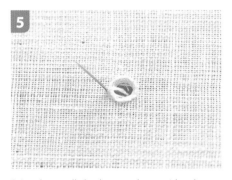

Bring the needle back up on the outside edge, right next to the first stitch. Again, give the stitch a gentle pull to make sure the stitch is tight around the edge of the eyelet.

Continue to work round the edge of the eyelet, bringing the needle up on the outside edge and taking it down through the middle. The stitches should sit close together with no gaps. Make sure to pull the stitches tight once you have taken them down into the hole. Pulling against the edge will help to open up the eyelet.

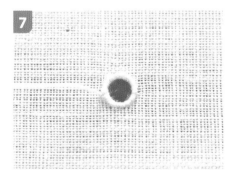

When you have worked all the way around the eyelet and are back where you started, bring the needle up on the outside as before and take the needle down into the eyelet to make the final stitch.

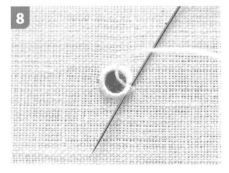

To finish off the thread, turn the frame over to work on the reverse. Right next to the last binding stitch, run the needle under a few stitches and pull tight. Do this for a second time a little distance away, then cut the thread.

Tiny Round Eyelet

With practice you can work beautifully neat, tiny round eyelets that are just millimetres in diameter. They are really delicate but still very effective.

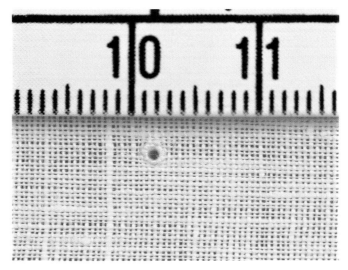

A tiny round eyelet, just 1mm wide.

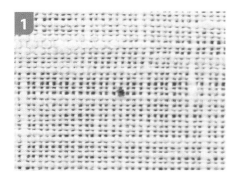

For really tiny eyelets, just mark a dot where the centre of the eyelet will be.

Work the double-running-stitch outline around this dot, making the stitches as small as you can. You may only need three or four stitches.

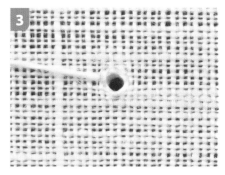

Make the eyelet hole with the stiletto, and stitch the eyelet as previously described. Finish the eyelet as before, taking extra care as the eyelet is so small.

LARGE ROUND EYELETS

Large round eyelets are created in the same way as small round eyelets, only this time the fabric is cut rather than stretched. This means much bigger eyelets can be created.

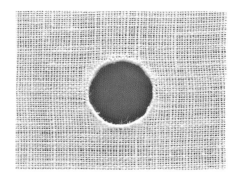

A large round eyelet.

Neatening the Shape

Larger eyelets are a bit trickier to keep round, and when complete, the stiletto is too small to help neaten off the shape. Depending on the size of the large eyelets, you could use a larger tool like a knitting needle or paintbrush to push through the eyelet to neaten off the shape. Whatever you decide to use, make sure it is clean before pushing it into the eyelet.

1 Start by drawing a circle using a circle template in blue pencil. Then work evenly stitched double running stitches around the circle. Then use the stiletto to make a small hole in the centre of the eyelet.

2 Then, with a sharp pair of scissors, cut from this central hole out to the double-running-stitch edge. Make as many cuts as you need to, creating small tabs. Be careful *not* to cut through the stitching.

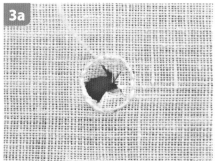

3a **3b** Fold the tabs of fabric back, away from the hole of the eyelet, until till you have a clean edge running round the shape of the eyelet. Then stitch the eyelet as before, bringing the needle up on the outside edge and taking it down through the central hole.

4 When the eyelet is complete and you turn it over to secure the threads on the back, if there are any tufts of fabric left visible from the tabs, trim these away as close to the stitching as you can.

SHAPED EYELETS

Eyelets can be worked to any shape, and not always round. In broderie anglaise you are more likely to encounter oval, leaf and teardrop shapes (*see* below). Of course, you can also create other shapes – have fun experimenting.

Oval

Oval eyelets are really simple and are basically worked in the same way as round eyelets. Draw the oval using an oval template and a blue pencil, and stitch the outline as previously described.

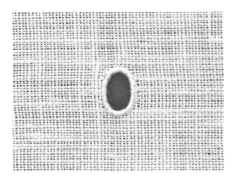

An oval-shaped eyelet.

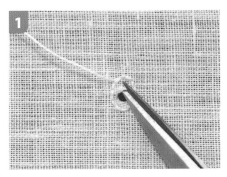

Make the initial hole in the centre of the eyelet with the stiletto as before. Then, with sharp scissors, snip into the oval at the narrowest parts of the curve. Take care *not* to cut the double running stitches.

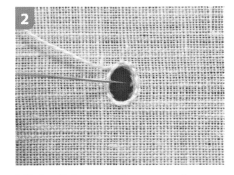

With the stiletto you can then open up the fibres within the oval eyelet, and fold back the larger parts of the tabs that have just been cut. Stitch the oval eyelet and secure the thread as previously described.

Leaf

Leaf-shaped eyelets are basically worked in the same way as oval eyelets, only now you need to accentuate the tips of the leaf, making them look nice and pointy. Trace the leaf shape using a blue pencil and stitch the outline as previously described.

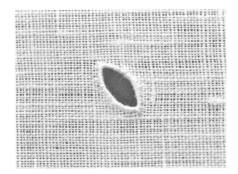

A leaf-shaped eyelet; notice the accentuated tips.

Make the initial hole in the centre of the eyelet with the stiletto as before. Then, with sharp scissors, snip into the tips of the leaf. Take care *not* to cut the double running stitches. Open up the shape of the eyelet and fold back the cut tabs.

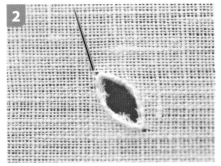

Stitch along one side of the leaf as previously described until you reach the tip. At the tip, rather than bringing the needle up just on the outside edge, bring it up slightly further away. This will make the stitch slightly longer, giving a nice, sharp point. Continue down the other side as before and complete the eyelet as previously described.

Teardrop

Teardrop eyelets are almost a combination of the oval and leaf eyelet, with one end curved and the other having a sharp tip. Trace the teardrop shape using a blue pencil and stitch the outline as previously described.

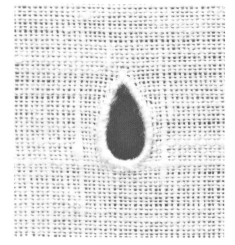

A teardrop eyelet.

Make the initial hole in the bottom curve of the eyelet with the stiletto as before. Then, with sharp scissors, snip into the tip of the teardrop. Take care *not* to cut the double running stitches. Open up the shape of the eyelet and fold back the cut tabs.

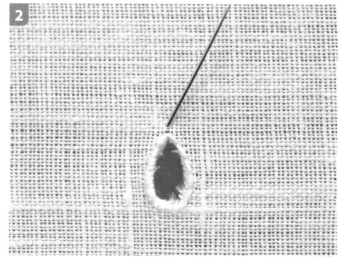

Stitch along one side of the teardrop as previously described until you reach the tip. At the tip, rather than bringing the needle up just on the outside edge, bring it up slightly further away. This will make the stitch slightly longer giving a nice, sharp point. Continue down the other side as before and complete the eyelet as previously described.

SHADED EYELETS

Shaded eyelets are even more eye catching due to the contrast between the eyelet hole and the dense padded stitching that binds the hole of the eyelet. Round and teardrop shapes are very traditional but try experimenting with other shapes too.

Round Shaded Eyelet

A round shaded eyelet.

Start by drawing the outlines for the shaded eyelet in a blue pencil, using a circle stencil or a template.

Work a row of evenly stitched double running stitches around both edges of the eyelet. The size of these stitches will depend on the size of the eyelet but they should be about 1mm in length. When complete, bring the needle back up to the surface in the shaded area of the eyelet.

This shaded area is now filled with long split stitches that form the padding. Try to make these stitches long on the surface and really tiny on the back, as this focuses the padding to the front of the embroidery. These stitches need to be worked in rows, working back and forth following the outlines of the eyelet until full.

Push the tip of the stiletto into the centre of the eyelet formed by the running stitches. Give the stiletto a twist until the fabric has been pushed out and reaches the double running stitches.

Anchor the old thread and introduce a new one, with the stab stitches being hidden in the shaded area. Bring the new thread up to the surface just on the outside edge of the eyelet at it widest point. Take the needle down through the hole and begin to stitch the eyelet as before, working across the widest area first.

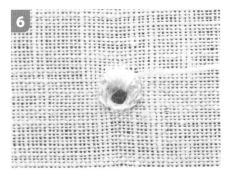

Take care that each stitch sits smooth and flat over the padding. Around this widest area, when bringing the needle up on the outside edge, leave really tiny gaps between a few of your stitches. This will help you to change the angle of your stitches as you work around the curve and prevent overcrowding in the centre of the eyelet. Continue round the eyelet and finish as previously described.

Teardrop Shaded Eyelet

This method was developed by Jenny Adin-Christie.

A teardrop shaded eyelet.

Draw the teardrop outlines in blue pencil and work the outlines as previously described.

Work the padding stitches in the shaded area as before. When complete, finish the thread in the shaded area. Then push the tip of the stiletto into the rounded area of the teardrop to make the eyelet hole.

Then, with sharp scissors, snip into the tip of the teardrop. Take care *not* to cut the double running stitches. Open up the shape of the eyelet and fold back the cut tabs.

Introduce a new thread, anchoring it in the shaded area. Then bring the needle up on the outside edge. Start to stitch the eyelet as before, beginning at the widest point. Make sure each stitch sits smooth and flat on the surface of the padding.

After two or three stitches, a wedge stitch is worked. This wedge stitch will help you to change the angle of the stitches in a small space, so the stitches follow the curve of the teardrop neatly. To do this, bring the needle up on the outside edge as before, then take the needle down through the padding stitches close to the edge, angling the needle down towards the previous stitch.

Continue round the eyelet, adding a wedge stitch every few stitches but only round the widest area. When you reach the tip, bring the needle up slightly further away from the tip to exaggerate the point. Continue down the other side and complete the eyelet as previously described.

Decorative Eyelets

Decorating/filling eyelets would usually fall under the technique of Ayrshire needlework, and are usually much bigger than broderie anglaise eyelets as there needs to be space in order to fill them. The number of ways you can fill an eyelet are numerous, so here I will show you a few simple ways using a few different techniques. With practice, you will soon be able to move on to more difficult, intricate filling stitches more prominent in Ayrshire needlework, and you can even design your own.

Shadow-Work Eyelet Oval

This type of decorative eyelet is so simple to stitch yet so effective. This decorative eyelet was inspired from a piece held in the collection at Chertsey Museum

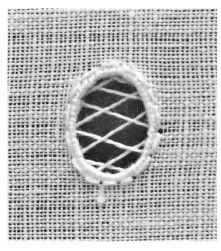

An oval-shaped eyelet with shadow-work decoration.

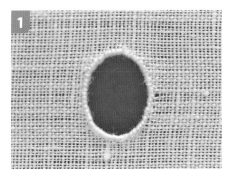

Stitch an oval eyelet as previously described, remembering that it is going to be decorated/filled, so make it on the larger side.

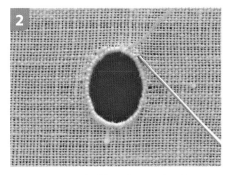

With a new length of thread secured at the top left-hand curve of the eyelet, begin to work the shadow-work stitch from one side of the eyelet to the other (following the instructions for shadow-work curves and points). The stitches should sit right on the outside edge of the eyelet.

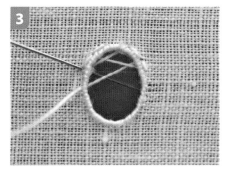

The first few stitches may not be visible as they sit under the top curve, but as you work down the eyelet the stitches will begin to cut across the eyelet. Make sure *not* to pull these stitches too tight, as fibres around the eyelet will become separated. When you reach the bottom of the curve and the shadow-work stitch is complete, fill in any gaps around the eyelet with fake stitches.

Shadow-Work Eyelet Circle

This is another example of a shadow-work eyelet, this time in circle form. Create a large eyelet as previously described, then follow the instructions for the double-backstitch circle in Chapter 8, placing the stitches just on the outside edge of the eyelet.

SEQUIN AND BEADED EYELETS

Though not very traditional, decorating small or large eyelets with a bead or sequin can be really effective and add a little sparkle to your whitework. Try to find beads or sequins that are white in colour or transparent, but using a silver spangle could also work. Whatever you choose to use, make sure that the bead or sequin is small enough not to fill the eyelet completely. After all, the whole point of making the eyelet in the first place was to see through it so you don't want to fill the eyelet completely.

A circle eyelet decorated with a transparent bead and sequin.

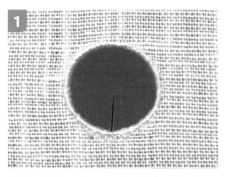

Stitch a circle eyelet as previously described, remembering that it is going to be decorated with a sequin, so make sure it is large enough to accommodate the sequin, and have room to spare. With a new length of fine lace thread, secure at the bottom and bring the needle out through the edge of the eyelet.

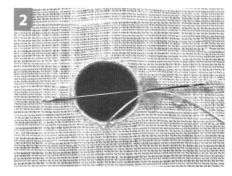

Thread the needle through the bottom of the sequin, followed by the bead. Then thread the needle back through the sequin through the top. The bead will then sit on top of the sequin and anchor its position.

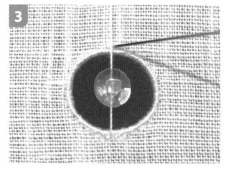

Lay the thread across the eyelet and manoeuvre the bead and sequin into the right position. I have centred mine, but you don't have to. When you are happy with the position, take the needle down on the opposite side of the eyelet and anchor with a tiny stab stitch to secure it in place.

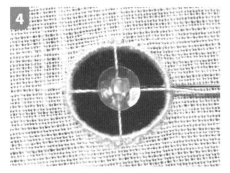

You could leave the eyelet like this with a single bar holding the bead and sequin in position. To fill and decorate the rest of the eyelet with bars, simply quarter the shape and continue dividing by adding new bars that sit underneath the sequin. Work a tiny stab stitch on the edge after each new bar and to move round to the next bar.

Tiny eyelets can simply be decorated with a bead. Stitch the eyelet as previously described, be it circle, oval or teardrop. With a new length of fine lace thread, secure at the bottom and bring the needle out through the bottom of the eyelet. Thread on the bead, then take the needle through the bead again. This extra wrap will help to keep the bead in position. Anchor the thread on the opposite side of the eyelet. If you choose not to work the extra wrap, the bead is left free to slide along the thread across the eyelet.

Needlepoint Filled Eyelet

Needlepoint eyelets are surprisingly simple to stitch and are a great way of drawing the eye into whitework designs. This sample is quite simple but with practice you can create highly decorative needlepoint eyelets. The trick is to have great control of your stitch tension.

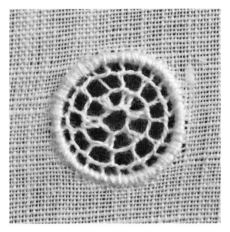

A circle eyelet filled with a simple needle-point filling.

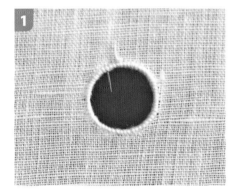

Stitch a large round eyelet as previously described. In terms of size you want to aim for about 1cm (⅓in) in diameter to make sure you have enough space to fill. Then introduce a strong lace thread, bringing the needle out into the centre of the eyelet through the overcasting stitches.

Then begin to work a twisted buttonhole stitch around the eyelet. To do this, slide the tip of the needle through the overcasting stitches. When the tip of the needle protrudes into the eyelet, wrap the lace thread over then under the tip of the needle, and then round the back and underneath the shaft of the needle.

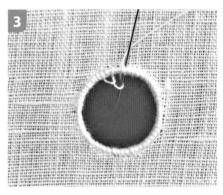

Pull the stitch tight so the twisted buttonhole sits about 2mm (¹⁄₁₆in) in from the edge of the eyelet. Then move on to make the next twisted buttonhole stitch.

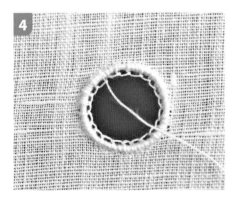

Continue all the way around the eyelet until you reach the first stitch. Make sure the stitches are all evenly spaced and are pulled to the same tension.

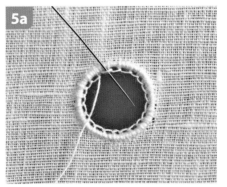

Next, take the needle down into the loop formed by the first twisted buttonhole stitch. Then work all the way around the eyelet by whipping around the inner edge of all the twisted buttonhole stitches, making sure to take the needle down into every buttonhole stitch.

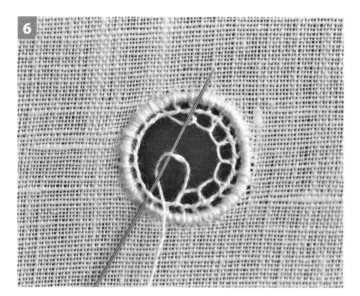

When you reach where you started, work round again, creating an inner row of twisted buttonhole stitch. This time, however, only make a new twisted buttonhole stitch in every other buttonhole stitch of the outer row.

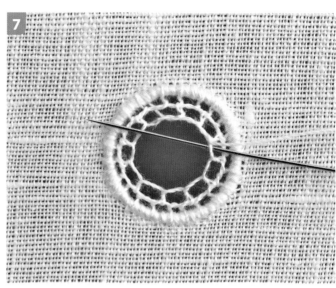

When that row is complete work, round again, whipping the new row of twisted buttonhole to strengthen it.

Work a final row of twisted buttonhole, again only on every other stitch of the previous row. This time, however, work two twisted buttonhole stitches immediately next to each other, before moving on to the next loop.

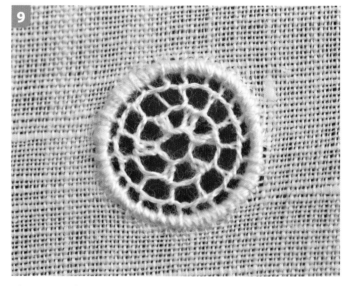

When you reach where you started again, whip the final inner row as before. Then weave through the stitches till you reach the edge of the eyelet and secure the thread in the edge of the eyelet as before.

Beading and Ladderwork

Beading and ladderwork are the terms used when rows, strings or chains of eyelets are worked very closely together and when finished it looks like a row or string of beads.

I have also included ladderwork in various other forms here too, as they create a similar effect, though different techniques are used.

Beading

Traditional beading is where a narrow length of eyelets are worked in a line and this line can be straight or curved.

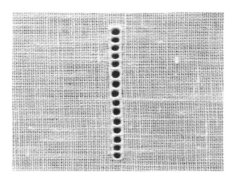

A sample row of straight traditional beading.

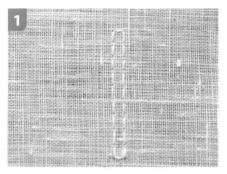

To start, outline the beading with a row of small parallel running stitches, making sure that there is a stitch at the top and bottom of the outline also. This form of beading looks best when worked in narrow delicate lines, so try to limit the width of this outline to around 5mm (⅕in).

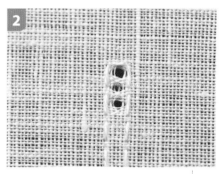

Then, starting at the top of the beading, use a stiletto to pierce a hole through the middle of the outline. Make one or two further down, leaving a few threads of the ground fabric between each hole. These holes are just a guide at the moment and may close up as you stitch, which is fine.

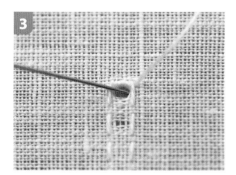

Introduce a new thread and bring the needle up right at the edge of the top left corner of the outline. Begin stitching/overcasting the first eyelet, taking the needle down through the hole and bringing it up again right on the edge of the outline.

When you reach the point where the first two holes are separated, make a stitch over to the opposite side, creating a bar. Then bring the needle back up through the second hole.

Overcast this bar and the threads of the ground fabric underneath from left to right, counting how many stitches you make so you can repeat that number for all the following bars. Then bring the needle back up right at the edge of the outline.

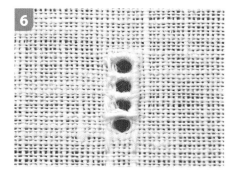

Continue in this way down the right-hand side of the outline, making new holes with the stiletto as you go. If you can, try to make sure that the number of ground fabric threads left between each hole is the same as the last. This will ensure a neat, even row of beading.

When you reach the end of the outline, complete the final eyelet like you did the first, round to the left-hand side of the outline and up to the first bar on this side. When the final stitch up to this bar has been made, bring the needle back up above this bar, ready to complete the next eyelet.

Continue in this way all the way up the left-hand side, trying if you can to mirror the stitches on the right, as this will ensure a neat, even row of beading. When you reach the top left corner, anchor and cut the thread as described previously. Then use the stiletto to push into every hole to neaten and round them all off.

This traditional beading can also be used create tapered beading, where it is larger at one end and the eyelets gradually get smaller in size, tapering down towards the other end. The lines of beading do not have to be straight either; they can be curved and undulating. You could also try starting large, tapering to small, then tapering back to large again.

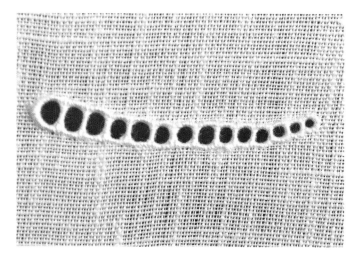

Tapered beading.

Chain Beading

What I call chain beading is where a row of individual eyelets are worked very close together. This could be in a straight, curved, wavy or offset line, but like a chain, with two or three stitches linking each eyelet together. Chain beading is a great way of adding depth to a whitework design; it draws the eye and, depending on the size and amount of eyelets to the chain, it can be delicate or bold.

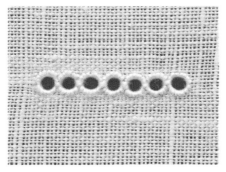

A chain of circle eyelets worked in a single strand of stranded cotton. Each of these eyelets is about 2mm (1⁄16in) in diameter.

1 Using a circle template, carefully trace the row of circles onto the fabric, making sure the widest point of each new circle just touches that of the previous one. Then begin the double-running-stitch outline to create a wave, stitching the bottom of one eyelet then the top of the next.

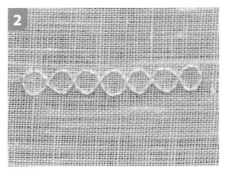

2 Stitch back in the opposite direction, filling in the other halves of each eyelet. Then stitch round the eyelets again in the same way, this time filling in the gaps to create a double-running-stitch outline. The way this is stitched gives a figure-of-eight effect.

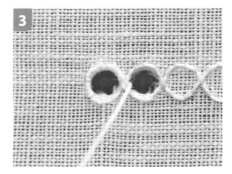

3 Using a stiletto, punch holes into the first two eyelets. Then, introducing a new thread, begin overcasting the first eyelet as previously described, starting on the left and travelling over the top of the eyelet. When you reach where the two eyelets meet, take the needle down into the first eyelet and back up through the second, creating two or three overcast stitches that join the eyelets together.

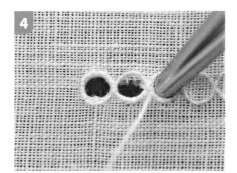

4 Continue round the second eyelet, this time overcasting the bottom half. Use the stiletto to punch the hole into the third eyelet, and again work two or three overcast stitches to join and strengthen these eyelets. Continue working in this wave-like way, overcasting the eyelets over the top then round the bottom. Try to keep the number of stitches joining the eyelets the same throughout.

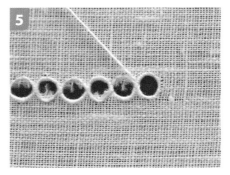

5 On the final eyelet, overcast all the way around till you reach where the two eyelets join. Make the final stitch, taking the needle down into the final eyelet, then pass underneath the join and bring the needle back up above the join, ready to stitch round the next eyelet. Continue in this direction, overcasting the other half of each eyelet and passing underneath each join to start the next. When complete, anchor and cut the thread as previously described.

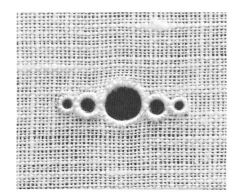

This technique also works if the eyelets vary in size, so you can create chains of eyelets that change size throughout the chain.

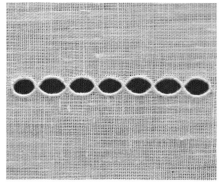

Oval or leaf-shaped eyelets can also be used in chain beading and are worked in exactly the same way. The exception being that you will have to snip into the oval or leaf shape as previously described to open up the eyelet.

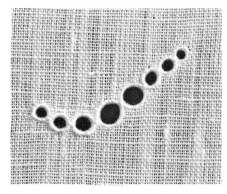

This sample shows an undulating row of chain beading with eyelets tapering in size throughout the chain.

Ladderwork

Ladderwork can be created using a few different techniques and stitches. As the title suggests, when finished, your stitches should have created something that gives the effect of ladder rungs. Depending on the techniques you choose to use, the effect can look very different.

Cut Ladder Technique

The cut ladder technique can create large, bold, open shapes. These can be even, straight, perpendicular shapes or can follow shapes on a design, curving and swelling following a design line. However, you need to make sure that the shapes are not too wide. For this sample I have chosen to overcast both the edge and bars but a buttonhole edge would work too; as for the bars, buttonhole or woven bars could also be used, like those in Chapter 6.

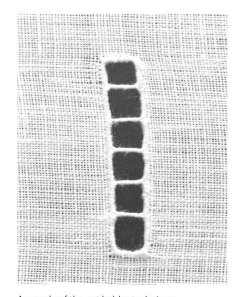

A sample of the cut ladder technique.

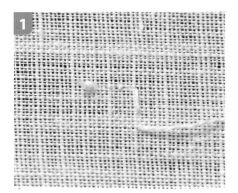

Start by anchoring the thread at the top of the shape. Then move down the right-hand side, making a small running stitches till you need to make your first bar.

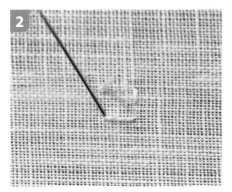

Make the first bar across the ladder by taking the needle down on the opposite side. Then bring the needle back up just above where you have taken it down on the same side.

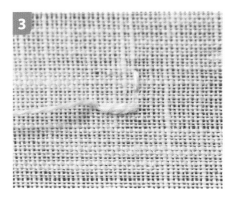

Make another two bars in the same way. You should end up with the needle on the surface on the left-hand side.

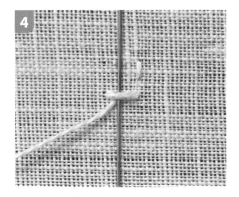

Overcast the bars, from top to bottom, grouping them together to make one bar. *See* the overcast bar instructions in Chapter 6.

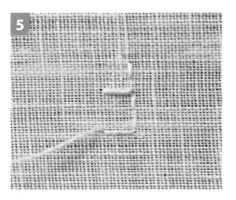

When the bar is overcast and you are back on the right-hand side, work down the side with running stitches as before, until you need to make the second bar.

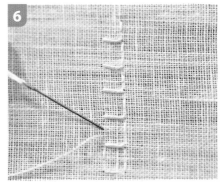

Create the second bar in the same way, then repeat all the way down the right-hand side, until you reach the bottom. Then work back up the left side with the running stitch, making sure it is in line with the end of all your bars.

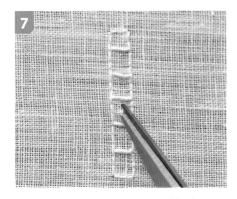

When you reach the beginning, work back around the shape again with running stitch, this time filling in the gaps to create a double-running-stitch outline all the way around. You can then very carefully cut through the centre of the shape, stopping just before the top and bottom ends. Take care not to cut the bars!

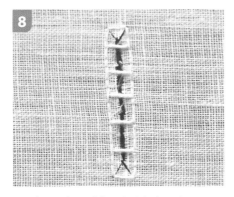

At either end, carefully snip right into the corners, creating a little triangle at each end.

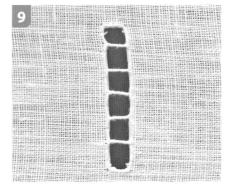

Use your finger to fold back the flaps towards the outer edges of the shape as close to the double-running-stitch outline as you can.

continued on the following page…

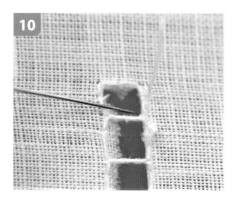

10

Starting at the top right-hand side, begin to overcast the edge. These stitches need to be very close together and all be the same size. When you reach a bar, take the needle down above it, then bring it back up below it to continue overcasting the next section. For more instructions on overcasting edges *see* Chapter 6.

11

When you reach the bottom right-hand corner, slightly extend the overcasting stitch so it creates a nice, sharp point around the corner. Then continue round the rest of the shape as before.

Spacing of the Bars

You need to make sure that the bars are worked fairly close together so that when you come to cut through the ladder later, the ladder does not bulge out of shape between the bars like this. You should aim to make the bars between 5–10mm (¼in).

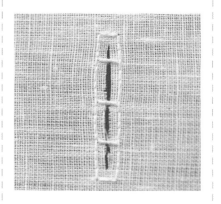

12

When the whole edge has been overcast, turn the frame over and carefully trim away any of the flaps that are still visible beyond the overcast stitches. Your cut ladder is now complete!

PULLED-LADDER STITCH

Pulled ladder is technically a pulled work stitch, but as it creates a line of beautifully delicate holes that give the effect of tiny eyelets that look like ladders, I am including it here. This technique can be worked in straight lines following the grain of the fabric, or curving, scrolling lines. This type of ladderwork is a very traditional stitch in whitework and is often seen being used in contrast to heavily worked areas of satin stitch.

See how the lines of ladder stitch sit neatly nestled between the satin-stitch leaves. Item 1813 from the RSN Collection.

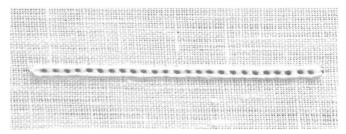

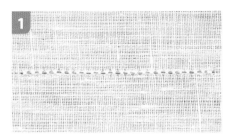

Pulled ladderwork, following the straight grain and worked in lace and coton à broder 30 thread. When you finish stitching and the ends have been secured, carefully push the very tip of a stiletto or a large tapestry needle through each hole to open and neaten them up.

Using a strong lace thread, work a row of evenly spaced backstitches, making sure to always take the needle down through a hole rather than through a thread of the ground fabric. Pull all of these stitches tight, opening up the weave of the ground fabric and creating tiny little holes. Bring the needle back up to the surface right at the end and just underneath this line of backstitch.

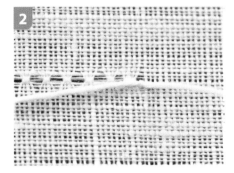

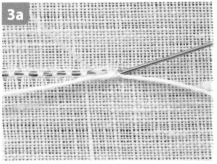

Introduce the new couching thread (*see* Chapter 9) – making sure it is long enough to lay along both edges with a bit extra at the ends – along the bottom edge of this line of backstitch. Using the lace thread, make a couching stitch over this new thread, taking the needle down into the last hole created by the pulled back-stitch. Then bring the needle back up through the next hole created by the backstitch.

Make a second backstitch over the first backstitch, wrapping and pulling tight again, increasing the tension on the backstitch to help keep the holes open. Then bring the needle up to the surface just below the couched thread and just underneath the next hole along.

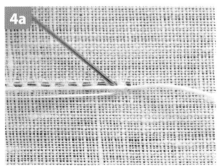

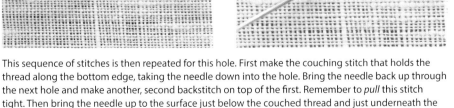

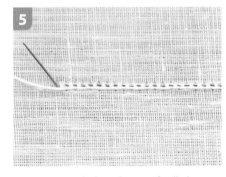

This sequence of stitches is then repeated for this hole. First make the couching stitch that holds the thread along the bottom edge, taking the needle down into the hole. Bring the needle back up through the next hole and make another, second backstitch on top of the first. Remember to *pull* this stitch tight. Then bring the needle up to the surface just below the couched thread and just underneath the next hole.

Continue to work along the row of pulled backstitches, repeating this sequence of stitches for every hole. Make sure to *pull* every second backstitch tight over the first, ensuring the holes stay clear and open. When you reach the last hole and have made the last second backstitch, bring the needle back up through the final hole.

continued on the following page…

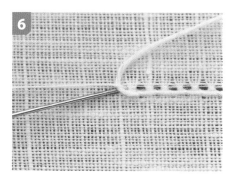

Catching Long Stitches

When you make the original row of backstitch, you will notice that the long stitches on the back are visible as they cut across the holes. When you work the couching stitches along the first edge, take the needle down into the holes, catching this long thread on the back within the stitch. This will pull it towards the edge and stop it interfering with the holes. If you miss any on the first edge, you can always catch them on the second edge.

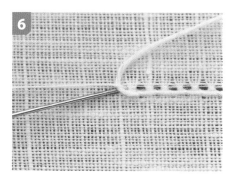

Now fold the couching thread round to the opposite edge of the backstitch, and make a couching stitch down into the edge to hold this fold in place.

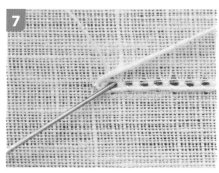

Then bring the needle back up just above the couched thread and the first hole on this side. The sequence of stitches is then repeated for every hole on this side, only this time you are making a third backstitch on top of the second backstitch. Make sure to *pull* every backstitch tight.

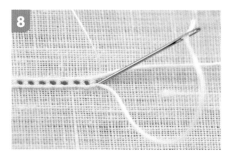

When both sides are complete, the ends of the couched threads can then be plunged by threading them through a needle and taking them through to the back, one at a time, but through the same hole.

On the back, lay each end of couched thread back on itself and very carefully make some oversew stitches, just catching the stitches on the back. Do this for about 1cm (⅓in), trying not to make any stitches that will interfere with the holes on the front. When both are tied back you can then secure and trim away any excess threads.

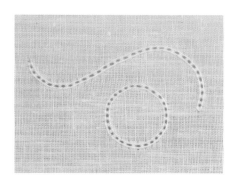

Pulled ladderwork in scrolling and circle shapes. When working pulled-ladder stitch on curving and scrolling shapes, you need to take extra care to make sure that when you work the first line of backstitch, the needle is taken down and brought up through a hole of the ground fabric. This ensures that even holes are created throughout.

If working ladder stitch in a circle, to make it appears that the circle has no start or end, rather than folding the couched thread round to work along the second edge, plunge both ends through the same hole on first edge. Then introduce a new couching thread for the second edge, and do the same again.

PUNCH STITCH

Punch stitch is also technically a pulled-thread technique but again I have included it here as, when worked in a single row, it gives the effect of tiny eyelets worked in an offset pattern. Punch stitch works best when it is worked following the grain, whether horizontal or vertical, but it can be used on soft curving lines too; it just takes a little more practice.

In this sample I have counted the threads of the fabric when creating the stitches (over six horizontal and ten vertical), but depending on the fabric and the shape/line you are trying to create, counting is not always necessary.

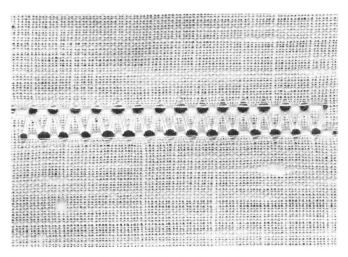

A sample of punch stitch worked following the grain line.

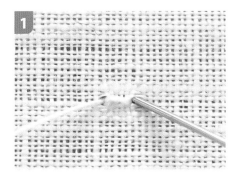

Make a small horizontal backstitch from left to right, making sure to go between the threads on the ground fabric. *Pull* the stitch tight so a small hole is created at either end of the stitch. Make a second stitch directly on top of the first.

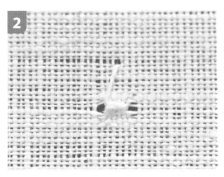

Then count ten threads up and three to the right, making a diagonal stitch from bottom left to top right. *Pull* the stitch tight.

Make a second stitch directly over the top, again pulling tight. Then count six threads to the left and bring the needle up to the surface. *Pulling* the second stitch tight opens up the holes being created even more.

Then work another two backstitches, one on top of the other over the six threads, *pulling* tight.

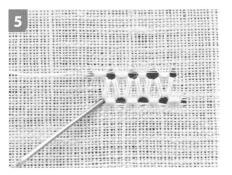

Then count ten threads down and three to the right, making a diagonal stitch from top left to bottom right. *Pull* the stitch tight. Make another stitch directly over the top. This sequence of stitches is then repeated till you have your required length of stitches.

CHAPTER 8

SHADOW-WORK

Shadow-work embroidery is a wonderful technique in its own right, and beautiful effects are created when working with shadow-work in colour, which is nowadays what it is most well known for. Traditionally it was worked in white thread on sheer muslin cloths and the like.

Applying shadow-work to whitework is really effective at adding depth and contrast to a design. The stitch used to create shadow-work is known as double backstitch. This is where the double backstitches are worked along each side of a narrow shape on the front, leaving the crossed herringbone-like stitches on the back, which creates the shadow effect.

There is also another technique called shadow-appliqué, where an extra layer of fabric is applied to the ground fabric with a decorative pin stitch (*see* the Shadow Appliqué section in this chapter), adding further density and contrast.

Many of the techniques in this chapter were first developed by Jenny Adin-Christie in her book *Fundamental Whitework Techniques*.

For these samples I have used organza as a ground fabric and a fine lace thread to stitch with.

PARALLEL LINES

Before working on more complicated shapes, practise and experiment stitching the double backstitch on parallel lines. This will help you to practise getting the double backstitches exactly opposite each other on either side of the shape, which is important to create the desired shadow effect. Also, as you work down the shape, gradually make the double backstitches slightly longer and this will make the herringbone on the back more open, allowing you to create different densities of shadow in one shape.

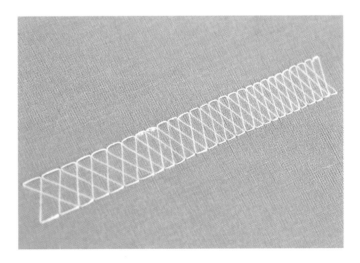

A finished sample of double backstitch worked in parallel lines. The stitches gradually increasing in length from small to large.

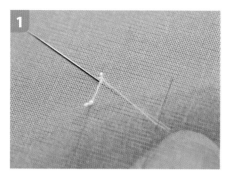

Start by drawing two parallel lines about 1cm (⅓in) apart in blue pencil. Anchor the thread with two tiny backstitches where you want the double backstitch to start on the left side of the shape. Bring the needle up to the surface below these two backstitches, ready to make the first double backstitch.

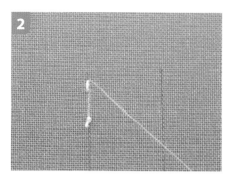

Make the first double backstitch on the left so that it covers these two tiny backstitches. For the purposes of this exercise, start with small stitches so you can gradually make them bigger as you work down the shape. This first stitch is 2mm (¹⁄₁₆in).

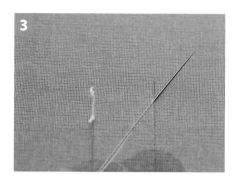

Bring the needle back up to the surface on the right and exactly opposite with the first double backstitch on the left.

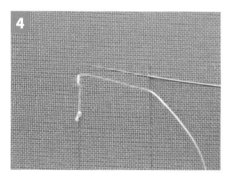

Make a second double backstitch on the right, the same length as the first.

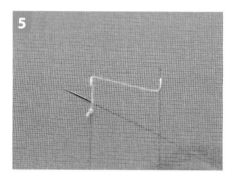

Bring the needle up on the left, a backstitch distance below the first stitch. If you can, try to pierce the trailing thread on the back, as this will stop the thread from moving around when the knot is cut off.

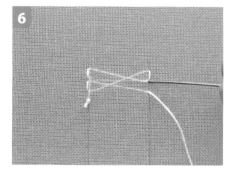

Make another double backstitch on the left, making sure that this stitch shares the same hole as the previous stitch. Then bring the needle back up to the surface on the right and exactly opposite, with this double backstitch on the left. Make another double backstitch on the right.

Take Care with Tightness

These double backstitches want to be tight, but make sure not to pull them too tight, as large holes will begin to appear between the stitches.

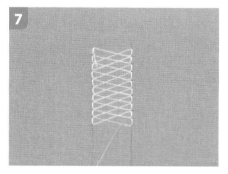

Continue working in this way, jumping across from one side to the other, creating new double backstitches each time. When you have worked down the shape a little way, begin to gradually make the double backstitches slightly longer.

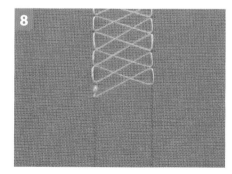

If you run out of thread midway through stitching a shape, bring the needle up to the left and secure the thread with two tiny backstitches as before. Make sure to work these stitches in place where the next double backstitch will cover them.

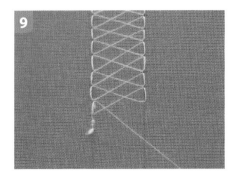

9

Anchor a new thread on the left in the same way as before, and in a place where a following double backstitch will cover them. Once secure, continue working the double backstitch as before.

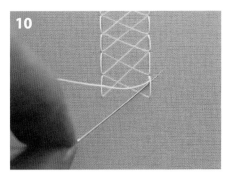

10

Continue as before, working down the shape and jumping from one side to the other, gradually making the double backstitches slightly longer. When you reach the end, the last double backstitch should be worked on the right-hand side of the shape. To secure the thread, work two tiny backstitches, hiding them underneath this final double backstitch. Any loose threads from previous anchoring stitches can then be cut away from the back.

Anchoring Stitches

Anchoring stitches should always be as small and neat as possible but this is especially important for shadow work, as the fabric is sheer. If possible, try to avoid having to introduce a new thread part way through a shape; if it is unavoidable, make the anchoring stitches as invisible as you can.

CURVES AND POINTS

Working double backstitch on curved, rounded and pointed shapes is done in much the same way. However, for the herringbone to look even throughout and follow the curves of the shape, the length of the double backstitches on either side of the shape need to fluctuate. The double backstitches worked on the outer edge of a curve are larger and the double backstitches worked on the inner edge of the curve are smaller. The most important thing to remember is that the bottom of the double backstitches on either side should always be level and at a 90-degree angle to the shape.

A sample of double backstitch worked on a curving and undulating shape with stitches varying in size where needed.

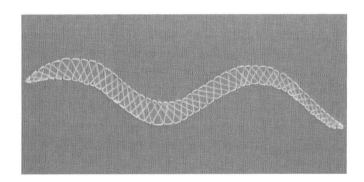

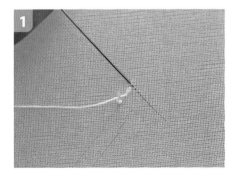

1

Anchor the thread in the same way as before, very close to the point on the left side of the shape. Make sure the two tiny backstitches will be covered by the first double backstitch. Then make the first double backstitch, taking the needle down at the very tip of the point.

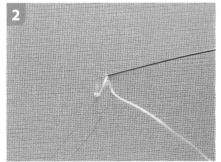

2

Make a second double backstitch on the right, also taking the needle down at the very tip of the point. These two stitches should share a hole at the point. Make sure the bottom of both these stitches are level with the 90-degree angle of the shape; this may mean that one is slightly longer than the other already.

continued on the following page…

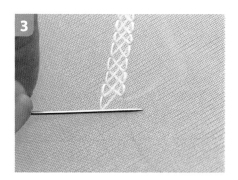

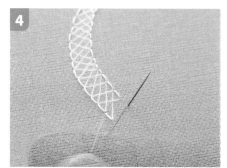

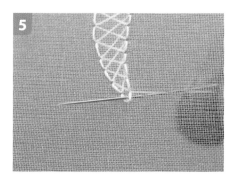

Continue working the double backstitches, jumping from one side to the next as before. A good trick for making sure the double backstitches are worked to the right length and are level with each other is to lay the needle flat against the fabric and at a 90-degree angle to the shape.

As you work down the shape you will see how the smaller and larger double backstitches on each side swap sides, as the curves of the shape change direction.

When you reach the end, work the final two double backstitches, with them sharing the same hole at the point. As before, hide the two anchoring stitches underneath the final double backstitch.

Size of First Stitches

Try not to make these first double backstitches too small. If you do, the points of shapes become very overcrowded and bulky, ruining the light effect that shadow work creates.

PETALS

Floral motifs are often used in shadow work. In nature, petals and leaves come in all shapes and sizes so this is the method used to create petals that have a point at one end, but are round at the other.

A sprig of three shadow-work petals on a backstitch stem.

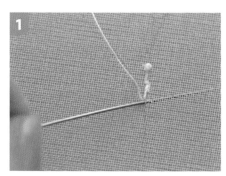

Start at the end with the point. Anchor the thread and create the point with the double backstitches in the same way as before. However, as the point is at the bottom of the shape, the stitches will be worked from the bottom to the top. For this shape, the double backstitch is first worked on the right, then on the left.

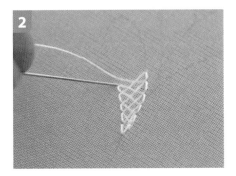

2

Continue working the double backstitch as before, working up towards the top of the petal shape.

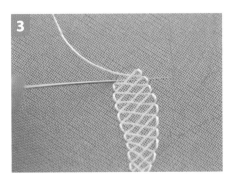

3

As you reach the curve, start to make the double backstitches slightly smaller.

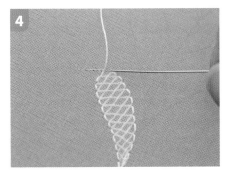

4

To complete the curve, bring the needle up at the top of the curve, making the last double backstitch on either side the same length. Secure the thread as before.

CIRCLES

Double backstitch can be used to create circles and voided circles. Large and small circles are made in the same way, but the size of the circle and the stitch need to be in proportion. The examples here feature large circles.

A sample of a double backstitch circle.

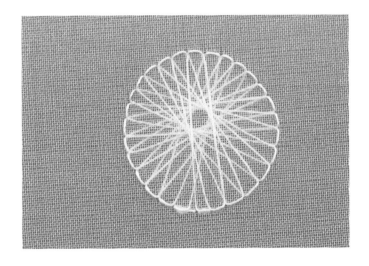

CIRCLE

1

Using a blue pencil, draw on a circle template. Secure the thread as before. Working clockwise, make the first double backstitch.

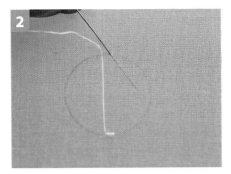

2

Bring the needle up on the opposite edge of the circle. Work the second double backstitch, keeping in a clockwise direction. The stitches should be the same size and directly opposite each other.

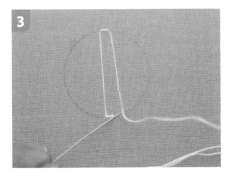

3

To make the third stitch, bring the needle back up, a stitch length to the right of the first double backstitch, working in a clockwise direction. The third stitch should share a hole with the second double backstitch.

continued on the following page…

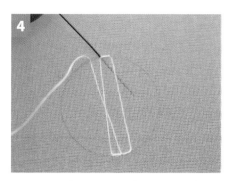

Returning to the opposite side, make your fourth double backstitch.

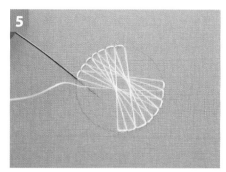

The idea here is to fill the circle with stitches, so you work in an anticlockwise direction, but with each double backstitch being worked clockwise. If you visualise the circle as a clockface, you will find that the two halves are simultaneously completed.

The double backstitches should meet when the circle is complete. If necessary, add another backstitch to fill any space. Secure the threads.

VOIDED CIRCLE

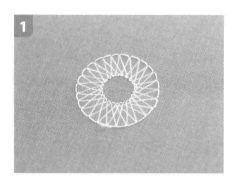

A sample of a double-backstitch voided circle.

Use a circle template and a blue pencil, and draw the design on the fabric. Secure the thread, then work a double backstitch along the edge of the outer circle in a clockwise direction.

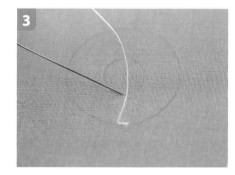

Then bring the needle up on the inner circle. Working clockwise, make another double back-stitch. This should be opposite the first stitch, but needs to be much smaller.

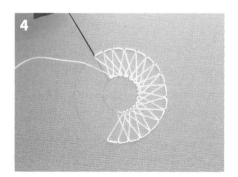

Continue working double backstitch evenly in a clockwise direction, moving from the outer to the inner circle.

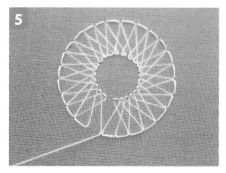

Once the circles are complete, the stitches should join up exactly.

To finish, secure the thread, bringing the needle back up through the same hole as the last stitch.

LARGER SHAPES

When using double backstitch it is important to remember that the long herringbone stitches that run across the back are what create the shadow effect. Though they are on the back they still need to look neat and be secure. Therefore some shapes that are very wide need to be worked in two separate halves, so that the herringbone stitches on the back do not become too long and loose. Again, shapes that are very long can also be divided, with areas being worked separately so they look as if they are folding back on themselves.

SEPARATE DOUBLE BACKSTITCH

Separate double backstitch is where a shape is divided in two, as it is too wide for the double backstitch to sit across the back neatly. This divide does not need to be even; one side can be bigger than the other or the divide can change as it works down the length of the shape.

Each half is stitched separately creating a double vein down the divide.

A shadow-work leaf shape that has been divided in half. Each half has been worked separately in double backstitch. The stitches on each half are different in size to create a different depth and density.

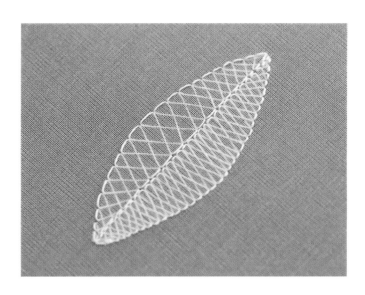

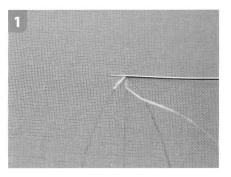

Begin by dividing your shape into two separate halves. These halves do not have to be even in size. Starting with the left side, anchor the thread as before and begin to work the double backstitch.

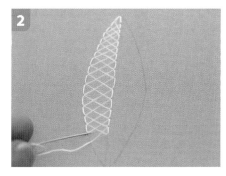

As you work down the shape you can change the length of the double backstitch to give a more open effect in the middle.

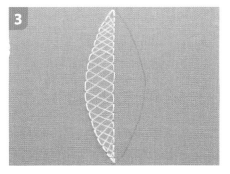

When the first half is complete, secure the thread as before.

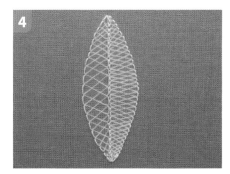

Work the second half in the same way. You can vary the size of the double backstitch to give different effects. In this example the second half has been filled with smaller even-sized double backstitches to give a denser shadow. Notice that where the two halves meet there is a double central vein.

COMBINED DOUBLE BACKSTITCH

Combined double backstitch is where a shape needs to be divided in two, as it is too wide for the double backstitch to sit neatly across the back. The divide does not need to be placed centrally and it can also change as runs through the length of the shape. The first half is worked in double backstitch with tiny backstitches being worked on the dividing line. The second half is then worked over the top covering the tiny backstitches of the first half, this creates a single vein down the dividing line.

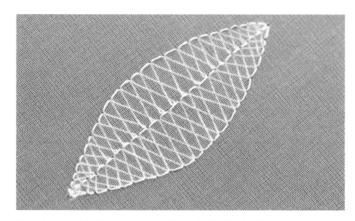

A shadow-work leaf worked in combined double backstitch.

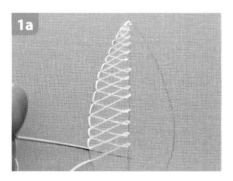

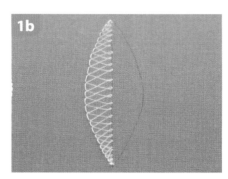

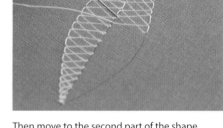

Use your blue pencil to divide your shape into two parts; these do not have to be of equal size. Secure the thread at the top of the left side, and start to work double backstitch. Be sure to make the double backstitch smaller on the right side of the shape, but keeping it opposite the middle of the larger double backstitch on the outside edge of the shape. Your aim is to keep the double backstitches even, although they are different sizes on either side.

Then move to the second part of the shape, and stitch as normal. The double backstitches down the centre of the shape are now over the small double backstitches, so they should not be visible.

JOINED DOUBLE BACKSTITCH

Longer shapes with lots of twists and turns can also be worked in double backstitch. Dividing these shapes into sections and working them separately can help to give an effect of the shape folding back on itself.

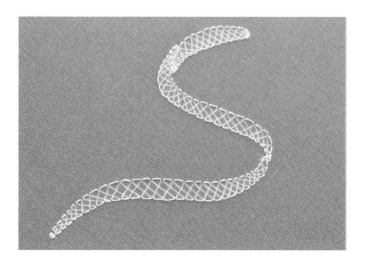

A curving and undulating shape that has been divided into three sections, each section being worked separately in double backstitch. See where the joins are, almost creating a turnover-like effect.

Shadow Appliqué

A sample of shadow appliqué.

Shadow appliqué is where another fabric is applied to the back of the sheer ground fabric with a small decorative stitch called pin stitch. Shadow appliqué is a great way of adding bold contrast to a design because you can create density in localized areas. In this sample I have applied a second layer of organza. However, different fabrics can be used depending on the density you are trying to create, for example, fine cottons and linen, other sheer fabrics, laces and silks, and printed or coloured fabrics.

Shadow appliqué is best worked with slightly larger shapes with simple outlines.

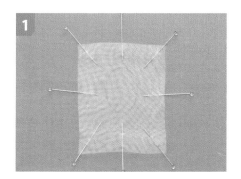

With a blue pencil, draw the design onto the front of the ground fabric. Cut out the piece of the fabric that will be applied to the back, and make sure that you cut it larger than the design shape. Lay the applied piece of fabric into position on the back of the ground fabric, matching up the grain lines as best you can. Then pin in place. Make sure the two layers are lying smooth and flat.

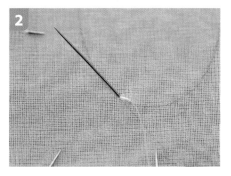

Anchor the thread as before on the design line. Pin stitch is then worked all the way around the shape, stitching these two layers together. To start the pin stitch, work two backstitches in the same place, hiding the anchoring stitches. These two backstitches should be about 2mm (1/16in) long.

continued on the following page…

Stitch Size

As a general rule, these stitches should be about 2mm (1/16in) long and you should try to keep them all the same length. However, depending on the design and shape, some stitches may need to be slightly smaller or longer in order to get around tight curves or to meet neatly at corners.

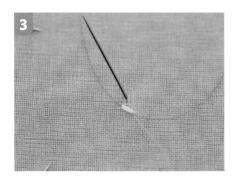

3

Then bring the needle up on the inside of the shape and at a 90-degree angle with the start of the two backstitches.

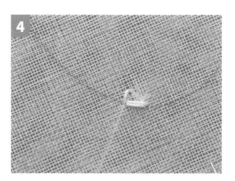

4

Make another stitch, taking the needle down through the same hole at the start of the two backstitches. This stitch should also be about 1–2mm (¹⁄₂₅–¹⁄₁₆in) long depending on the size of your shape. These stitches should not eat into the edge of the shape too much. You should be able to see the thread trailing diagonally across the back.

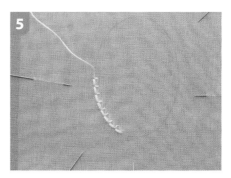

5

Then repeat, starting with the two backstitches, one on top of the other. Try to make all the stitches the same size, and make sure that the backstitches share holes. Depending on the design, the angle of the stitch worked into the shape will change as you follow the shape around, and you should always see the faint shadow of the thread trailing diagonally across the back.

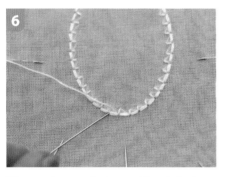

6

When you have worked around the whole shape, the stitches should meet up exactly, but you may need to make your final two backstitches slightly longer or shorter in order for this to happen. You can then anchor the thread, hiding the stitches underneath the final two backstitches.

7

Then remove the pins and turn the work over. From the reverse side, very carefully cut away the excess applied fabric, trimming very close to the stitched outline. Take your time and be careful not to cut the stitches.

Lace/Appliqué Scissors

Try using lace/appliqué scissors for cutting away the excess applied fabric. The rounded end guards against cutting anything you do not want cut. If you do not have a pair of these then sharp, curved embroidery scissors work just as well; you just need to take a little more care.

Experimenting with Shadow Appliqué

Because shadow appliqué is effectively attaching two pieces of fabric together, this allows you to trap small objects between the two layers. This could be anything from spangles and sequins, to ribbon, loose threads or even dried flowers and leaves. Whatever you decide to trap between the two layers needs to be flat and very thin, otherwise it will bulge out and put strain on the pin stitch and on the delicate fabrics used. In these samples I have trapped a pressed and dried daisy, a collection of loose spangles and a length of folded and twisted silk ribbon.

A sample of shadow appliqué with a daisy trapped between the two layers.

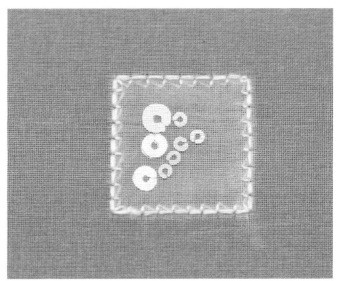

A sample shadow appliqué with loose spangles trapped between the layers.

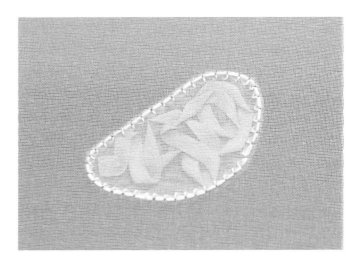

A sample of shadow appliqué with a small length of pink silk ribbon trapped between the two layers.

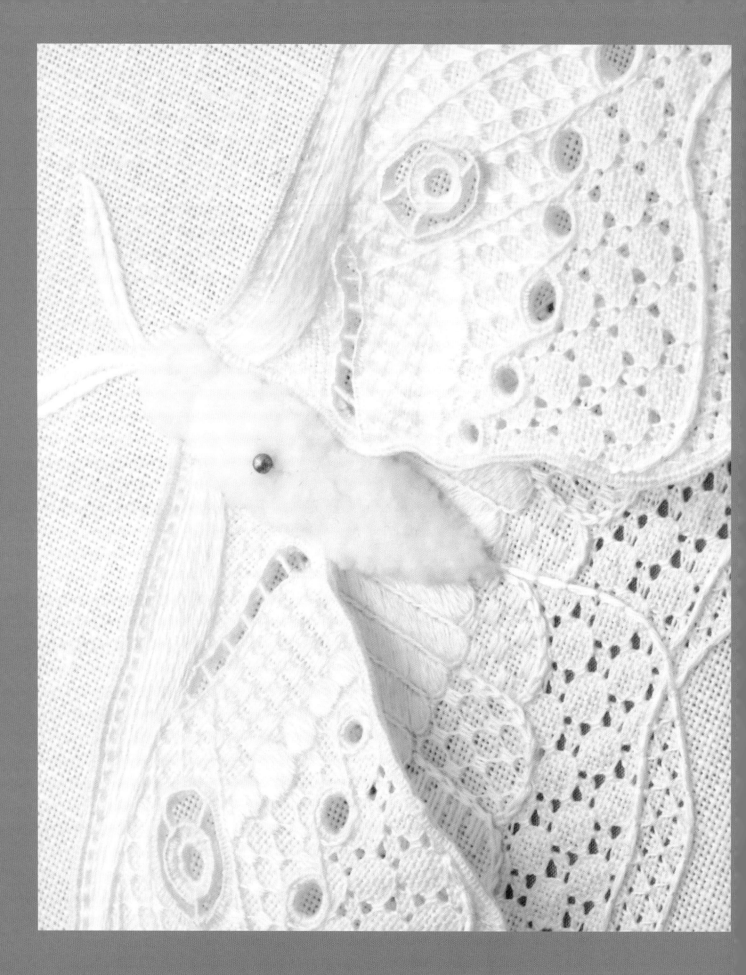

CHAPTER 9

SURFACE AND DECORATIVE STITCHES

The stitches included in this chapter are not exclusive to whitework and they are used in lots of other embroidery techniques. However, when combined with traditional whitework techniques, these stitches help create texture and add weight and depth to designs; they also create borders, outlines, tendrils and flourishes that enhance designs and bring whitework embroideries to life. These stitches can be worked in any thread, from fine lace threads to chunky perle cottons.

For most of these samples I have used a coton à broder 16 thread. The trailing and long and short samples have been stitched with a single strand of stranded cotton.

SECURING THE THREAD

Securing the start and end of your embroidery thread correctly and neatly is really important. This is especially the case in whitework, as the ground fabrics are often fine and sheer, so any messy or loose stitching on either the front or back of the work will be easily noticed. This is the waste-knot method – it is quick, neat, easy and secure. It creates a minimal amount of bulk on the back of the work and ensures that there are no nasty knots left at the end. The waste-knot method can be used for any type of thread but bear in mind that if you are using very fine lace or silk threads you may need an extra stitch or two to make sure they are really secure.

Professional Practice

All of the stitches/threads in this chapter and indeed throughout this book have been secured using the waste-knot method.

This is because it is quick, neat and secure and it doesn't require you to turn your frame over, as it is all worked from the front. Working this way in a professional environment is very important as there can be numerous embroiderers working on the same frame at the same time. If threads were being secured on the back, everyone would have to stop stitching to turn the frame over so one stitcher could secure their thread every five minutes – not very productive.

So even if it is only you stitching it is still good working practice to use the waste-knot method when securing the start and end of your threads.

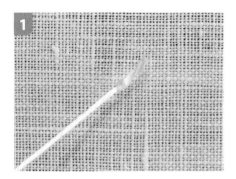

1

Before you start to secure the thread you need to make a knot in the end of the thread. There are many ways of doing this so just use the method you find easiest.

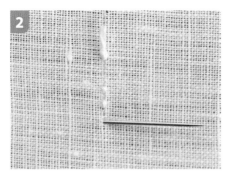

2

To secure the thread, take the needle down into the fabric a little way in from the start of the design line; the knot should sit on the surface. Make two very small stitches (I call these stab stitches) close together, just inside from the start of the design line. Then bring the needle up at the start of the design line to begin your chosen stitch. It is important that these stab stitches are worked in a place that will be covered with embroidery, such as on a design line or inside an area that will be completely filled with stitch.

3

When the needle is back on the surface and you are ready to start your chosen stitch, the knot can now be cut away as it is the two stab stitches that are anchoring the thread. When you are ready to finish the length of thread, again make two small stab stitches in a place where they will be hidden by other embroidery. If you are working on a line and have no other place nearby to finish the thread, simply hide the finishing stab stitches underneath where you have just stitched. Be careful not to disturb the embroidery stitches by angling the needle out from underneath the stitches. Bring the needle and remaining thread back up to the surface and cut away the excess thread as close the surface as possible.

STEM STITCH

Stem stitch is a really useful stitch in whitework. It creates fine scrolling lines that are great for tendrils and flower stems but also creates a simple rope-like effect for outlines on pulled-work shapes. Depending on your choice of thread, stem stitch can be fine and delicate or bold and weighty.

Outline Stitch

Stem stitch also goes by another name: outline stitch. It can get confusing but the simplest way to think about it is like this. Stem stitch is worked with the loop always on the right of the needle, making the stitch bottom left to top right. Outline stitch is worked with the loop always on the left of the needle, making the stitch from bottom right to top left. It does not matter which stitch you use but once you have started, continue to use that stitch till you reach the end of the shape or line. If working with curves, the stitch will always look neater if the stitch is worked with the loop on the outside of the curve.

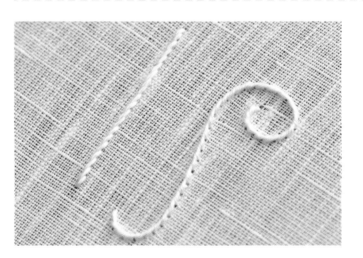

Samples of stem and outline stitch. The straight line has been worked in stem stitch and the curved line has been worked in outline stitch.

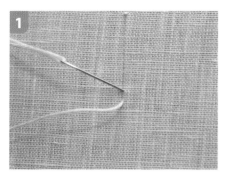

1

To start, bring the needle and thread up to the surface at the beginning of the design line. Take the needle down into the fabric about 3mm (⅛in) away to make the first stitch. Do not pull all the thread through; leave a small loop on the surface.

2

Bring the tip of the needle back up to the surface halfway along this first stitch. From the back, pull the thread so the loop closes and sits flat against the surface of the fabric. Then pull the needle and thread out of the fabric and up to the surface.

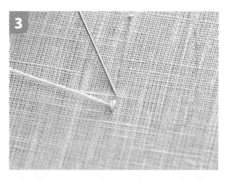

3

Make the next stitch the same length as the first. Remember to leave a loop on the surface.

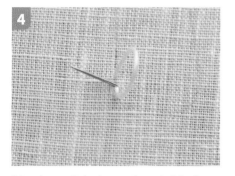

4

Bring the needle back up at the end of the first stitch (this should be halfway along the second stitch). Close the loop by pulling the thread from the back. Then pull the rest of the needle and thread through to the surface.

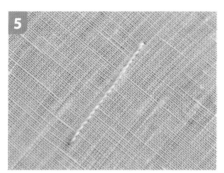

5

Continue working in this way till you reach the end of the line. Make sure to keep the loop on the same side of the needle for every stitch. This will ensure that the rope-like effect is continuous the whole way along the line of stitching.

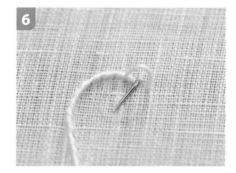

6

When working stem stitch (or outline stitch) around curves, it will look neater and create a smoother line if the stitch is worked with the loop on the outside of the curve.

CHAIN STITCH AND LAZY DAISIES

Chain stitch is another great stitch for creating outlines and stems. It creates bold and textured lines but still looks intricate and delicate when worked in a fine thread.

Lazy daisies are simply individual chain stitches. They can be worked separately to fill shapes or create leaves on a stem or grouped together to give the effect of flower petals.

A line of chain stitch, a lazy-daisy flower and individual lazy-daisy filling stitches.

1

Start by bringing the needle and thread up to the surface at the beginning of the design line. Take the needle back down through the same hole and pull the thread through to the back, but leave a small loop on the surface.

continued on the following page…

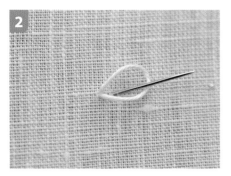

Bring the needle back up to the surface about 3mm (⅛in) away. This is the start of the second chain stitch. Make sure to bring the needle back up inside the loop of thread on the surface.

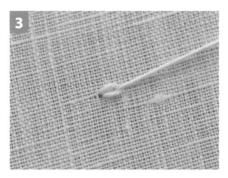

Pull this stitch so the loop on the surface will close around the working thread. Be careful not to over-pull the stitch; if you do the chain will look thin and stretched.

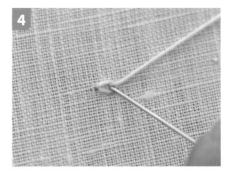

Now take the needle back down through the same hole; this should be inside the loop of the first chain stitch. Pull the thread through but leave a small loop on the surface.

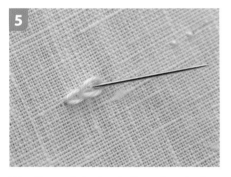

Bring the needle back up to the surface about 3mm (⅛in) away. This is the start of the third chain stitch. Make sure to bring the needle back up inside the loop of thread on the surface. Pull the stitch tight so the loop closes around the working thread. Continue working in this way till you reach the end of the line or shape.

To end the row of chain stitch, at the last stitch take the needle down outside the last loop. This secures and anchors the last chain. If the row is not complete and you need to introduce a new thread, secure the new thread further along the design line, continue the line of chain stitches by bringing the needle up through the loop of the last chain stitch and continue. This will give a single line of unbroken chain stitches.

Stitch Tension

Try to pull each stitch to the same tension. That way, each chain will be uniform.

Lazy daisies are worked in the same way. Start by bringing the needle and thread up to the surface of the work in the place where you want the lazy daisy to sit. Take the needle back down through the same hole and leave a small loop on the surface.

Bring the needle back up to the surface a short distance away (lazy daisies can have varying sizes depending on the effect you are trying to create). Make sure to bring the needle up inside the loop and pull the stitch tight.

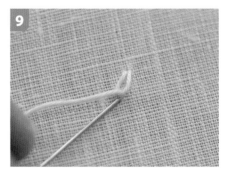

Then take the needle back down on the outside of the loop. This secures the lazy daisy.

Split Stitch

Split stitch is a really useful stitch in embroidery. It creates lovely delicate and fine lines for tendrils and outlines. It is also used as a preparatory stitch for long and short and satin stitches, as it creates a strong foundation for the other stitches to sit around and on top of. It is also a really quick way of filling shapes and can be used as a padding method when working padded satin shapes; this is known as long split stitch.

A line of split stitch.

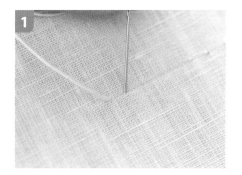

Begin by bringing the needle and thread up to the surface at the start of the design line. Take the needle back down a stitch distance away, about 3mm (⅛in).

Pull the stitch tight so it sits flat on the surface of the fabric.

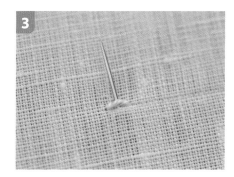

Bring the needle back up to the surface, coming up halfway along the first stitch and piercing the thread.

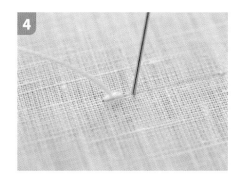

Make a second stitch that is the same length as the first. Pull the stitch tight and bring the needle back up through the middle of the second stitch, piercing the thread. Continue in this way with each new stitch emerging through the middle of the previous one.

Backstitch Method

You can also work split stitch using the backstitch method. This is where you split each stitch in a backward motion from the surface rather than from underneath. I find the method illustrated gives a much neater finish as there is less thread on the back.

Backstitch

Backstitch is really quick and simple. It is great for outlining shapes and works really well if you do not want to create too much decoration.

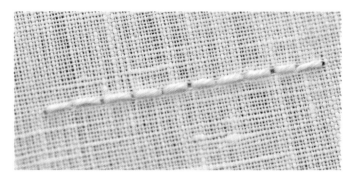

A row of backstitch.

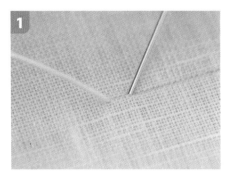

Start by bringing the needle and thread up to the surface at the start of the design line. Make the first stitch by taking the needle back down a stitch distance away, about 3mm (⅛in) .

Bring the needle back up to the surface a stitch distance away. Make the second stitch by taking the needle back down into the end of the first stitch.

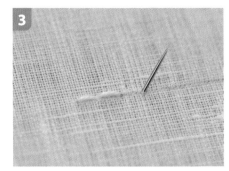

Bring the needle back up a stitch distance along the design line. To make the next stitch, take the needle down through the end of the previous stitch. Although you are moving forward along the design line, the stitches are made with a backwards motion. Repeat until you reach the end of the design line.

Backstitch can also be used to create a dense background texture when stitched in rows very close together and following a shaped outline, like the top two petals of this pansy. RSN Collection Box A3 415.

Open Fly Stitch

Open fly stitch is not often seen in white-work but I think it creates a really beautiful texture and is perfect for tendrils, sprigs, ferns and emulating snowflakes. In this sample I have kept it simple by keeping all the stitches the same size and equal distance apart, but experiment with this stitch to see what different effects you can create.

A row of open fly stitch.

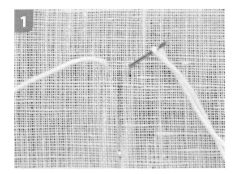

When working open fly stitch you need to start at the top of the design line and stitch down towards the bottom of the design. To start, bring the needle up just above and on the left side of the design line. Take the needle back down on the right of the design line as though to make a horizontal stitch.

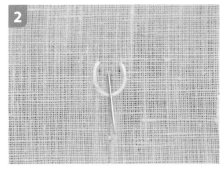

Pull the thread through, leaving a small loop on the surface. Bring the needle back up to the surface at the top of the design line and above the loop. Pull the thread tight so the loop closes around the working thread and a V shape is created.

Secure this loop by making a vertical stitch down along the design line. The length of this straight stitch will determine the distance between each V in the open fly stitch.

Bring the needle back up on the left-hand side, just underneath the tip of the V created by the first stitch. Take the needle back down on the right of the design line as though to make another horizontal stitch.

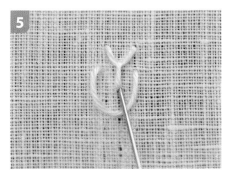

Pull the thread through, leaving a small loop on the surface. Bring the needle back up to the surface on the design line and through the same hole of the first vertical stitch. Pull the thread tight so the loop closes around the working thread and a V shape is created. Make the next vertical to secure this loop. Continue working in this way to create a continuous line of open fly.

Detached Fly Stitch

Detached fly stitches are individual open fly stitches that can be used to fill shapes, adding texture and pattern. They also work really well when stitched on the sides of tendrils and stems as they look a little like small leaves or sprouting twigs.

A single detached fly stitch.

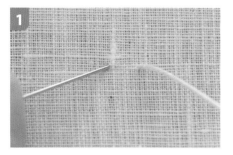

Bring the needle up to the surface in the place where you want the detached fly to sit. Take the needle back down as though to create a horizontal stitch. Pull the thread through, leaving a small loop on the surface.

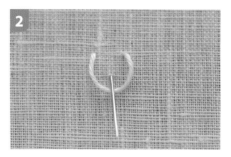

Bring the needle back up in the middle of this stitch and slightly further away and inside the loop. A small distance away will create a shallow V and a larger distance will create a more acute V.

Pull the thread tight so the loop closes around the working thread and the V is created. Secure the stitch by taking the needle down on the outside of the loop.

Seeding

Seeding is often used in whitework as it creates a soft shading-like quality that is simple yet very effective. In these samples I have kept it very simple but this stitch is great to experiment with. Try varying stitch lengths or working them densely packed fading to spaced out.

Bring the needle up in the area where you want to work the seeding. Make a tiny stitch in any direction and bring the needle back up to the surface. Continue to make tiny stitches in random directions till you have filled the desired area. Make sure that the stitches are all evenly spaced and the same size.

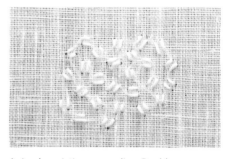

A simple variation on seeding. Double seeding is worked in the same way, only two parallel stitches are worked at the same time. The stitches should all be the same size and evenly spaced.

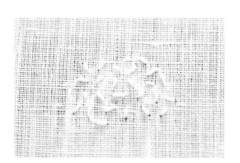

An area of seeding.

FRENCH KNOTS

French knots are a great stitch to use in whitework. When worked spaced apart they create texture and can fill areas to give a soft shaded effect. They can also be worked clustered together to fill spaces, which gives a rich texture and density that adds weight to designs. Stitching French knots clustered together is perfect for the centre of flowers. French knots can be worked in any thread; a single strand of stranded cotton will create tiny delicate French knots and a perle cotton will create really chunky French knots.

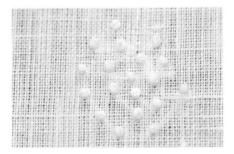

French knots.

Start by bringing up the needle and thread in the position where you want the French knot to sit. Hold the needle in one hand and parallel with the fabric. In the other hand, hold the thread fairly close to the surface of the fabric.

Then wrap the thread over the top of the needle from front to back. Make sure to only wrap the thread once!

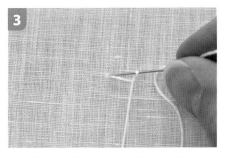

Place the tip of the needle back into the fabric a very small distance away. Be careful not to put the needle through the same hole where the thread is emerging from. If you do, the French knot may disappear through the fabric when pulled tight. Keep hold of the thread that is wrapped round the needle.

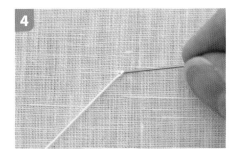

With the tip of the needle in position, pull the working thread tight round the needle and the knot will slide down the needle to sit on the surface of the fabric. Once the knot is in position, keep the tension of the thread tight.

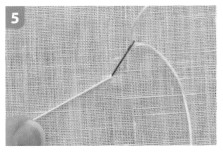

From the back, pull the needle and thread through. Only let go of the working thread at the last moment as the stitch tightens. This will ensure you have a neat and tight French knot.

Tiny French Knots

To make tiny French knots, use fine threads or a single strand of stranded cotton. To make larger French knots, use a thicker thread or multiple strands of stranded cotton in the needle. Make sure to only wrap the thread round the needle once.

A single French knot.

Clustered French knots.

BULLION KNOTS

Bullion knots are also a brilliant stitch for adding texture and dimension to pieces of whitework. They can be spaced apart or clustered together depending on the effect you are trying to create. They can be a little tricky to get right at first, so practise with a thicker thread to begin with as it makes them easier to work. Then try using finer threads to create small and delicate bullion knots. Also try experimenting with the length of bullion knots to create different textures.

Scattered bullion knots in different sizes.

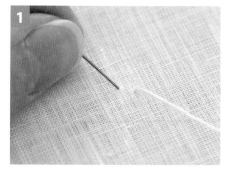

Bring the needle and thread up in the position where you want the bullion knot to sit. Take the needle back down a stitch length away. This length will depend on the required size of the bullion knot. Any more than 1cm (⅓in) in length and the bullion will be more difficult to work neatly.

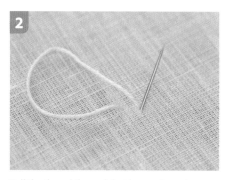

Pull the thread through but leave a large loop on the surface. Bring the needle back up through the same hole where the stitch started but do not pull the needle all the way through. Hold the needle in position with one hand from underneath.

With the other hand, wrap the loop around the needle several times. At this point keep the tension quite loose.

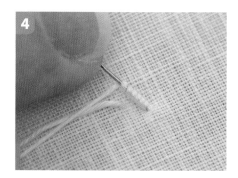

To check you have the right amount of wraps to fill the length of the bullion knot, pull the tension on the thread tight and lay the needle down flat along the stitch length. There should be enough wraps round the needle to reach the point where the thread enters the fabric.

Extra Wrap

I always add an extra wrap round the needle just to be sure I get nice, plump bullion knots.

When you have the right amount of wraps, keep the tension on the thread tight and push all the wraps down the needle so they sit on the surface of the fabric neatly on top of each other. Pull the needle gently through the wraps, trying to keep the tension on the wraps as tight as you can.

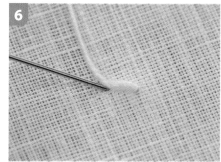

Keep tightening the stitch by pulling the working thread till the loop on the surface completely disappears. This can take some time to get right as you will need to readjust the tension of the wraps to get a tight, neat and even knot. To finish, take the needle down at the end of the stitch.

BUTTONHOLE STITCH

Buttonhole is a really versatile stitch and is used in lots of whitework techniques. It can be used as the foundation for outlining shapes as it creates and binds edges; it can also be used simply as decoration. It can be worked in any thread and the length of the buttonhole stitch can be whatever you wish. In this sample I have used coton à broder 16 but a finer thread would create a more delicate buttonhole stitch.

Buttonhole stitch can also be worked within any shape to create things like petals or leaves.

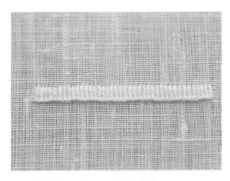

A straight line of buttonhole stitch.

Buttonhole leaf.

To make the first stitch, bring the needle and thread up at the start of the design line. Take the needle back down a stitch distance above and slightly to the right. Pull the stitch tight, leaving a small loop on the surface.

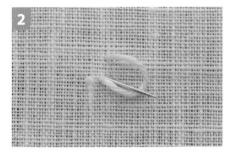

Bring the needle back up on the design line just next to the start of the first stitch and inside the loop. This should also be directly below where the needle was taken down.

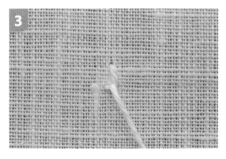

Pull this stitch tight, down and in the direction the buttonhole is travelling. This will ensure you get a neat and even edge to the buttonhole stitches.

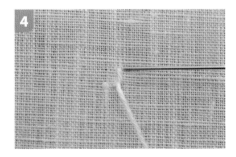

Make the second stitch by taking the needle down, above and slightly to the right of where the thread emerges from the fabric and the first stitch. Leave a small loop on the surface.

Bring the needle back up on the design line just next to the start of the previous stitch and inside the loop. This should also be directly below where the needle was taken down. Continue in this way till you reach the end of the design line or the area you wish to fill.

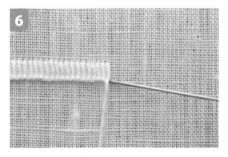

To secure the end of a thread or to finish the buttonhole stitch, take the needle down on the design line, on the outside of the loop made by the last stitch. This stitch over the last loop secures the whole row of buttonhole stitches. To introduce a new thread, secure it further along the design line and continue the buttonhole stitch as normal by bringing the needle up inside the loop of the last stitch.

COUCHING

Couching is used in lots of embroidery techniques but in whitework it is great for edging pulled-work shapes and creating slightly raised outlines. It can follow any shape and curve and can be fine and delicate or bold, depending on how many threads are being couched down. In this sample I have used six strands of stranded cotton in the core and one strand to couch with.

Core Strands

If using stranded cotton and needing multiple strands for the core, you need to separate each strand, then gather them back together. This is so you lose the twist the cotton has when it is cut from the skein, especially if you are using more than six strands for the core. If you are using thicker threads like perle or coton à broder, just cut as many strands as you require for the core and bunch them together to create the core.

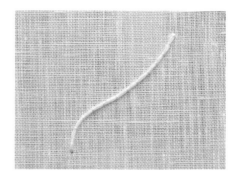

A wavy line of couching.

Start by bringing the needle and couching thread up to the surface at the start of the design line. Lay the core threads on the surface of the fabric along the design line. Make sure you have enough length of core threads to leave a tail of about 5–6cm (2in) at either end of the design line. Take the needle down over the top of the core threads, making a tiny stitch that will hold the core threads in place.

Continue to make these tiny couching stitches over the core thread at intervals of about 3mm (⅛in). These stitches should all be the same size and distance apart. They should also be at a 90-degree angle to the core threads. If working around a tight curve, work the stitches closer together to create a flowing line. When making these couching stitches, angle the needle up and out from under the core threads and back down towards and underneath the core threads.

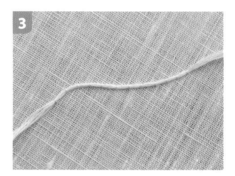

When couching the core threads it is important to make sure that the core threads are lying flat against the surface of the fabric. If you hold the core threads tight as you stitch, this will help to keep the core threads flat against the fabric and also stop them from twisting.

4 As you reach the end of the design line, thread the core threads into a needle with a large eye (such as a chenille needle). Then take this needle down into the fabric at the end of the design line. If you have lots of threads in the core, separate them into smaller groups and pull them through to the back separately. Do the same with the core threads at the beginning of the couching.

5 To secure the ends of the core threads on the back, start a new thread and run it through the stitching on the back. Then lay the core threads back on themselves. Starting at the end, oversew the core threads on the back for 1–2cm (½–¾in). These oversewing stitches should be quite close together.

6 When the core threads are secure cut away any excess thread. The securing process is the same for both ends of the couching.

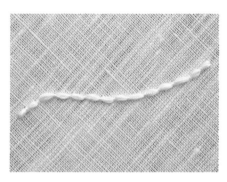

Ballooned couching. This is worked in the same way as ordinary couching, only the core threads are not pulled tight. They are left slack to create this slightly bobbled effect.

TRAILING

Trailing is another form of couching. In trailing, the core threads are completely covered by the closely worked couching stitches, creating a bold cord-like effect, which is great at adding depth to whitework designs. Trailing can be tapered, which creates beautifully smooth and flowing lines, which are perfect for outlines, lettering, floral stems, scrolling and borders. Working smooth, neat trailing takes a lot of practice, so to make it easier, start with a fairly thick core of twelve strands of stranded cotton. You can then experiment creating finer, bolder and tapered trailing.

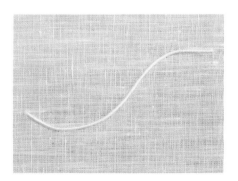

A wavy line of trailing with an even twelve-strand core.

Number of Strands

When deciding how many strands to include in the core for trailing, separate the single strands and group them back together. Twist these strands tightly in between your fingers and see how much the twisting compacts the threads. Lay them against the fabric to see the effect. You can then decide whether to add or remove some strands.

Start by cutting the length of the core threads, making sure you include enough excess thread in the length. I would suggest a minimum of 10cm (4in) for each end of the trailing. As before, you need to separate each strand then group them back together. Then thread up the core threads into a large-eyed needle (such as a chenille needle) and tie a knot at the end. Take the needle down into the fabric away from the start of the design line and in a place that will later be covered by stitch. Bring the needle and thread back up to the surface at the start of the design line. Do *not* cut the knot.

Move the core threads to one side and introduce the couching thread a little way in from the start of the design line. In this sample I have used one strand of stranded cotton, but other threads can be used. Trailing couched with one strand of stranded cotton will be very smooth as all the couching stitches blend together. Trailing couched with a thicker thread will be slightly more textured as each individual couching stitch will be more noticeable.

Lay the core threads over the design line and on the surface of the fabric. With your non-stitching hand, hold the core threads under tension. You need to keep the core threads under this tension for the whole time you are stitching. Couch over the core threads, keeping the couching stitches really close together so none of the core threads show between them. The stitches should be worked at a 90-degree angle to the core threads.

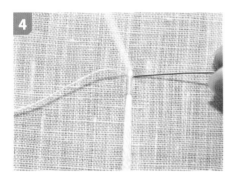

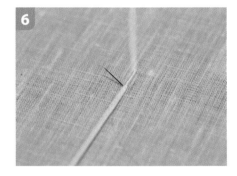

Work the couching stitches back towards the beginning of the design line first, to secure the end. When couching, angle the needle up and out from under the core threads and back down towards and underneath the core threads. This will ensure that your trailing has a really tight, neat and rounded form with clean edges.

When you reach the point where the core threads emerge from the fabric you may notice that the trailing line becomes slightly finer. This is fine; just make sure the end is completely covered with couching stitches. It helps if you work two or three small couching stitches just past the end as these give a smoother finish.

Bring the needle and thread back up to where you started couching. Secure the couching you have just completed with two tiny stab stitches. Work these stab stitches on the design line and they will be hidden by the trailing. Now continue couching the core threads following the design line and keeping the tension on the core threads.

Thread Management

When working a line of trailing, it is best to get the whole lot completed in one sitting. If you stop halfway through, when you come back your stitch tension and the tension you had on the core threads are not always the same. You will also need to change the working thread more regularly as worn thread is very obvious in trailing. This is known professionally as thread management.

Continue couching the core threads along the length of the design line. Just before you reach the end of the design line, stop couching and thread the core threads into a large-eyed needle (such as a chenille needle) and take them down through to the back of the work.

With one hand underneath the frame, keep the tension on these core threads while holding them out of the way. Continue to couch over the core threads as before till you reach the end. Work a few extra stitches right at the end to completely encase the core threads.

To finish, turn the frame over and simply cut away the excess core threads flush against the fabric and the end of the stitching (do this at both ends).

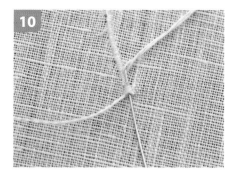

To secure the couching thread, carefully run it through the stitching in reverse a couple of times and trim away.

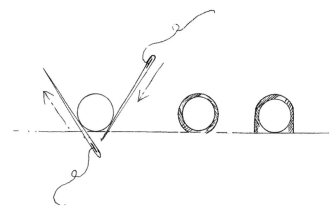

An illustration showing how to angle the needle when working trailing.

TAPERED TRAILING

Tapered trailing is created in much the same way as regular trailing but, as the title suggests, it is tapered so there are a few things that need to be worked differently. Whether it is at the start of the design line or right in the middle of the design line, you always need to start the couching at the thickest part of the trailing. In this sample the thickest part of trailing has a core of eighteen single strands of stranded cotton; the finest part has only three single strands of stranded cotton.

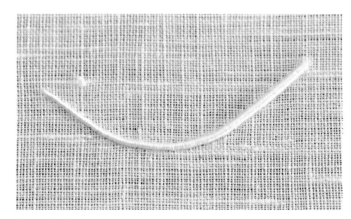

Tapered trailing.

continued on the following page…

Start the trailing in the same way as before, gathering all the core threads together that will form the thickest part of the trailing. Thread up the core threads into a large-eyed needle (such as a chenille needle) and tie a knot at the end. Take the needle down into the fabric away from the start of the design line and in a place that will later be covered by stitch. Then bring the needle and thread back up to the surface at the start of the design line. Do *not* cut the knot.

Lay the core threads over the design line and start couching the core threads where the trailing will be at its thickest. Remember to angle the needle and to keep a nice tension on the core threads as you stitch. When you want to start tapering the trailing, fold the core threads back on themselves. Separate the number of threads you wish to remove from the bottom of the bunch of core threads and hold them under tension. With sharp scissors, cut these threads away very close to where they emerge from the core.

Then lay the remaining core threads back over the design line and continue couching, removing core threads as you wish till you reach the end of the design line. If you started in the middle of the design line, go back to where you started and repeat for the other half. The ends of the tapered trailing are finished and secured in the same way as before.

Smooth Tapered Trailing

For smooth and gradual tapered trailing I would suggest cutting two or three strands from the core each time, but if you want your tapered trailing to be more dramatic cut a few more. If using stranded cotton as your core I would use three single strands as a minimum for the core. It is always worth stitching a little practice sample first to see the effect before working on a final piece.

ROWS OF TRAILING

Multiple rows of trailing can be worked next to each other and can create some really great effects. It does not matter if the trailing is one size or tapered, or if the different rows of trailing are different sizes.

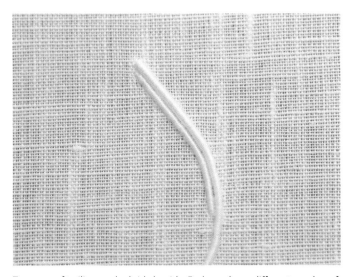

Two rows of trailing worked side by side. Each row has a different number of threads in the core to add more depth.

1

Work the first row of trailing following the previous instructions. Then introduce the core threads for the new row of trailing in the same way as before, but make sure to bring the new core threads up very close to the first row of trailing.

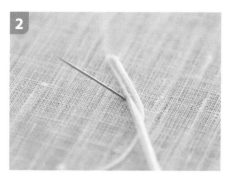

2

Couch the new row of trailing in the same way as before but make sure to bring the needle up on the outside of the new row of trailing, angling the needle out from underneath.

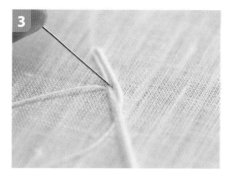

3

Take the needle back down in between the two rows of trailing, but make sure to angle the needle back down, towards the first row of trailing. This makes sure that the new row of trailing hugs the first row of trailing tightly. When the new row of trailing is complete, plunge the end and secure as before.

INTERTWINING TRAILING

Trailing, whether tapered or not, is fantastic at creating lettering, scrolls, curves and tendrils. In whitework you often see trailing intertwining and merging, which looks really beautiful. The trailing is worked in the same way as before, the lines of trailing just cut across each other or merge. The following instructions will show you how to create a really neat join.

Intertwining trailing.

1

Stitch the rows of trailing following the previous instructions. Just before one row of trailing crosses another, stop couching. Thread the core threads into a large-eyed needle (such as a chenille needle), and take the needle down, angling the needle underneath the already existing row of trailing. Bring the needle back out on the other side, angling the needle out from underneath the existing row of trailing.

2

Pull all the core threads back through to the surface and continue couching as normal until you reach where the lines of trailing cross each other. Remember to keep tension on the core threads while you stitch. Make the final couching stitch on this side and take the needle down. Pass the needle underneath the cross section on the back, and bring the needle back up ready to continue couching on the new side.

Long and Short

Long and short is a really versatile stitch and is used in lots of different embroidery techniques. In whitework it creates areas of dense, bold white, which contrasts really well with the fine fabrics and stitches that are used in whitework. This helps add depth and interest to designs. Long and short can be worked in a number of ways – which way you choose will depend on the design and the area that is going to be stitched. In these samples I have used one strand of stranded cotton but other threads may be used.

Straight Long and Short

What I call straight long and short is the whitework equivalent to tapestry shading. It is worked like tapestry shading in that all the stitches follow one direction; unlike tapestry shading, however, the direction does not have to be vertical. It can be in any direction through the middle of a shape. Also the stitches are not shaded, as all the thread is white, so the direction of the stitches is important as they will reflect light differently.

A simple leaf shape filled with straight long and short. See how all the stitches run straight through the shape from tip to tip.

Begin by preparing the area that is going to be filled with long and short with a split-stitch outline (*see* the instructions for split stitch earlier in this chapter). If a point needs to be created, work up one side as normal. To start the next side, work a backstitch first that shares the same hole as the last stitch (this creates a really sharp point). Then continue with the split stitch down the remaining side.

To stitch the first row, start by bringing the needle and thread up inside the shape and in a central position towards the top of the shape. Make the first stitch by taking the needle down over the split-stitch edge. To create a sharp point, extend this stitch slightly further than the split-stitch outline.

For the next stitch, bring the needle up again within the shape and just next to the first stitch. This stitch needs to be a different length than the first, so you need to bring the needle up slightly below or above where the first stitch emerges. Take the needle back down against the split-stitch outline, angling the needle down towards the split-stitch outline and previous stitch.

4

Bring the needle back up inside the shape to make the next stitch, making sure it is not in the same position as the first two stitches. Continue working in this way to one side of the shape. All these stitches should fit snugly together with no gaps in between.

5

With one side complete, come back to the middle and work the other side in the same way. This is the first row complete. Notice that all the stitches are different lengths but have been worked straight and in the same direction. Try to keep the length of the stitches as random as possible, as this gives the smoothest finish.

6

To stitch the second row, start in the middle of the shape as before. Bring the needle up about one third of the way into the first row. If you can, try to split the first stitch in the first row. Do not worry if you cannot split this first stitch but you should aim to try and split as many stitches as you can.

7

Then take the needle back down into the fabric, following the direction of all the other stitches. Bring the needle back up in the first row just next to the previous stitch but either slightly below or above it. Take the needle back down into the fabric, making another stitch and remembering to vary the stitch lengths.

8

Continue to work in this way across one half of the row. When you reach the edge, make sure to work the stitches so the needle goes down over the split-stitch outline, remembering to angle the needle as you do so. Then return to the middle and work the other half in the same way.

9

Work in this way for as many rows as the shape requires. On the final row, bring the needle up, splitting the stitches of the previous row. Then take the needle back down on the outside edge of the split-stitch outline. When complete there should be no split-stitch outline visible, there should be no gaps between the stitches and the outline should be smooth and neat.

Stitch Length

The average length of the stitches in long and short will vary depending on the size of the shape you are filling. The size of the shape will help to set the scale for the average stitch length. If you have a small fiddly shape, the stitches need to be fairly small as you need at least two rows of long and short, and working small stitches helps in getting round, tight curves. For larger shapes, the stitches can be slightly longer as this gives a smoother finish and means the long and short won't look heavy and overstitched. However large the shape though, any long and short stitch should never be more than about 1cm (⅓in) in length

NATURAL LONG AND SHORT

Natural long and short is where the long and short stitches follow the natural direction and form of the shape or area that is being filled. The stitches will change angle as they are worked through the shape, adding movement and texture. You can use a blue pencil to draw in direction lines that the stitches will follow. These will help you to change angle as you work through the shape.

Natural long and short. Notice how the stitches are angled in towards the centre of the leaf. As the stitches are worked in rows, the gently changing angle of the stitches means that they smoothly converge into one central point at the bottom tip of the leaf.

Start by preparing the area with the split-stitch outline as before. To stitch the first row, bring the needle up inside the shape and in a central position towards the top of the shape. Take the needle back down on the outside edge of the split-stitch outline. Then bring the needle up slightly higher than where the first stitch emerged, angling the needle out from under the first stitch. This will help to change the angle as you work across the shape.

Continue working in this way to one side of the shape, gently fanning out the stitches till you reach the correct angle. You can also bring the needle up directly underneath the previous stitch before taking the needle down over the design line, which will also help to gently fan out the stitches. The stitches will be slightly closer together where they emerge from the fabric than on the outside edge. Then come back to the centre and work the other side in the same way.

When working the second and subsequent rows, like before, the needle is brought up through the previous row and taken back down into the fabric. When working these rows the stitches should all be angled slightly into the centre to keep the angle. This is done either by angling the needle down underneath the previous stitch or by taking the needle down directly below the previous stitch. Always remember to keep the placement of the stitches varying and random to create a smooth finish.

PLANNING LONG AND SHORT

When using long and short stitch in a whitework piece you need to think carefully how that stitch is going to look when finished. Long and short will fill an area densely with stitch, but it will also add dimension and texture. The direction the stitches are worked can change how the shape will look when finished and this is where straight or natural long and short come into play. Before you start stitching an area of long and short, always draw up a stitch direction plan first. You may need to do a few before you have one you are happy with, but this will be your guide as you work through the shape to make sure your stitch angles are correct. This will also be your guide to mark the stitch angles on the linen if you choose to do so. If you do this, make sure to always use a blue pencil.

The following images show the stitch directions for the leaf samples on the previous pages, but also for the rabbit shown on the front cover. See how the natural long and short gives the leaf shape more dimension and makes it look more delicate and life-like, whereas with the rabbit motif both the straight and natural long and short work equally well. Carefully planning small details like this is what will pull your design together and bring it to life.

Leaf motif with natural long and short stitch direction.

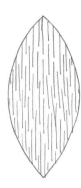

Leaf motif with straight long and short stitch direction.

Rabbit motif with natural long and short stitch direction.

Rabbit motif with straight long and short stitch direction.

Close up detail of the stitched rabbit motif showing the detail of the natural long and short stitch.

CHAPTER 10

SATIN STITCH

Satin stitch and all its variants are widely used in many different types of embroidery, not just whitework. Yet satin stitch works so well when used in conjunction with the other whitework techniques because it creates smooth, solid areas of tone that create contrast to the textures and openness of the other stitches.

You see satin stitch used widely with cutwork, broderie anglaise and Ayrshire embroideries, and the contrast between the areas of open work and the satin stitch is very satisfying. Like many of the other stitches included in this book, working satin stitch in whitework will help you to practise and refine your stitching technique. Mistakes and slightly fluffy or wonky stitches show up more easily in whitework. The aim is to create a smooth and shiny surface on your satin stitch.

The techniques explained in this chapter were first developed by Jenny Adin-Christie.

SATIN-STITCH DOTS

Stain-stitch dots look as though they are the opposite of eyelets. They are an excellent stitch in whitework because they are versatile, quick to work, and very useful. They can be used in a range of sizes, and can be padded or not. They are particularly effective when worked around an eyelet centre so create a flower-like effect.

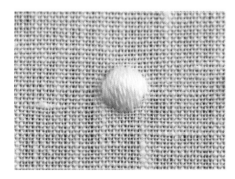

Satin-stitch dots are really quick and simple to achieve, and can be used for many different things. Visually they are the opposite of eyelets and can be worked in various sizes; they can be padded or unpadded. They look great when worked around an eyelet centre as they look like little petals.

Two dots, each a different size but both worked with two layers of padding. For the smaller dot on the left, the final layer of satin has been worked in a single strand of stranded cotton. For the larger dot on the right, the final layer of satin has been worked in coton à broder 25.

Start by drawing the circle outline onto the fabric using a sharp blue pencil and a circle template. Then outline the circle with split stitch using a single strand of stranded cotton. You can use this thread for the padding, or if using a thicker thread for the padding, anchor and then cut this thread away.

To start the padding (anchor the new thread if using one), make a vertical stitch in the centre of the circle. The direction of the stitch should go from the bottom of the circle to the top. Make sure to leave a little gap between the split-stitch edge of the circle and this first padding stitch. Then bring the needle back up to the surface just next to where you have just taken it down.

Make a second vertical stitch, just to the side of the first. This time the direction of the stitch should go from the top of the circle to the bottom. Doing this creates a very small stitch on the back of the embroidery, which means the padding is focused to the front for maximum effect.

Then make a third padding stitch on the opposite side of the central stitch. The direction of this stitch should be from the bottom to the top of the circle. This completes the first layer of padding. Make sure that when the first layer is complete there is a little halo of visible fabric between the stitches of the first layer of padding and the split-stitch outline, as this is where the second layer will sit.

You can now start the second layer of padding by bringing the needle up on the left, just to the inside of the split-stitch outline. Now make a horizontal stitch across the centre of the circle, taking the needle down on the right-hand side, just in inside the split-stitch outline. This is the first stitch of the second layer of padding.

Then bring the needle up just above this stitch, ready to make the next. Work the rest of the padding stitches on the second layer in the same way as the first, travelling back and forth across the circle, leaving only tiny stitches on the back. When all the padding stitches are complete, secure the thread within the circle and cut away the thread.

To create smooth and even-domed padding for your dot, you need to make sure there is an equal amount of padding stitches on either side of the first central stitch on each layer of the padding. Depending on the size of your dot, you may need more stitches on either side of the central stitch than I have shown here; that is fine. Just make sure that the final layer of padding is worked right up to the split-stitch outline.

Fresh Thread

For the final satin-stitch layer, regardless of whether you are using the same type of thread that you used for the padding, always start with a fresh new thread. This will ensure you get a lovely smooth shine to the satin stitch.

Anchor the new thread within the padding. Then bring the needle up on the edge of the split-stitch outline at the centre of the bottom of the circle. Take the needle down on the opposite side of the circle, angling it underneath the split-stitch edge in order to make the first satin stitch. Bring the needle back up slightly to the left, angling it out from underneath the first satin stitch.

All the stitches are worked in the same direction. Make the next stitch slightly to the left of the first by angling the needle down towards the split-stitch outline and underneath the previous stitch. You want to keep the edge of the dot as smooth and round as possible so angle the needle as you stitch.

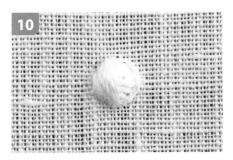

Continue to complete the left side of the dot until all of the split stitch is completely covered on that side and you have a clean, smooth and rounded edge. As you work this side, count how many stitches you worked after the first central stitch as you want to replicate that on the right side.

The right side of the dot is worked in exactly the same way as the left. Come back to that first central stitch and begin the right side of the satin stitch from there. Angle the needle out from underneath and back down towards the previous stitch as before. Repeat as closely as possible the stitching on the left hand side, so you create a smooth and even dot.

When the dot is complete, turn the frame over and secure the thread on the back by sliding the needle through the stitches on the back a few times. Then cut off the thread.

Good Working Practice

When the left side is complete, work two securing stitches within the padding before continuing to the right side. Doing this means that if something goes wrong with the right side and you need to unpick, the left side will be safe.

PADDED SLANTED SATIN, WITH SATIN STITCH PADDING

Using the satin-stitch method for creating the padding when working a simple padded satin-stitch shape is really quick and simple, especially if you use a thicker thread to stitch the padding. This method creates a smooth, slightly domed padded shape that is slightly higher in the centre, sloping down gently towards the edges. It is very important to work out the layers for the padding before you begin to stitch, as you need to make sure you leave enough room to get all the padding layers in; you also need to make sure that the final layer of padding is stitched in a different direction to the final layer of satin stitch, or the two layers will sink into each other. In this sample the slanted angle of the stitch is

A simple leaf shape worked in slanted satin with satin-stitch padding.

bottom left to top right, but the same rules apply if you were to stitch the slanted satin in the opposite direction. The final layer of slanted satin in this sample has been worked in stranded cotton.

A diagram showing how the layers of padding are worked out in order to make sure the final layer of padding and the final layer of satin are not worked in the same direction.

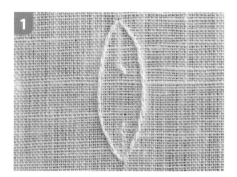

Start by outlining the shape with split stitch, using a single strand of stranded cotton. You can work the securing stitches within the shape as these will be covered with padding. You can use this thread to work the padding stitches but using a single strand of stranded cotton for padding this way will be very slow to work and will create very gentle padding. I always try to use thicker thread like a coton à broder or perle thread for padding.

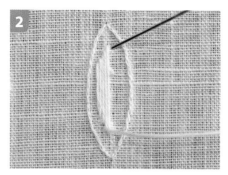

Begin to work the first layer of padding, starting in the centre at the widest or longest part of the shape. Continue to work to one side, making sure to stitch back and forth across the shape, leaving tiny stitches on the back of the embroidery. Make sure to leave a big enough gap between this first layer of padding and the split-stitch outline, ensuring there is enough space to fit all the other layers in.

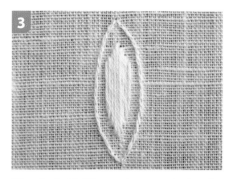

When the first half is complete, come back to the first stitch and on the other side, fill in the first layer of padding in the same way. As best you can, you need to try to have the same number of stitches either side of the central stitch, as this will give an even layer of padding.

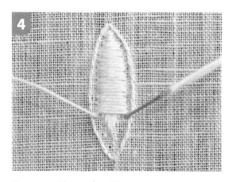

The second layer of padding is worked over the top of the first in the same way. Only this time, change the angle of the stitches. Again, start in the middle at the widest or longest part and fill in one half. Then come back to the centre and fill in the other half to complete the second layer. Make sure to leave a halo of fabric visible in between this second layer and the split-stitch outline.

Stitch Direction Rule

If you are a seasoned stitcher and your slanted satin stitch has just never been quite right, this trick might be just what you need. For those who are just starting out, this might make slanted satin stitch easier for you.

Always start at the widest part of the shape, which will be somewhere in the middle. Starting and setting the 45-degree angle in the middle of the shape means you have only got half the chance of changing the angle by the time you reach the end.

From this middle point, to fill in the top half of the shape, bring the needle up on the right-hand side leaving a tiny gap between the previous stitch. Then take the needle down on the left-hand side, angling the needle down underneath the previous stitch.

The direction of the stitch should be opposite to the direction in which the stitches are travelling.

Next fill in the bottom half of the shape. To do this, bring the needle up on the left, coming down slightly and leaving a tiny gap between the previous stitch. Then take the needle down on the right, angling the needle up underneath the previous stitch.

This guide works for slanted satin stitches worked in either direction and for many different shapes, and even if the angle changes.

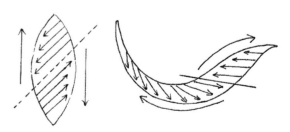

A diagram showing how the stitch direction rule works for a simple satin shape and a more complicated curving sating shape.

5 The third and final layer of padding can then be worked in the same way as the first two, but again make sure to change the angle of the stitches. The padding stitches of this final layer should sit just inside the split-stitch outline so that the whole shape is filled with padding. When complete, secure the thread within the padding and cut away the thread.

6 The final layer of satin stitch can now be worked, so begin by securing the new thread within the padding. Bring the needle just to the outside edge of the split-stitch outline, and make the first slanted satin stitch so it will sit across the shape at its widest point at a 45-degree angle, taking the needle down just on the outside edge of the split stitch on the opposite side.

7 Next complete the bottom half of the shape. When pulling the needle up on the left, leave a small space after the previous stitch. This will help to keep the angle as you stitch and stop it from flattening as you continue to stitch.

8 When taking the needle down on the right, make sure to angle the needle up towards the previous stitch, as this too will help to maintain the angle of the stitches and ensure a smooth, clean outline.

9 Keep stitching in this way, filling in the bottom half of the shape, maintaining the 45-degree angle as you go. When you reach the tip of the shape and are making the final stitch, bring the needle up just beyond the split-stitch edge to accentuate the point. Then take the needle down on the right again, sliding the needle underneath the previous stitch and through into the padding. Doing this helps tuck in that final stitch, giving a nice, sharp point. You can then secure the thread within the padding.

10 The top half of the shape can now be stitched in the same way. Only this time you need to bring the needle up on the right-hand side of the shape, leaving a tiny gap between the previous stitch. Then take the needle down on the left, angling the needle down towards the previous stitch. Accentuating the tip for the final stitch is also done in the same way as the bottom half, only as the satin stitch is now complete, take the needle through to the back.

11 With the slanted satin stitch complete, and looking smooth and even on the surface, the best way to secure the working thread is to turn the frame over and slide the needle through a few of the stitches on the back, then cut the thread

PADDED SLANTED SATIN, WITH LONG SPLIT-STITCH PADDING

Jenny Adin-Christie developed the method for the long split-stitch padding. This method takes a little more time to build up the layers; however, using a thicker thread for padding will make this easier. Choose for yourself where the padding is focused, so one side or one end of the shape could be padded higher than the other. This method still creates a smooth slightly domed finish, but now the dome of the padding does not have to be in the centre. Again, it is very important to work out the layers of padding before you begin as you need to make sure that they are smooth, even and gradual. Otherwise, when you work the final layer of satin, you will find that they do not sit flat and smooth on the surface of the padding underneath.

In this sample the slanted angle of the stitch is bottom left to top right, but the same rules apply if you were to stitch the slanted satin in the opposite direction. The slanted satin stitch in this sample has been worked in coton à broder 25.

A simple leaf shape worked in slanted satin with long split-stitch padding.

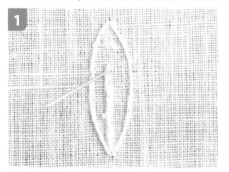

Use a single strand of stranded cotton to outline the shape in split stitch. Then use a thicker thread like a coton à broder or perle thread for the padding. Anchor the thread inside the shape. Start at the bottom, and sew a row of long split stitch through the centre of the shape. Long split stitch is worked in the same way as ordinary split stitch, but with the stitches slightly longer on the surface and the needle pulled back up through the end of the previous stitch, rather than the middle. This concentrates the longer stitches on the surface, which makes the padding, and the smaller stitches on the underneath, which creates less bulk on the back.

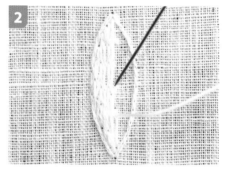

Complete one half of the shape first by working rows in long split stitch, back and forth across its the length. Keep the stitches similar in length, and the rows tightly together, and work all the way up to the split stitch outline. When one half of the shape is full, go back to the centre and complete the other side. This is the first layer of padding.

Subsequent layers are worked in the same way. Begin each new layer of padding directly on top of the layer below. Each new layer should end just inside the layer below it, leaving a little of the row beneath visible. This will ensure you create padding that is smooth and domed and gently slopes down towards the edges. The final shape of the padding will depend on where the layers start, which could be in the centre again or just off to one side.

When all the padding is complete, thread up and secure the thread you are going to use to stitch your final layer of slanted satin. Follow the same instructions for working the final layer of slanted satin as previously described. Make sure to angle your needle to get the smoothest shape and edges, and secure on the back in the same way.

Here you can see how all the layers of long split-stitch padding sit on top of each other and a smooth domed effect has been created. The padding in this sample is very simple and domed in the centre but practise and experiment to see what different padding effects you can create.

Padded Slanted Satin, on Curving Shapes

Working slanted satin on a shape that curves and rolls, though a little more challenging, is worth the practice as it looks beautiful in whitework and is often used for long flowing leaves or grasses and monogrammed letters. Because the angle of the stitches changes, as you work through the shape you need to work wedge stitches, which help the slanted satin to change angle without the stitches on the inside curves becoming overcrowded. This sample has been worked in coton à broder 25.

A curving and widening shape worked in slanted satin with wedge stitches, and padded in the long split-stitch method.

1

I would advise that you sketch the changes of angle on paper before you start to stitch. This will help you know where wedge stitches need to be worked to change the angle more quickly. If not you could end up with a lumpy end to the shape, which you may then have to unpick.

2a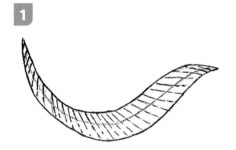

2b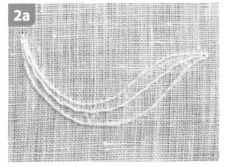

Outline the shape as before, using a single strand of stranded cotton. Then, using a thicker thread (like coton à broder or perle) and the long split-stitch method, create the padding for the shape. Make sure that the padding follows the lines of the shape, and that when complete, all the layers build up to create a smooth, curved dome to the shape.

3

When the padding is complete, the next step is to start the slanted satin stitch. Begin at the widest point of the shape, bringing the needle up just outside the split stitch outline, and taking the needle back down on the opposite side of the shape, setting the angle. Although the shape is not even and the angle is going to change, try to get this first stitch at a 45-degree angle.

4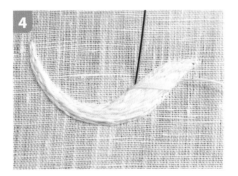

If there is one, always choose the simplest and most straightforward half to complete first, so you can get into the flow of stitching before tackling the trickier half. Remember to angle the needle as you work to create a smooth, clean outline and follow the tips for slanted satin stitch to make sure you are stitching in the right direction to maintain the correct angles. For this part of the shape, the change in angle is only slight, and this can be achieved by making slightly bigger or smaller gaps in between each stitch as you bring the needle up and take it down.

5

Come back to where you started and remember that you will now be stitching in the opposite direction so need to bring the needle up and take it down accordingly. This half of the shape has a very dramatic angle change as it curves down and round, so to help achieve this, wedge stitches will need to be used. A wedge stitch is made by bringing the needle up through the padding, and angling it out from underneath the previous stitch. Take the needle back down just to the outside of the split-stitch outline as before.

continued on the following page…

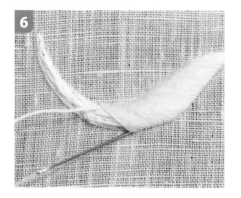

6

You can work as many wedge stitches as you need to in order to help change the angle smoothly and quickly, and they can be worked anywhere throughout the shape. Just make sure that either side of each wedge stitch you have at least one satin stitch, as this will help the wedge stitches to blend in and the change in angle to look smooth and invisible.

Twisting and Untwisting Thread

Many embroiderers unknowingly have the habit of either twisting or untwisting the thread as they work. This is not usually an issue, but with satin stitch, as you want to create a smooth, flat, shiny surface, this is something to watch out for. If you notice that your stitches are becoming over-twisted, take the needle through to the back of the work, drop the needle and let it hang; it will untwist by itself. If you notice that your stitches are becoming untwisted, bring the needle up to the surface and twist the needle in your fingers until the twist in the thread tightens up again. This is usually only noticeable if you are using thicker threads like coton à broder and perle.

VOIDED SATIN SHAPES

Voided satin shapes are a simple but very effective way of creating some extra detail and dimension in whitework embroidery. Voids can be created on tiny petals and leaves but also on larger areas of satin too. Creating voids does take some practice so start simple before moving on to more complicated shapes.

A simple small petal shape worked in slanted satin with a void down the lower centre half.

Start by outlining the shape with split stitch. Then work a row of split stitch just next to the line where the void will be placed.

Work long split-stitch padding, following the shape, making sure not to cover the split stitch that indicates the void.

Start the satin stitch just above where the top of the void starts. This allows you to work a few stitches next to each other, to set the angle, before you start stitching the void. When you reach where the void starts, bring the needle up on the outside edge as before. Then take the needle straight down next to the row of split stitch that indicates the void.

Continue working these half-length stitches, creating the void. Make sure to maintain the angle as you work down the shape.

When you reach the bottom tip, slightly extend the final stitch to ensure you have a nice, sharp point.

Come back to where you started and complete the satin stitch that covers the top half of the shape. Make sure to keep the same angle all the way through the shape.

With the top half complete, it is now time to work the second half of the void. This is done in exactly the same way as before. Take care not to disturb the satin stitches worked on the first half when taking the needle down. Make sure to keep the angle so it is the same on both sides of the void.

Work down the void, ensuring all the spilt stitches are covered. When you reach the bottom, angle the final stitch underneath the slightly extended stitch to ensure the sharp tip is maintained. Secure the thread and your voided satin petal is now complete.

HISTORICAL SATIN-STITCH SHAPES

If you look at historical and traditional whitework pieces that have satin worked on them, you will notice that the satin stitch cuts across the shape at 90 degrees rather than using a slanted satin at 45 degrees. This is the traditional way to work satin stitch and if you wish to work your satin stitches in this way that is absolutely fine. However, I find I create a much smoother and more elegant-looking shape by using the slanted-satin method, which is why I have focused mainly on the slanted-satin method. If you choose to work in the traditional method, the technique is very much the same as the satin-stitch dots, only the stitches are horizontal rather than vertical.

Here I have worked a few samples to show how shapes can look different, with something as simple as a change in the stitch angle.

When coming up with your own designs, showing different versions of the same thing is not only good practice in terms of stitching and technique, it also creates interest. For example, if you have three satin-stitch flowers, work each one in a slightly different way. Below are some more samples of more traditional satin-stitch petal shapes for inspiration.

A traditional piece of whitework, showing areas of satin stitch being worked at a 90-degree angle across the shapes. Whitework pocket bag from the RSN Collection (item E141).

Two undulating leaf shapes, both worked in satin stitch. On the left you can see the slanted-satin method and on the right you can see the traditional method.

Two simple petal shapes, both worked in satin stitch. On the left you can see the traditional method and on the right you can see the slanted-satin method.

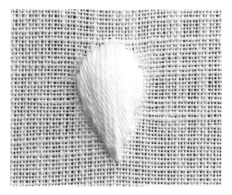

A sample showing a simple rounded and padded petal shape with the satin stitch cutting across the shape vertically.

A sample showing a simple rounded and padded petal shape with the satin stitch fanning out and round from the middle, with a void down the centre.

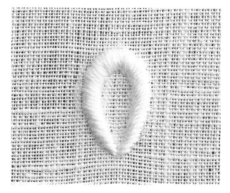

A sample showing an open rounded and padded petal shape with a large void in the middle. The satin stitch fans out and round from the centre.

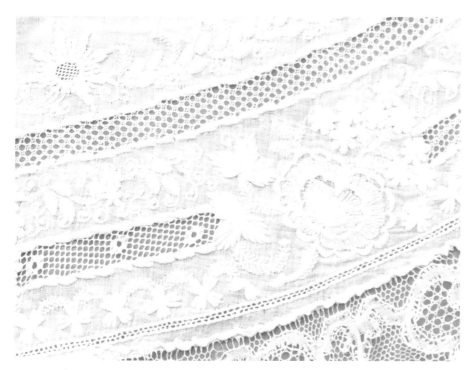

A nineteenth-century Pelerine 1830-40, worked in Ayrshire embroidery, showing multiple different ways in which satin stitch could be utilised. (From the Olive Matthews collection, Chertsey Museum MT.1264)

CHAPTER 11

COMBINING TECHNIQUES AND PROJECTS

In their own right, each of the whitework embroidery techniques create beautiful pieces of work. But when whitework techniques are combined harmoniously, truly spectacular embroideries, showing texture, depth, tone and technique can be created.

Understanding how to combine whitework techniques takes practice, not only because certain techniques work better together when done in a certain way, but also because the choice of fabric you choose to use is important too, along with which stitches need to be worked first and where.

At the beginning of this book, Chapter 2 goes through what types of fabric are best chosen when stitching a certain whitework technique. When combining techniques, though, how do you know which one to pick? Unfortunately there is no right or wrong answer to this, as any design could have any number of different techniques and stitches and you need to take all into consideration when choosing your fabric.

However, here are some points to think about that will make your decision easier.

Does the design have pulled- or drawn-thread areas? If the answer is yes, then you need to make sure that you pick an even-weave fabric to show these pulled and drawn stitches at their best.

Does the design have areas of cutwork or large eyelets? If the answer is yes, then you need to pick a fabric that has a close weave in order to support the stitches that support the large areas that will be cut away.

What does this mean for your choice of fabric and for your design? Well, it means that you need a closely woven even-weave fabric such as 55TPI Kingston linen, as it suits the needs of all your stitches. However, it means that the pulled and drawn areas will be more difficult to work, as the threads could be trickier to count. It is also worth bearing in mind that as the fabric is a closer weave, the pulled and drawn stitches will be much smaller, finer and more delicate in appearance, which may have an effect on which pulled or drawn stitches you choose to use.

Test Samples

Before starting a final piece of embroidery, I always work a few samples of some of the stitches I am planning to use to see how they look in terms of texture and scale, but also to see how easy they are to work on my chosen fabric.

The small projects on the following pages have been designed to introduce you to how some of the whitework techniques can be combined and, because they are combined, how they need to be worked. These will give you a firm understanding of the order of work and a good foundation to start from and begin to develop your own whitework designs.

PROJECT 1

1970s WALLPAPER FLOWERS

This project is fairly simple, combining pulled- and drawn-thread stitches and eyelets, along with a number of surface stitching to finish off and complete the design. It is perfect if you are new to combining whitework techniques.

I have worked this sample on 25TPI Edinburgh linen but it would be just as effective if it was worked on a finer evenweave fabric too.

The following instructions give the details of which stitches go where and how I have counted them, but feel free to experiment and try your own stitch variations.

Tonal drawing for the wallpaper design.

Stitch plan for the wallpaper design.

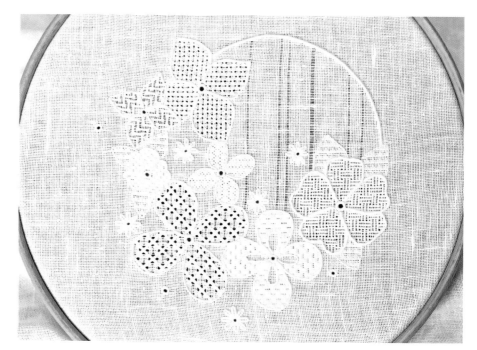

The finished 1970s wallpaper flowers.

What You Will Need

Equipment

+ 8in bound ring frame
+ Tissue paper
+ Blue pencil/water-soluble pen
+ Tapestry needle size 28
+ Embroidery needle sizes 10 and 12
+ Sharp embroidery scissors
+ Design template

Materials

+ 25TPI Edinburgh linen (or evenweave fabric of your choice)
+ Fine white lace thread
+ Anchor/DMC coton à broder 25
+ Anchor/DMC stranded cotton

Transfer the design onto the linen using the tracing method. (For this design I used a blue pencil, but choose whichever tool you prefer.) Do not transfer the straight vertical lines for the drawn threads; these need to be tacked. Insert the linen into the 8in ring frame with a piece of tissue covering the design. When the frame is tight, tear away some of the tissue, revealing the centre of the design.

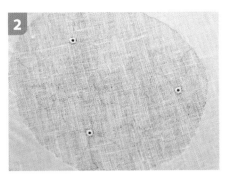

Using a tapestry 28 needle threaded with two strands of stranded cotton, work a counted full eyelet in the centre of the three largest flowers. The counted full eyelet is counted over four threads.

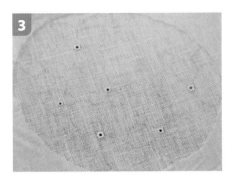

Then move on to the three medium flowers. In the centre of each, work a counted full eyelet, this time counting over three threads.

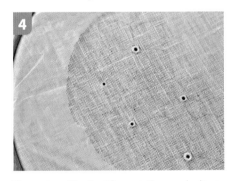

The centre of the final flower is then worked in a counted full eyelet, this time counting over two threads. Again, use the tapestry 28 needle and two strands of stranded cotton to do this.

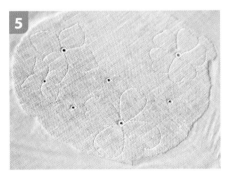

The next step is to work the double-running-stitch outline around the four flowers that are to be worked in pulled-thread stitches and pulled-satin stitches. Use a fine lace thread and a size 10 or 12 embroidery needle to do this.

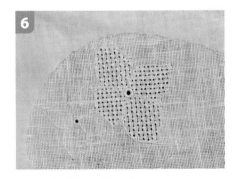

The petals of the first large flower can now be filled with the pulled stitch honeycomb, counting over three threads. Notice how on each of the two opposite petals the pattern has been worked either horizontally or vertically. Keep using the fine lace thread, but change the needle for the tapestry 28.

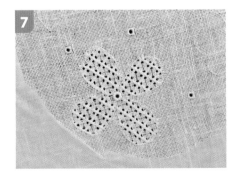

The petals of the second large flower can then be filled with the pulled pattern open trellis, counting over six threads. Again, use the tapestry 28 needle and the fine lace thread.

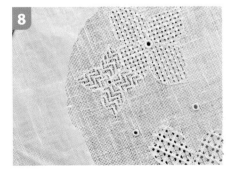

Keep using the tapestry 28 needle, but now thread it with a single strand of stranded cotton. Fill the petals of the small flower to the left with pulled-satin pattern 2 (*see* Chapter 4), counting four stitches over three threads.

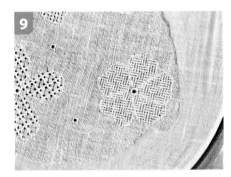

The petals of the large flower on the right can then be filled with pulled-satin pattern 3 (*see* Chapter 4), counting seven stitches over three threads. Again, use the tapestry 28 needle and a single strand of stranded cotton to do this.

continued on the following page…

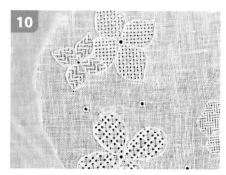

The petals of the three filled flowers on the left can then be outlined. First, the smaller petal is outlined in stem stitch, using a single strand of stranded cotton. The petals of the two larger flowers are then outlined with couching. Use a single strand of coton à broder 25 as the core and the fine lace thread to couch it down.

The small four-petal flower can then be filled with counted-satin pattern 3 (see Chapter 4), counting over two, four, six, four, two and so on. Use the tapestry 28 needle threaded with a single strand of stranded cotton to do this. Notice how, on each of the two opposite petals, the pattern has been worked either horizontally or vertically.

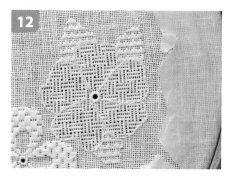

Still using the tapestry 28 needle and a single strand of stranded cotton, the three leaves of the large flower on the right can now be filled with counted-satin pattern 1 (see Chapter 4), counting over two, three, four, three, two and so on.

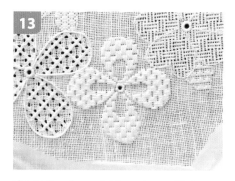

The medium four-petal flower is now filled with counted-satin pattern 5 (see Chapter 4), counting three stitches over six threads. Notice how, on each of the two opposite petals, the pattern has been worked either horizontally or vertically. Keep using the tapestry 28 needle but change the thread to a single strand of coton à broder 25.

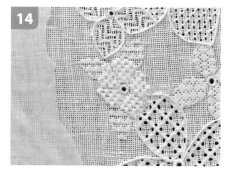

The petals of the small flower on the left can also then be filled with counted-satin pattern 5, but this time counting two stitches over four threads. Again, use the tapestry 28 needle and coton à broder 25 to do this. This time notice how the direction of the pattern changes for each petal. When the petals are complete, the leaves can then be filled with counted-satin pattern 1, counting over two, three, four, three, two and so on, stitched with a single strand of stranded cotton.

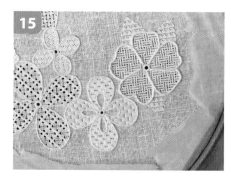

The petals of the large and medium flowers on the right are then outlined in couching. The large flower uses six strands of stranded cotton as the core and a single strand to couch. The medium flower uses four strands of stranded cotton as the core and a single strand to couch. The leaves of the large flower can then be outlined in stem stitch using a single strand of stranded cotton.

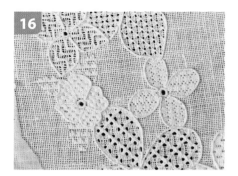

16

The petals of the medium flowers on the left can then be outlined in couching. Both use a single strand of coton à broder 25 as the core and a fine lace thread to couch it down. When they are both complete, the leaves for the medium flower can then be outlined with stem stitch using a single strand of stranded cotton.

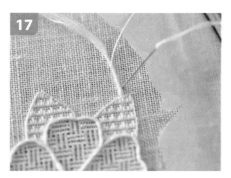

17

When all the flowers are complete you can then tear away more of the tissue to reveal the final areas of the design. The arch that joins the two large flowers is worked in trailing. Use twelve strands of stranded cotton for the core and a single strand of stranded cotton for the couching. Start the trailing just ahead of the leaf on the right-hand side, then work back towards the leaf, anchoring and completing the start of the trailing.

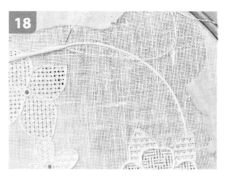

18

Then continue from where you started, following the arch up and over to the left to where it ends at the top left flower. Make sure to pull the core threads tightly as you work, to ensure a neat, smooth and even curved line of trailing.

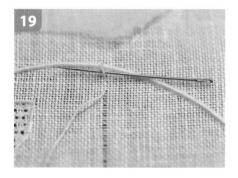

19

The next step is to slightly slacken the fabric in the frame, and begin withdrawing the threads for the drawn lines. You can place the design template back underneath the fabric to find which threads need to be withdrawn. Do this carefully and remember to make the cut in the middle of the line.

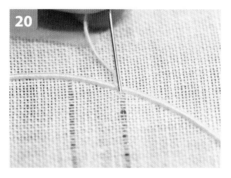

20

When the threads have been withdrawn, as they butt up to previously worked stitches, the threads can be taken through to the back of the work and trimmed from the back. I left my withdrawn areas plain as a design choice but feel free to decorate them as you wish.

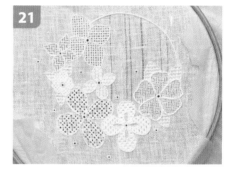

21

Tighten the fabric back up in the frame and stitch the final eight counted full eyelets. Each one is stitched in two strands of stranded cotton and is counted over two threads.

The final step is to work eight lazy-daisy stitches around five of the counted full eyelets, creating the tiny petals. When these are complete, your 1970s whitework floral wallpaper is finished and ready to be mounted.

Well done!

22

Tonal drawing for the swallow design.

Stitch plan for the swallow design.

The finished whitework swallow.

PROJECT 2

WHITEWORK SWALLOW

Though still quite simple, this project is a little more complicated, as more whitework techniques and advanced stitches have been included, such as cutwork, eyelets, satin and long and short. The aim of this is for you to be able to practise some of the more complicated whitework techniques in small areas before moving on to a more adventurous design. It will also help you to understand the importance of the order of work. This design is perfect if you are just learning to combine techniques and stitches.

I have worked this sample on Kingston 55 because of the cutwork elements.

What You Will Need

Equipment

+ 8in bound ring frame
+ Tissue paper
+ Blue pencil/water-soluble pen
+ Tapestry needle size 28
+ Embroidery needle sizes 10 and 12
+ Sharp embroidery scissors
+ Design template

Materials

+ Kingston 55 linen (or even-weave fabric of your choice)
+ Fine white lace thread
+ Anchor/DMC coton à broder 25
+ Anchor/DMC stranded cotton

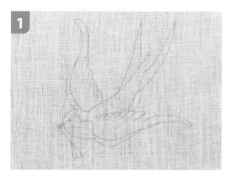

1 Transfer the design onto the linen using the tracing method. (For this design I used a water-soluble pen, but choose whichever tool you prefer.) Insert the linen into the 8in ring frame with a piece of tissue covering the design. When the frame is tight, tear away some of the tissue revealing the design.

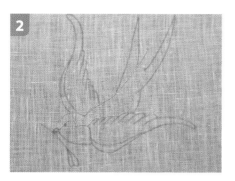

2 Following the design lines, outline the top of the swallow's body and head with double running stitch.

3 Fill the shape in with a pulled-thread stitch of your choice. I used honeycomb darning counted over three threads. Work the pulled-thread stitch in the lace thread, remembering to start in the middle of the shape across the widest point.

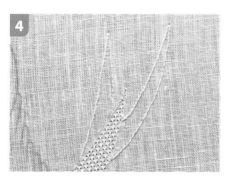

4 Outline the two tail feathers in split stitch using a single strand of stranded cotton.

5 Fill both tail feathers with long and short stitch. The direction of the stitches should follow the gentle curve through the shape. Remember to start at the tip and extend the first stitch slightly in order to create a nice sharp point at the tip of each feather.

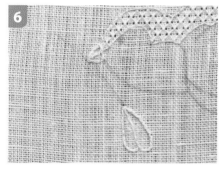

6 Outline the beak and the leaf in split stitch, using a single strand of stranded cotton. Include the split stitch through the centre of each shape, which indicates the void.

7 Using coton à broder 25, pad the top half of the beak and the right-hand side of the leaf using the long split-stitch method. The beak is so small that a single layer is enough, but for the leaf work two or three layers.

8 Work slanted satin across the left side of the leaf, using a single strand of stranded cotton. Make sure to angle the needle down underneath the split stitch that cuts through the middle of the leaf so a gap will not appear between the two halves. Remember to start the satin in the middle to set the angle and follow the rule for slanted satin (*see* Chapter 10).

9 Then work slanted satin across the padded half of the leaf in the same way, only the stitches lay across the shape in the opposite direction. When you work this half, make sure to angle the needle down underneath the central line of split stitch in order to create a clear and sharp void.

continued on the following page…

10

Work slanted satin in the beak in the same way, first completing the bottom half, then the top. Again, try to make a clear, sharp void. The satin on the beak is also worked in a single strand of stranded cotton.

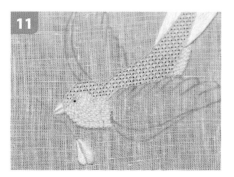

11

Work the tiny eyelet in a single strand of stranded cotton for the eye. Then, using coton à broder 25, work rows of backstitch, filling in the bottom half of the head and body of the swallow.

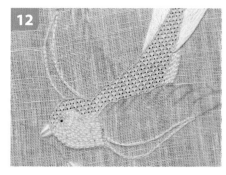

12

Prepare the outlines for the cutwork with two rows of double running stitch, worked in a single strand of stranded cotton, on each wing.

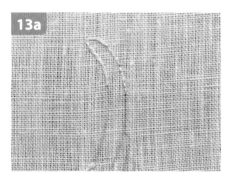

13a

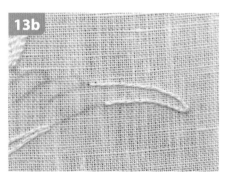

13b

Then outline just the tips of each wing with split stitch, worked in a single strand of stranded cotton. This is where the long and short stitch will be worked, but only on the tips of the wings.

14a

14b

Work the long and short stitch on each wing in a single strand of stranded cotton. The direction of the stitches should follow the gentle curve of each wing. When the split-stitch edge is covered, gently fade out the long and short stitches to give a natural and smooth fade, rather than a hard line.

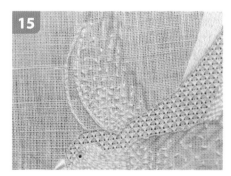

15

Starting at the base of each wing, work seeding stitches. First have them worked closely together and evenly spaced. Then as you work through the wing, gently start dispersing them, working them slightly further and further apart as you reach the outer feathers. The seeding stitches themselves should all be the same size.

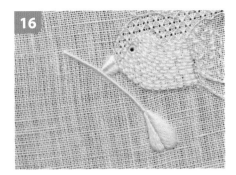

Complete the row of trailing for the branch of the leaf. Starting at the tip, working down towards the leaf. I used four strands of stranded cotton for the core thread and a single strand to couch with.

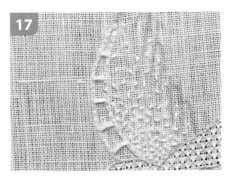

Then work the bars that support the cutwork, five on each wing. The two longest bars having an added picot. I chose to work buttonhole bars but overcast or needle woven would work just as well. The bars are worked in a single strand of stranded cotton.

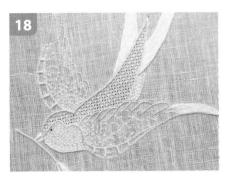

The remaining outlines can then be worked in stem or outline stitch. I chose to use coton à broder 25 for the body and head of the swallow and a single strand of stranded cotton for the wings.

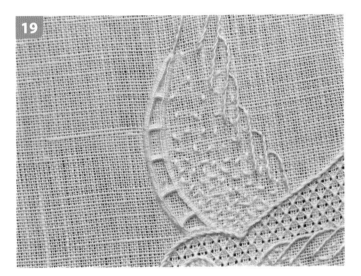

Finally, work the buttonhole edging around the areas of cutwork, using a single strand of stranded cotton.

Then, very carefully and with a sharp pair of embroidery scissors, cut away the areas of fabric in each wing, revealing the cutwork. Do this slowly and keep trimming bit by bit, till you have a neat, smooth and even edge. Your stitching is now complete!

Well done!

CHAPTER 12

DESIGNING AND PLANNING FOR WHITEWORK

A blank, white piece of paper can be a daunting prospect when trying to design a piece of embroidery, no matter what the technique, and there is no right or wrong way to start designing for whitework. As whitework includes so many different techniques and stitches it can hard to understand which different whitework techniques work well together, and if combining different techniques and stitches in one piece, how to get them to work in harmony with each other. The design and planning can make or break a piece of embroidery, which is why it is so important to spend the time making sure it is well balanced and that there is a clear order of work for you to follow when you start stitching. Remember there is no one right way to design whitework; it is only through practice that you will find the way that works for you. There are many things to think about and to take into consideration when designing for whitework and this chapter will go through each stage of my design process, breaking it down and explaining each step, so you can learn how to do it for yourself.

WHERE TO START

When starting to think of a whitework design, there are a few things to consider and questions you can ask yourself first that will make the design process much easier.

The first thing to ask is are there any specific whitework techniques and stitches you want to use? If yes, then great! Make a list of them to use as a check list against your design or image. If not, no problem, you can allow the design to inform your stitch choices.

The main difficulty in design for whitework is that there is no colour. Instead, you need to be thinking about texture, tone and depth, and how the different techniques and stitches will work together and complement your design.

A close-up of an eighteenth-century whitework cap crown showing multiple whitework techniques including pulled thread and pulled satin, buttonhole, eyelets, satin and shadow work.

The Design

Designing for embroidery can be daunting but you do not need to be an artist to do it. If you have not designed your own embroidery before, start small and simple. The first step is to gather a collection of images or things that inspire you. This could be books, postcards, images from the internet, other pieces of embroidery, wallpaper or items from nature such as leaves, flowers or shells.

Start your design by drawing or tracing a few elements from these reference images or objects on different pieces of tracing paper. You can then lay these bits of tracing paper on top of each other, rearranging their position till you have a basic motif that can be developed and refined.

At this point, do not go into too much detail; all you need is a rough sketch. I always find that once I have marked the paper, even if it is just a wavy line, the rest of the design comes more easily. For me, the easiest and quickest way is with a pencil, rubber and a piece of paper, but there is some excellent computer software out there that makes designing on your computer really quick and easy.

Points to Remember

⊹ Think about the techniques you want to use and what shapes they work well in or can create. For example, pulled-thread areas work best in open areas with simple outlines, rather than tight fiddly areas.

⊹ What fabric would work best for this design depending on the techniques that are going to be used? If there are a lot of pulled-thread stitches worked into the design, this would tend to lead towards a more open-weave fabric so that it is easier to work. If you also have heavy areas of satin and cutwork, however, you will need a finer weave in order to support these stitches, in which case a compromise is needed – choose a fabric that has a close weave to support the satin and cutwork, but that you can still easily count for the pulled-thread stitches.

⊹ Which areas of the design do you want to stand out? What techniques or stitches would work well in this area? Remember, areas of high contrast draw the eye.

⊹ Smaller details can be worked in satin or eyelets, or a combination along with any other surface stitches.

⊹ Long flowing lines would be great worked in trailing, slanted satin, couching, beading or ladderwork.

⊹ Open areas in the design, such as eyelets and drawn thread, will draw the eye as they create a darker tone.

⊹ Pulled thread can be worked freely or encased in an enclosed shape that is outlined. Pulled thread works best in larger open areas with simpler outlines, as more complicated shapes make the counting and starting of new rows more complicated.

⊹ Different pulled-thread patterns create different textures by opening the weave of the fabric in different ways. Using a pulled-thread stitch will create a slightly darker tone.

⊹ Pulled-thread stitches are counted, so make sure that you can still count the threads of your chosen fabric if it has a closer and finer weave.

⊹ Drawn thread works great as borders but can also work well within designs. Drawn threads will leave a band or bands of a dark tone.

⊹ Remember that drawn thread can only be worked horizontally or vertically through the design, and when threads are withdrawn in both directions in the same area, a square void will be left.

⊹ If the design has a lot of linear elements then drawn thread will work well for those areas.

⊹ Drawn-thread technique removes threads from the ground fabric one thread at a time, so it is easier to work on an even-weave fabric with a lower TPI. Drawn thread can be worked on finer fabrics, but more care needs to be taken when removing the threads.

⊹ Cutwork is best worked on a fine, closely woven fabric that is able to support the heavy stitching that will support the cutwork area. Large areas of cutwork can be created so long as they are supported with enough bars or brides.

⊹ Shadow work is best used on transparent fabric but it can also be worked on denser fabrics too. The shadow created will just be less obvious.

⊹ Symmetrical designs can be challenging but not impossible.

Inspiration can come from anywhere so look at books, photographs, prints, postcards and nature.

Initial design motifs drawn on tracing paper so they can be moved around until the best composition is found.

A rough design sketch in pencil.

When you are happy with your rough design, the next step is to refine it. For this I find a lightbox invaluable. By laying the rough sketch on the light box and a new sheet of paper on top, you can quickly and easily redraw the design, making sure all the design lines are smooth, clean and sharp. I would use a sharp HB pencil for this. When complete, this is what I would call the original design. Trace this original design again, on a new piece of paper, but this time using a fineliner pen; this is what I would call the hard copy.

This hard copy can then be scanned into your computer or photocopied. Drawing to the correct scale can be difficult so at this point, if you need or want to, you can always resize the image before printing it out. Print several copies out as you will need a number of different copies for each stage of planning.

Image Copyright

There is no shame in tracing some elements from other designs or images from books or the internet, but you need to think about the image copyright. Copyright is a very grey area but it is always worth considering and you should never copy anything directly without the original artist's permission.

THE PLANNING

Now that the design is complete, the next step is to plan the embroidery, and this encompasses many things from techniques, stitches and order of work to threads and materials. Unfortunately there is no one set of rules, as each design is different and therefore so will each stitch plan, order of work and choice of materials. I hope to be able to guide you into making the right decisions using this list of things to think about and the following design processes.

STITCH PLAN

The first thing to do is a stitch plan. Start with an open mind and let the design help you to choose. If there is a technique you want to include but you cannot find a place for it, alter the design slightly so you can include it, or save it for your next piece.

When choosing techniques and stitches, let the design guide you. Large open areas lend themselves to pulled thread or counted-satin stitches, whereas small detailed areas could be satin stitch or cutwork, and long flowing lines could be tailing or ladderwork. Think about the different shapes and areas in your design and imagine what stitches would look like there. When working on my stitch plans I always have numerous whitework books and samples around me so I can flick through and study them, which helps me visualize which stitches will work best for my new design.

Using one of the photocopies of your design, begin to make notes of where you think stitches could go. I find it helpful to roughly sketch the stitches in place on the design to give me a better idea of how they would look. This does not have to be particularly accurate; it just gives a rough idea of what the textures will look like. For example, you can roughly sketch in place what the pulled-thread patterns will look like, or the stitch direction for areas of satin stitch.

I find it easier to start with the main feature of the design and work out from there, deciding on the stitches for the larger open areas first, then moving on to the smaller details and elements and finally choosing the outline stitches and surface decoration stitches at the end.

When you are happy with the stitch plan, label it as your final stitch plan so you know this is the one you need to follow when stitching. The stitch plan may change once you have started stitching but it is good to have a clear guide to start off with.

A traced hard copy of the design using a light box and fineliner pen.

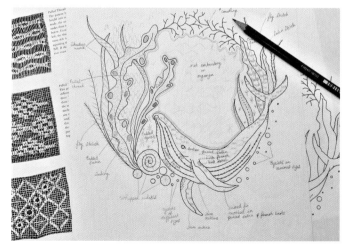

A design with a rough version of a stitch plan, with notes, doodles and sketches of stitches, to show what stitches will go where and what they could look like.

TONAL DRAWING

With a stitch plan in place, the next step is to understand how your design is going to work tonally. This can be tricky to visualize, as how do you define tones within your design when everything is white?

Well, one way of doing just that was ingeniously thought up by Sally Saunders (Royal School of Needlework (RSN)). She realized that by using different shades of blue to represent the different tones created by the different techniques and stitches, you could colour in your design, using the stitch plan as a guide for where each of the blue shades should be placed. Though in blue, this would create a tonal drawing of the design allowing you to clearly see how the techniques, tones and textures would be balanced throughout the design.

The blue tonal scale works like this. Colour in your design as follows:

- Darkest shade of blue – areas of cutwork, the holes in eyelets, beading and ladder stitch
- Medium shade of blue – areas of drawn thread
- Light shade of blue – areas of pulled thread and pulled satin
- Very pale blue – areas of background fabric with no stitching
- White – areas of surface stitching such as satin and counted satin, trailing, shadow work and other decorative surface stitches.

A tonal drawing of the design, showing how the tonal texture and depth are spread throughout the design. Use the stitch plan as guide for where each shade of blue should be placed.

Layers of tracing paper, each with its own section drawn on so when combined, the whole design comes together. For visual clarity I used a different coloured pen or pencil for each layer but you can just use a black fineliner pen.

An alternative way is to use multiple pieces of tracing paper. On each piece, trace the parts of the design that use the same technique. For example, for the first piece, trace all the areas of pulled thread, for the next do all the areas of cutwork and eyelets, for the next do drawn-thread areas, and so on.

When all the areas have been traced you should be able to lay all the sheets of tracing paper on top of each other and have a complete design. Make sure to label each piece of tracing paper so you know what stitch or stitches each piece is supposed to represent.

ORDER OF WORK

Next comes the order of work, which is very important. Remember there is no single set of rules that you should follow for every whitework design, as each one is different with different techniques and stitches being used. However, here is a simple guide you can use as a starting point.

Using another of the photocopies of the design, number each part of the design in the order that it needs to be worked. This may change once you start stitching but it is helpful to have a clear plan to start off with.

1. If the design has areas of pulled thread, pulled satin or counted satin, these should be worked first. If the pulled thread is in an enclosed shape, remember to outline the shape in double running stitch first.

2. You can then begin to stitch the outlines on the design whether they be in stem, couching, trailing or any other surface stitch.

3. All other areas of surface and decorative stitching can then be worked. This includes areas of seeding and fly stitch to satin and shadow work.

4. If your design includes them, next work any areas of ladderwork or beading.

5. If included in the design, the eyelets can now be worked. I always start off with the smaller ones and then move on to the bigger ones.

6. Areas of cutwork can be stitched next but when they are complete *do not* cut them yet!

Design with the numbered order of work.

7. Drawn thread should always be one of the last features to stitch, whether it is embedded in the design or used as a border. This is because as you are removing threads, you weaken the structure of the fabric. Remember to slacken the fabric in the frame to remove the threads, and remove all of them in one go. When all the threads have been removed, tighten the frame again in order to work the decorative drawn-thread stitches.

8. At this point all the stitching should now be complete. If there were areas of cutwork in the design, slacken the fabric in the frame again and trim away all the areas of the ground fabric that need to be removed. On the back you can then trim away the excess organza from areas of shadow-appliqué.

THREADS AND FABRICS

The final stage before you can start stitching is to choose which fabric and threads are going to bring your design to life. In Chapter 2, I explained which fabric is best used for each individual technique. If the design combines techniques, though, how do you decide which is the best fabric to use? Again, there is no right or wrong answer and there will have to be a compromise somewhere. That said, here are a few things to consider to help you make the right choice for your design.

- If pulled- or drawn-thread stitches make up part of the design then the fabric you choose needs to be an even weave in order for the patterns to be worked correctly. However, if areas of cutwork and eyelets are also included, then the fabric needs to be a closer weave to withstand the surface stitching and support the cut-out areas. This means that the counting of the pulled and drawn threads becomes more difficult.

- Which technique or stitch is the most prominent or makes up the main feature of the design? If one technique is more dominant than the rest, choose a fabric that works better for this technique.

- How good is your eyesight? Will you be able to count the threads of a very fine fabric if combining pulled or drawn with areas of cutwork?

- What is your stitching ability? If you are a beginner, start simple; if you are a more advanced stitcher, experiment and use finer fabrics.

When you have decided on the fabric, you can then go through the design and decide which threads will be worked where and for what stitch. Remember there is no colour in whitework, so the aim is to try to create different textures and tones with the threads.

When your design is complete, you have worked out the stitch plan, order of work and chosen your fabrics and threads, it is time to start framing up and stitching! As you work, make sure to keep all of these drawings, plans and notes to hand so you can easily refer back to them as you stitch. You have spent time doing them so use them; they are there to guide you through your embroidery. Also, if you make changes as you work, note them down so you can remember in future.

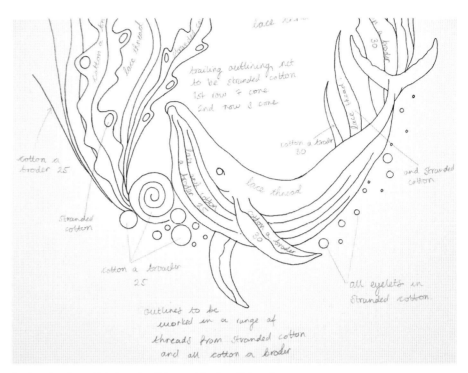

Design showing which threads will be used for the stitches chosen.

READY TO STITCH

With all the planning complete, you are now ready for the truly exciting part: the stitching. Here is a quick and simple guide from start to finish of all the processes you need to go through, and in what order, to create a beautiful piece of whitework.

1. Design.
2. Stitch plan.
3. Tonal drawing.
4. Order of work. Use the guide above to help but the order of work really depends on what is included in your design and where it is placed.
5. Choose threads and fabrics.
6. Wash your hands!
7. Frame up the fabric using the frame and framing-up method of your choice. Make sure the frame is drum-tight.
8. Using the hard copy of the design, very carefully transfer the design on to the fabric. Remember, if you have any vertical or horizontal straight lines in your design these need to be tacked using a light blue thread and following the grain line.
9. Wash your hands again!
10. Start stitching.
11. Take breaks and wash your hands regularly.
12. Tighten your frame every time you sit down to stitch.
13. Finish stitching.
14. If needed, wash your whitework.
15. Wash your hands again.
16. Mount your whitework.
17. Frame your whitework and show it off!

CHAPTER 13

WASHING AND MOUNTING WHITEWORK

As you have dedicated so much time and effort to creating and stitching your embroideries, the final step is to present and preserve them in the best way possible. There are many different ways of mounting embroidery, but there are a few limits with whitework embroidery, as everything is white and you want to keep it that way for as long as possible. Therefore you may not want to turn your delicate and beautiful whitework into something like a pincushion that is going to be poked and handled till it turns grey!

This chapter will go through the best ways to care for your embroideries, along with a few traditional mounting options that can be considered for whitework embroidery.

CHECKING YOUR WORK

When I finish a piece of embroidery, I always cover it up and leave it for a day or two before I begin the mounting process. Coming back to look at it with fresh eyes after some time away always makes a difference. Check over the whole piece of embroi-dery, first looking for any stray or trapped tacking threads. Although they should have been worked in pale blue thread, you need to make sure they have all been removed.

Then check for any visible design lines. Again, these should have been worked in a blue pencil or water-soluble pen. If you used the water-soluble pen, this is no problem as they will disappear when the work is washed. If you used a blue pencil, you have two options. The first is to work an extra outline or some sort of stitching to cover them completely. The second is to just leave them, in the hope that they will fade slightly in the washing process. The fact that they have been worked in blue will make the white look brighter anyway, and hopefully just look like a shadow created by the stitching.

You then want to check for any areas that need extra work, such as missed stitches, or anything that could be redone to achieve a better result. Ideally, anything like this should have been done at the time of stitching but now is your last chance. If you are not happy and you leave it, you will always know that it is there! Then check the back of the work to make sure there are no stray or long trailing threads, or any threads

Close-up of whitework embroidery with trapped black fibres caught within the stitching.

that need tying back.

Finally, look over the whole piece front and back, checking for any stray fibres. You will be surprised by what you find, whether they are caught in the stitching or just lying on the surface. If caught in the stitching, use a pair of tweezers to carefully pull them out. If lying on the surface, use a piece of low-tack tape, like Scotch tape, to gently lift them away from the surface. If using tape, *never* rub it across the surface of the fabric or the embroidery, as this will damage and cause matting on the surface of the stitching. Always place the tape on the surface of the embroidery with a little pressure, then lift straight off.

Washing Whitework

Whichever method you choose to mount your whitework, washing it before you do so will help it look its best. Even if you think your embroidery is white when finished, washing it will brighten it and you will really see the difference – especially if you have been working on a piece for a long time.

If you have worked in a slate or roller frame you can keep the embroidery in the frame to wash it. Just make sure you unroll all the fabric so the frame is as big as it can be before washing. If you have worked in a ring frame then you need to remove it from the frame before washing.

Removing Water-Soluble Pen

If you used a water-soluble pen to draw on the design, this needs to be removed before washing it to make sure that the ink from the pen does not react with any of the chemicals when washing.

If the embroidery if still in the slate frame, use a clean sponge. Soak the sponge in cold water and gently dab it on the surface of the embroidery, focusing especially on the areas where the pen is visible. You may need to do this a few times till the pen has all disappeared. Make sure *never* to rub the sponge across the embroidery. Always gently dab the surface.

If the embroidery is out of the frame, fill a clean basin or washbowl with water. Place the embroidery flat on the surface of the water and let it sink naturally. Keep an eye on it and when the ink has disappeared you can remove it. If the embroidery is too big for the basin or washbowl, you can fold it so it fits in.

Wired Shapes

If you have any wired shapes on your piece, you need to wash the embroidery before these are attached or the paper around the wire will disintegrate and ruin the embroidered wired shape.

The Final Wash

This process for washing can be used on many different types of embroidery or textile, old or new. However, if washing non-whitework items, always test and make sure that the dye from coloured threads and fabrics does not run before washing. The idea of washing whitework on completion, particularly while on the frame, was developed by Jenny Adin-Christie at the Royal School of Needlework (RSN).

Finished whitework swallow with much of the blue pen outlines already removed with water.

In the Frame

If you worked your embroidery in a slate or roller frame you can keep it in the frame to wash it, but before washing commences you need to make sure the fabric is completely unrolled. This is so you can wash the embroidery and the fabric around it without the water interacting with the webbing at the sides or bottom and top of the frame. When the fabric is unrolled, you will need to tighten the frame back up again so it is smooth and flat. Make sure not to tighten it too much, especially if there are areas of drawn thread, for example. Also remove any tissue paper that was attached to the frame in order to protect your work while stitching.

Textile Cleaners

Restore and Vulpex are conservation-grade textile cleaners that you can buy and use at home. Note that these have their own specific instructions on the amount needed per litre of water used.

Place the frame in or on a clean basin, bath or shower. Fill a separate jug or container with lukewarm water and add a little washing detergent, and a small amount of Calgon powder. Mix until the detergent and Calgon powder are completely dissolved.

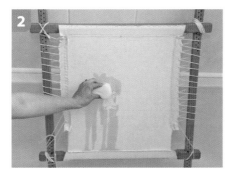

Wearing gloves, soak a clean, soft sponge in the mixture. Then gently dab the sponge on the surface of the embroidery and surrounding fabric. Start in the middle and work outwards, making sure the embroidery is completely soaked through to the back. If there are any areas that you notice have started yellowing or greying, try to focus on these areas, going over them again and again. When the embroidery is wet it will look like it has discoloured. Do not worry; this is normal and it will lighten back to normal as it dries. Do the same on the reverse of the work.

When the surface of the embroidery and surrounding area is completely soaked through, leave it for about half an hour or so to let the mixture work. If there are bubbles on the surface of the embroidery from the detergent, that is absolutely fine. If you notice that some areas still look dirty, go back and gently dab over them again.

While the embroidery is soaking, throw away the detergent mix and thoroughly clean the sponge so no detergent mixture is left in it. Clean the jug and fill it up with lukewarm water again. Repeat the dabbing process, this time with just the water, washing away the detergent from the surface of the embroidery and fabric. Repeat this as many times as needed, until there is no detergent mixture left on the surface of the embroidery.

Fill the jug one more time with cold water and, from the top, gently pour it over the fabric so it falls and soaks down through the embroidery to the bottom. If you like, you can buy distilled water for this final step, as it is free from impurities and limescale. Cold water works just fine, though.

Finally, leave the embroidery somewhere safe and clean to completely dry. You can use a clean white towel to dab the surface to try to remove any excess water. You do not need to cover the embroidery while it dries; just make sure nothing touches the front or back of the embroidery while it is drying. Only remove the embroidery from the frame when it is completely dry, which should take at least a few hours.

Out of the Frame

If you worked your embroidery in a ring frame, you need to remove it from the frame before washing. This is because you cannot control how the water soaks into the fabric and you do not want any wet wood from the ring frame touching the fabric and discolouring it, especially if you plan on mounting the embroidery afterwards.

Fill a clean sink or washbowl with lukewarm water. Add a little washing detergent and a small amount of Calgon powder. Mix until the detergent and Calgon powder are completely dissolved. Wearing gloves, lay the embroidery flat on the surface of the water and let it sink naturally. You may need to fold the edges of the fabric in to fit it in the sink or washbowl.

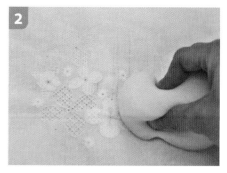

When the embroidery is fully submerged, leave it to soak for half an hour or so. If you notice any areas that are particularly grubby after thirty minutes, lay the embroidery on a clean white towel. With a clean sponge soaked in the detergent mix, gently dab on the surface of the grubby areas. Then place the embroidery back into the detergent mix and let it soak for another 15 to 30 minutes.

When the time is up, carefully remove the embroidery onto a clean white towel. Throw away the detergent mix and rinse out the sink or washbowl. Fill with lukewarm water and place the embroidery back in. You will need to repeat this a few times till the detergent mix has been completely soaked out of the embroidery. For the final soak, if you like, you can use distilled water as it is free from impurities and limescale, but tap water will still work just fine.

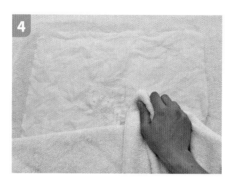

Finally remove the embroidery from the sink or washbowl and lay it flat on a clean white towel. Carefully dab the surface of the embroidery with a second clean white towel, trying to remove as much excess surface water as possible. Leave to dry for fifteen minutes or so to allow as much of the excess water to dry out.

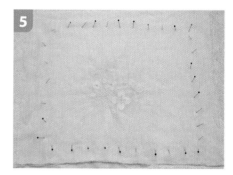

Before allowing the embroidery to dry completely, lay out a new clean white towel and place the embroidery flat on the surface. Pin the edges of the embroidered fabric to the towel, stretching the fabric slightly as you do so, making sure the embroidery is not distorted at the same time. Doing this will help the embroidery to dry flat without any creases and will help prevent the need for ironing or pressing when it is completely dry. If you do need to iron the fabric after it is dry, do so very carefully, starting on a low heat with only a little pressure, and using a pressing cloth.

Mounting

The process of mounting is just as important as the embroidery design and stitching process. There are many ways to mount embroidery and you need to make sure you pick the right one for your piece so that it will be preserved in the best possible way for generations to come. You can always have your pieces framed professionally but this is expensive and you cannot always be sure that a framer will take the same care you would over your painstakingly stitched embroidery, especially when glue is involved. With practice, you will do just as good a job (and better) mounting on your own at home. The main thing is to make sure you use the correct equipment and buy the best mounting materials you can afford. Using conservation-grade materials will give your embroidery a longer life span when mounted and framed, and prevent slow discolouration, damage, wrinkles and sagging.

Most importantly when mounting, you need to make sure all the surfaces you work on are clean, and that you cover the area where you are working with acid-free tissue paper to protect your embroidery from dirt and damage throughout the mounting process.

Mounting over Card

Mounting your finished embroidery over card is the most secure and accurate way of presenting and preserving your embroidery, even if you do not chose to frame it afterwards. The following pages will go through each process of mounting your embroidery over card using the herringbone method, how to back the board when you have mounted your embroidery, and

Finished whitework moth embroidery. Mounted in an entomology frame box, which is deep enough to accommodate the 3D wired wings.

A whitework moth mounted over card to look like an entomological piece.

how to lace the back of your mounting if the tension loosens over time and wrinkles start to appear.

Choosing the Right Fabric to Cover the Card

Usually when mounting embroidery you would just cover the mount board in a medium-weight calico as this would be completely covered by the embroidery. However, as many of the whitework fabrics are transparent in varying degrees, you would be able to see the calico showing through, and the colour of the calico would make your whitework look yellow, dirty and faded. This is why for mounting whitework you cover your board in a coloured cloth of silk, cotton or fine linen. If you choose to use a silk or fine linen, I would always cover the board in calico first, then cover the calico with the fine silk or linen. If using cotton or a heavier-weight fabric, it is fine to just cover the board in that.

Blue in varying shades is the ideal colour to choose as it makes the whitework look whiter and brighter. However, you can use other colours like reds, purples and greens. The aim is to choose a coloured fabric that will enhance the embroidery, showing it at its best. Try to avoid orange and yellow colours as this will make the embroidery look yellow, dirty and fading. When choosing the fabric, it can help to take some of the samples and practice work with you so you can lay it on top of the coloured fabrics and get a better idea of how much colour will show through the differently worked areas.

Things You Will Need

- Finished embroidery. If worked in a slate frame, keep it in the frame and under tension. If worked in a ring frame, remove it from the frame and carefully iron and press any creases in the surrounding fabric.
- Coloured silk, cotton or linen to cover the card and that will show through the embroidery.
- Fabric to back the board when the embroidery has been mounted. This could be a closely woven cotton or silk, and in a colour or print that complements the embroidery on the front.
- Acid-free tissue paper
- White acid-free mount board. This comes in a few different thicknesses. I prefer to buy the 2mm (1⁄16in) thick mount board and cut pieces of card and glue them together. You can buy the thicker card, which is about 5mm (1⁄5in) thick, but this is much harder to cut accurately.
- Cutting mat
- Stanley knife
- Set square
- Long metal ruler to cut against
- Sharp HB pencil
- Conservation glue ideally, but otherwise use PVA
- Fabric scissors
- Soft sandpaper
- Pins
- Buttonhole thread
- Curved needle
- Four pieces of plain paper

Cutting and Covering the Mount Board

The first thing to do is to decide the dimensions for the finished, mounted embroidery. If you worked the embroidery in a slate frame, it is best to keep it in the frame so you can take accurate measurements. If you worked in a ring frame, lay the embroidery on a flat surface. Leave a margin of at least 2.5cm (1in) around the whole design, measuring from the widest part of the embroidery on each side. You can leave a bigger margin than 2.5cm (1in) – it all depends on the scale and intricacy of the design – but generally you should not need more than a 5cm (2in) margin.

Lay four sheets of paper around the design, following this margin to create a window. This will give you an idea of what the embroidery will look like when mounted. Move these pieces of paper around, changing the size of the margin till you are happy with how it looks. As a general rule, the margin should be the same on all four sides but you may prefer certain designs to be set to one side or corner.

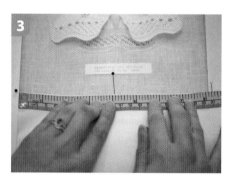

Pin the paper in place following the grain of the fabric as best you can. Then measure and find the middle point on all four sides, marking these points with pins. Then find the dimensions by measuring from side to side and top to bottom from these points. Makes sure to take note of the dimensions accurately before you forget them.

Carefully draw out the dimensions of the card onto the white acid-free mount board. If using the 2mm (1⁄16in) thick card you need to cut two pieces of card that are exactly the same size. If using thicker mount board, just draw one. Use a set square to make sure that all four corners are square and all the edges are straight.

Using a long metal ruler and a sharp Stanley knife, very carefully cut out the two pieces of card. When cutting, use long stokes going from the top to the bottom and make sure the blade is cutting into the card at a 90-degree angle. You will need to run the blade through the card a few times to cut through accurately. Make sure to line up the ruler exactly with the marked lines, laying the ruler on top of the area of card you want to keep so the ruler will protect it. Keep one hand firmly on the ruler at all times when cutting to stop it from moving around.

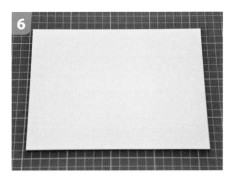

When both pieces of card have been cut, lay them on top of each other on a clean flat surface and check they fit perfectly. If there are any rough edges, these can be sanded down and smoothed away with the sand paper. If the cards do not fit perfectly, for example if one is slightly bigger than the other or one edge is not quite straight, it best to re-cut the card from scratch. Do this as many times as needed till all four sides lay perfectly together side by side.

The two pieces of card can then be glued together using the conservation or PVA glue. The glue should sit just inside the edges of the card and across the middle, so they are glued firmly together. Try not to use so much glue that it splurges out the edge when the card is put together or it begins to soften and warp the board. Place the glued boards on a clean, flat surface, cover with tissue paper and place some heavy books on top to keep them flat. Leave to dry, ideally overnight.

Cut a piece of your chosen backing fabric or calico that is about 10cm (4in) bigger than the mount board on each side. Iron the fabric if needed to remove any creases. Lay the mount board centrally on top of the fabric. Along one of the longest sides, run a line of conservation or PVA glue, leaving a margin of about 3cm (1¼in) from the edges of the card. This is a very important step as you will need this margin later.

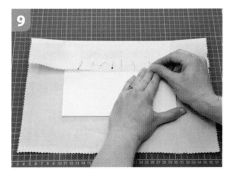

Fold the fabric around the edge of the board, pressing it into the glue. Starting in the middle, use pins to hold the fabric in place while the glue is drying. Starting from the middle, pin one side first, pulling the fabric tight as you do so; then come back to the middle and do the same on the other side.

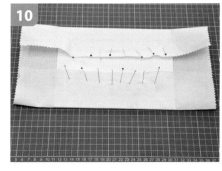

When the first long side is complete, repeat the process on the opposite side. This time you need to make sure the fabric is pulled very tight across the front of the board. Before folding the fabric back, rest the glued and pinned edge against your leg so you can pull tightly on the fabric against your leg. Then press the fabric into the glue and pin in place from the middle to either side. Leave the glue to dry completely before moving on to the next step.

continued on the following page…

Remove the pins from the first two sides and trim away any excess fabric. Then trim away the excess fabric from the corners by cutting up at about a 45-degree angle, to about 4mm above the edge of the card. Do this at all four corners.

Open out these flaps so they lie flat on the surface you are working on. Then, starting at the corners and leaving the excess 4mm at the first corner, cut at a 45-degree angle again, cutting away the remaining excess fabric so you have a shape that looks a bit like the fold of an envelope. Do this at all four corners.

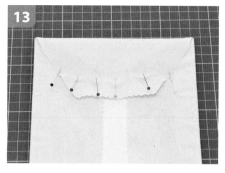

With the final two sides of the fabric cut, you can now glue them down as described above, making sure to fold the 4mm excess fabric at each corner in first. This is your last chance to get the fabric tight around the board so make sure to pull on the fabric as you fold it round and glue and pin in place. To check that the fabric is tight enough, run your finger over the front of the board. If a bubble forms in the fabric in front of your finger, you need to unpin and pull tighter before the glue dries. When you are sure it is tight enough, leave it to dry overnight. You can then trim away any excess fabric from the top and bottom edges.

When the glue is completely dry, remove the remaining pins. If you have covered the card with calico, you now need to repeat this process, covering the calico with the coloured silk or fine linen.

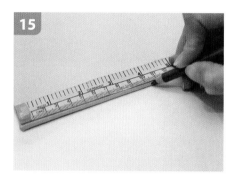

Next, with a blue pencil, mark the centre point on each edge of the covered mount board. These marks can then be matched up to the centre points on the four sides of your embroidery, which were marked with pins earlier.

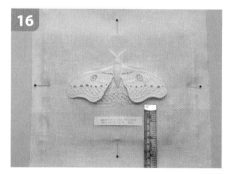

Pin the embroidery to the card, making sure to centre it first by matching up the four central points on the card to the four central points on the embroidery. Make sure to push the pins into the edges of the card. Double check that the embroidery is centred onto the card by measuring the rebate on each side before moving forward.

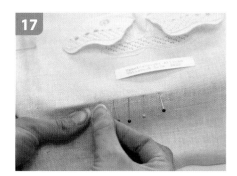

17

On one side, starting from the middle, continue to add pins spaced about 1.5cm (½in) apart till you reach the edge of the card. Then come back to the middle point and do the other side. As you pin, you need to pull on the fabric so that the grain line of the fabric runs straight with the edge of the board. The grain on whitework fabrics is usually much easier to see so if the grain is not quite straight it should be obvious.

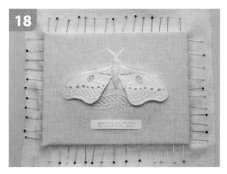

18

When the first edge is pinned all the way along the edge, do the same for the opposite side. Then repeat for the two remaining sides. When all four sides are pinned, the grain should run parallel with the edges of the board and the fabric should be pulled quite tightly across the board.

Use a Table

For the following steps, it helps to have the edge of the board resting at the edge of a table, with the fabric hanging over the edge. This makes pulling the fabric much easier as you can pull it down over the edge of the table and get a much better tension.

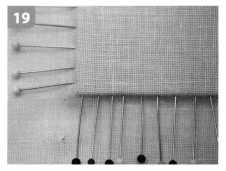

19

Starting from the middle point and working outwards, on one side of the board, remove the central pin and pull the fabric tight, then replace the pin. You should be able to pull the fabric so at least one or two grains of the fabric fall off the edge of the card. Continue to pull the fabric tight, following this new grain along the edge of the card. The pins need to be much closer together now, around 5mm (⅕in) apart. This will help control and keep the tension even along the edge of the card.

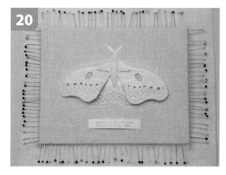

20

Repeat this on the remaining three sides. When finished, the grain should run parallel with the edges of the board on all four sides and the embroidery should be tight across the board. To check if it is tight enough, run a *clean finger* across the surface of the fabric along the edges of the card. If a bubble appears in front of your finger, it is not tight enough and you will need to repeat this process, pulling the fabric tighter again. When this stage is complete you are now ready to start stitching!

Caution with Tightening

If the embroidery has shadow appliqué, or large areas of cutwork or drawn thread etc., do not pull the fabric too tight, as you do not want to distort the shapes, tear the fabric or create holes that are not supposed to be there. As long as the fabric is tight across the surface and there is no bubbling or waving, it is tight enough.

Herringbone Method

Before you start stitching, lay the embroidery face down on a clean sheet of acid-free tissue paper. This will protect the embroidery as you work.

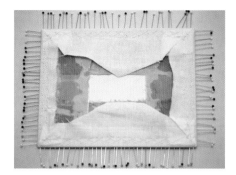

What the herringbone method looks like when complete.

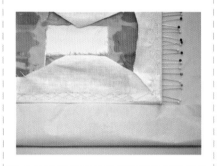
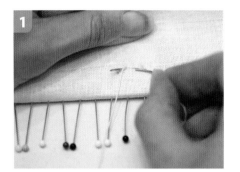

To start stitching, thread up a long length of button thread into a curved needle and tie a knot in the end. Starting in the middle along one of the longer edges, use your non-needle hand to fold and pull the fabric tight around the edge of the card. Cast on the button thread, focusing the stitches to sit inside the 2.5cm (1in) rebate between the edge of the card and the line of glue. Then cut off the knot.

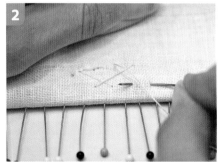

As you stitch, you need to continuously pull tight on the fabric with your non-needle hand to retain the same tension on the fabric. Start working the herringbone stitch, making sure that the needle goes through both the embroidery fabric and the fabric used to cover the card. The herringbone stitch is again focused in that 2.5cm (1in) rebate around the edge of the board. Make sure not to take the herringbone too close to the edge of the card.

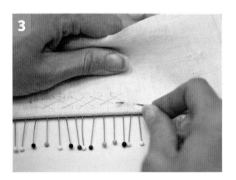

As you work the herringbone, you need to make sure that the stitches are in-line or cross over with each other, top and bottom, to ensure that there is an even and consistent tension on the fabric all the way around. If gaps are left, this can cause the fabric to slacken on the front of the board. Work along this first side but stop stitching about 5cm (2in) before you reach the first corner. *Do not anchor the thread.*

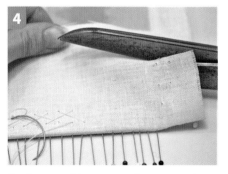

Cut the excess fabric away at the corner, making sure to leave just under 5cm (2in) along each side at the corner. This is so the corner can be folded and fit inside the area that you have already stitched.

The fabric at the corner can now be folded back and mitred. To start, fold in the corner of the fabric so that the edges of the fabric are square to the board. Hold this fold in place with a pin near the corner of the fabric.

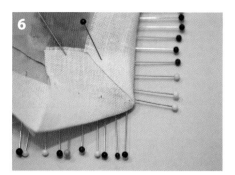

6

Then fold in one edge of the fabric so that the fold cuts across the corner at a 45-degree angle. Make sure that the excess fabric underneath the fold is smooth and flat. The fold should sit right up to the corner of the board. Use a pin to hold this fold in place.

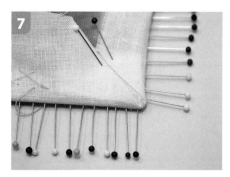

7

Repeat with the other edge of the fabric. Towards the top of the fold, at the raw edges of the fabric, the folds should meet. At the corner of the board there may be a small gap in between the fold. This as fine and will disappear later. Keep refolding as many times as you need till you are happy that your mitred corner is as neat as it can be.

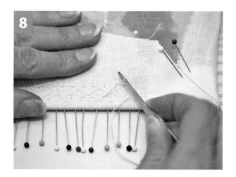

8

Before you continue to stitch the corner, you need to go back and tighten up all the stitching you have done so far. This is a very important step, as the stitches need to be very tight in order to control the tension of the fabric around the board. Use a mellor or large tapestry needle to pull each stitch tight. If the fabric puckers at each stitch, do not worry.

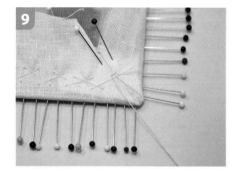

9

Continue working the herringbone all the way up to the folded mitre, continuing to pull all your stitches very tight. Then jump across to the opposite edge of the corner, making a stitch towards the corner; again, make sure to pull this tight. At the top of the mitre, work a few anchoring stitches across both of the folds of the mitre. This will secure the tension of your stitches so far. *Do not cut the thread.*

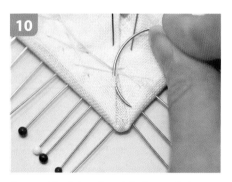

10

On one side of the mitre, slide the needle into the fold and make a short stitch, bringing the needle back out through the fold on the same side. It is important to make sure that the needle goes in and comes out of the fold of the fabric on the same side.

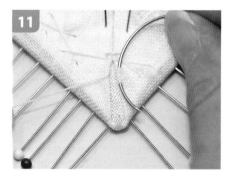

11

Take the needle across to the other folded edge of the mitre and do the same again. When you take the needle down on this side, try to take the needle through the fold just slightly behind where the thread emerges on the opposite side. This will create a tiny backwards diagonal stitch. This is known as slip stitch.

Slip Stitching

The reason for taking the needle slightly behind where it emerges from the previous stitch when slip stitching is so that a small backwards diagonal stitch is created. When this stitch is pulled tight, it sits horizontal and becomes invisible.

If the stitch was made horizontal to begin with, when pulled tight it would pull forward, creating a forwards diagonal stitch that would be visible.

continued on the following page…

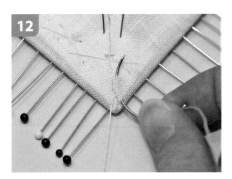

12

Continue working in this way, jumping across from fold to fold until you reach the corner. Then pull your thread tightly away from the corner – the two folded edges should pull together with no stitches visible. Take the needle back into the corner on the opposite fold, bringing it up towards the top of the mitre. Pull the stitch tight and the fabric will pull together around the corner, completing the mitre. Work a few anchoring stitches to secure the stitching of the mitred corner.

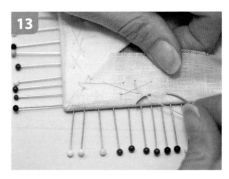

13

Continue the herringbone along the other edge of the board, and so on. Make sure to pull the fabric tight as you work around all four sides. Remember, every time you complete a section of stitching, use a mellor to tighten up all your stitches before anchoring the thread. All four edges and corners are completed in the same way.

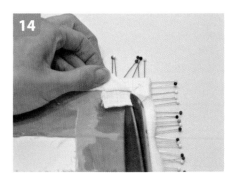

14

When all four sides and corners are complete, you can trim away any excess fabric, trying to keep an even rebate all the way around. This should be about 5cm (2in) or so. Then lift up the corners and trim away the fabric underneath to reduce any unwanted bulk. When you do this, be careful not to cut any of your stitching.

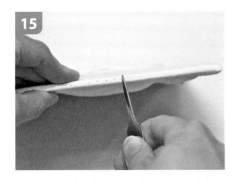

15

The pins can then be removed from around the board. You will see lots of tiny pinholes all the way around the board. To remove these, gently run a mellor or large tapestry needle around the edges of the board, realigning the grains of the fabric and closing up the pinholes. Now the herringbone is complete, leave it for a day or so before moving on to the next step. This allows the embroidery to relax if it is going to, which may mean it needs to be laced before you attach the backing.

Lacing

Lacing is a process that re-tightens the tension of the embroidery around the mount board after the mounting process is complete. Some pieces will never need to be laced, whereas others may need to be laced before the backing goes on. Others still may not need lacing for years after they have been mounted, as over time the tension has slowly slackened and wrinkles have started to appear.

You really only need to lace the back of a mounted piece of embroidery if wrinkles or sagging appear on the front. You do not even need to lace the whole of the board; you can focus the lacing only where it is needed. Lacing can also be worked in both directions across the board if needed.

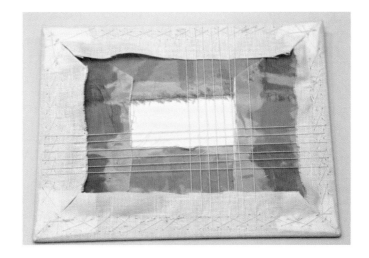

Showing how the back of the embroidery should look when it has been mounted over card with excess fabric trimmed away, and lacing has been worked in both directions in order to tighten a small section on the front.

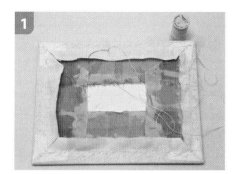

Lay the embroidery face down on a clean piece of acid-free tissue paper. Thread up a curved needle with button thread but do not cut the thread from the spool.

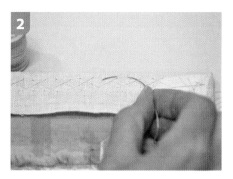

Make a small, straight stitch parallel to the edge of the board and about 5mm (⅛in) in length. This stitch needs to sit in the gap between the herringbone stitches and the edge of the board.

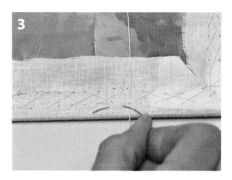

Then jump across to the other side of the board and make another stitch in the same way. There will now be a long stitch that sits across the back of the board. Continue working in this way, jumping from one edge of the board to the other, making your stitches about 5mm (⅛in) apart. As you run out of thread, reel more off from the spool.

When the lacing along these two sides is complete, anchor the thread. This needs to be done very securely as it needs to hold the tension for all of the lacing.

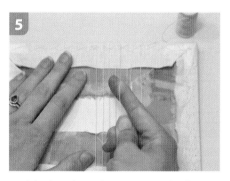

Work backwards to where you started pulling the excess thread tight across the board. You need to try to pull evenly on each stitch, so do not pull too tightly the first time round. Do this two or three times, pulling a little tighter every time.

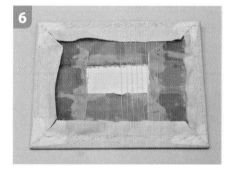

Check the front of the embroidery to make sure that any wrinkles have disappeared. Cut the thread from the spool, leaving yourself enough so you can thread it in a curved needle to anchor the thread without losing any of the tension. When this is done, cut any excess thread away.

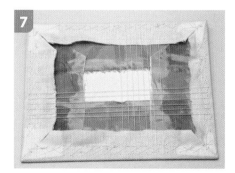

If there is still wrinkling on the front, work the lacing stitches again, but this time working on the other two edges of the board so that the lacing is worked in the opposite direction.

Applying the Backing Fabric

The last step of mounting is to apply fabric to the back of the board to cover up all the excess and folded fabric, herringbone and lacing stitches on the back. The best fabrics to use are mid-weight cottons or sateen fabrics, but silks and linens can also be used if they are heavy enough. These can be any colour or pattern you like, but if you have fabric left over from covering your board, you could easily use that.

The backing fabric needs to be as tight as it possibly can be across the back of the embroidery, as this is a final fail safe. If over the time the glue fails or the herringbone stitches lose their tension, it is this backing fabric and slip stitching that will support the embroidery and keep it tight around the board. If the backing is loose, the embroidery will loosen too and wrinkles and sagging will start to appear.

First, cut the chosen fabric so that it is about 5cm (2in) bigger than the mounted embroidery on all four sides. Then press the fabric to remove any creases. Along one of the longer sides, fold the fabric under 5cm (2in), making sure the fold follows the grain of the fabric.

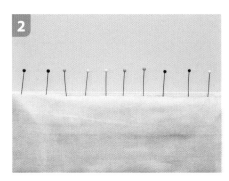

Place the embroidery face down, then centrally place the folded edge of the fabric along one of the longer sides of the mounted embroidery. Starting in the middle, pin the edge of the fold into place, leaving an even 3mm (⅛in) rebate from the edge of the board. As you pin outwards from the middle, make sure to pull the backing fabric tight as you go. Your pins should be about 2.5cm (1in) apart.

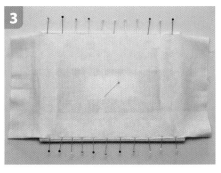

Fold under the fabric on the opposite side of the board, this time just slightly more than 5cm (2in). Again, starting in the middle, pull the fabric tight across the board and pin along the fold. The rebate between the fold and the edge of the board should be the same 3mm (⅛in) Run a *clean finger* across the surface of the backing fabric between the two pinned sides. If a bubble appears in front of your finger then you can pull tighter still.

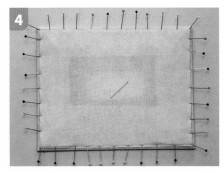

Fold and pin the remaining two sides in the same way. Along each of the four sides, the fabric should be folded following the grain and there should be an even rebate of 3mm (⅛in) all the way around.

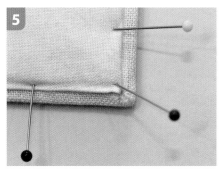

Add a pin in each of the corners, making sure that the fold is neat and makes a 90-degree angle. The rebate at the corners should be the same 3mm (⅛in). Before stitching, make sure the backing fabric is tight enough in both directions by running a *clean finger* along the surface. If a bubble appears, you need to re-pin the fabric tighter.

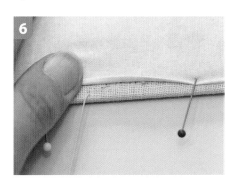

Starting in the middle along one side, thread up a long length of button thread in a curved needle and anchor the thread on the back of the mounted embroidery, hiding the stitches underneath the backing fabric. Cut off the knot and bring the needle out just outside the folded edge of the backing fabric.

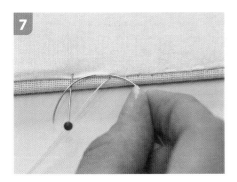

7

Then slip stitch the folded edge of the backing fabric to the back of the mounted embroidery. The stitches should be no more than 5mm (⅕in) in length. Make sure to take the needle down just slightly behind where it emerges from the previous stitch. This will create a slightly back-wards diagonal stitch. Make sure to pull each stitch tight in the direction that you are working, as this will help all the slip stitches disappear.

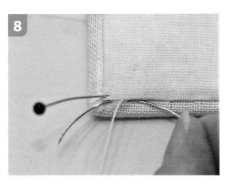

8

Continue working in this way along the first side. When you reach the corner, you need to bring the needle up through the mounted embroidery about 1–2mm (½₅–¹⁄₁₆in) away from corner of the folded backing fabric.

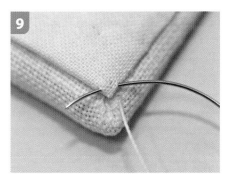

9

Remove the pin from the corner and take the needle through the folded edge of the backing fabric, cutting across the corner and bringing the needle back out in the same position on the opposite side of the corner. Pull all the thread through.

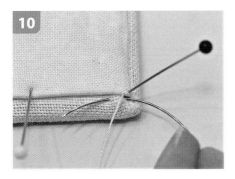

10

Replace the pin, making sure that the corner is pinned as it was before with an even rebate. Turn the embroidery then continue slip stitching along the new edge. If you stitch right into the corner rather than across it, the corner of the fabric becomes rounded and distorted, and pulled out of position when the thread is pulled tight.

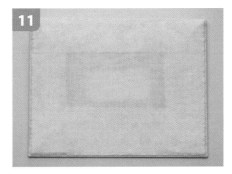

11

Continue slip stitching round the rest of the board, working each of the corners in turn in the same way. When you reach where you started, anchor the thread, hiding the stitches under the backing fabric before cutting any excess thread away. Then remove all the pins. If there are pin marks left around the edge of the backing fabric, use a mellor and gently rub them away as described previously. The mounting process is now complete!

Mounting in a Hoop

Smaller pieces of embroidery can also be mounted into embroidery hoops. These come in many shapes and sizes, from the traditional round to oval and square or even octagonal. Mounting in an embroidery hoop is a much quicker and cheaper way to mount your embroideries but it does not preserve them quite as well as mounting over mount board would. You will find that the tension slackens off much more quickly when mounted in a ring frame, so you may need to re-tighten and rework the stitching sooner than you would think.

When mounting whitework in an embroidery hoop, you will need to choose a lining fabric to sit behind the embroidery. This is because whitework fabrics are translucent and many of the stitches create small or big holes. If you do not line the embroidery when mounting, you will be able to see through it to all the stitching at the back, which does not look professional.

Things You Will Need

- Embroidery hoop to mount in
- Finished embroidery. If worked in a ring frame, remove it from the frame and carefully iron and press any creases in the surrounding fabric.
- Coloured silk, cotton or linen to line the embroidery with
- Fabric to back the embroidery when mounted. This could be the same fabric you used to line the embroidery with.
- Acid-free tissue paper
- Fabric scissors
- Pins
- Buttonhole thread
- Curved needle
- Embroidery needle
- Screwdriver

1970s whitework wallpaper mounted in a ring frame.

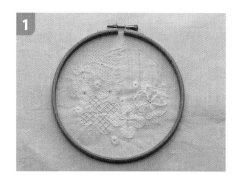

Place outer ring of the embroidery hoop on a piece of acid-free tissue paper, with the screw at the top. Then place the embroidery face down onto the hoop. Turn to check that the embroidery is placed centrally in the hoop.

Lay it back on the tissue face down, keeping it in the same position. Then lay the lining fabric on top of the embroidery. Push the inner ring of the hoop into the outer ring. Turn the hoop over to check the positioning again. If happy, work around the hoop pulling both the embroidery and the lining fabric tight.

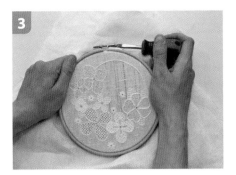

3 When the fabric is as tight as it can be, use a screwdriver to tighten the screw at the top of the hoop as much as you possibly can. This will help keep the tension in the hoop.

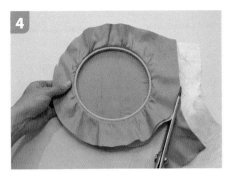

4 Place the embroidery face down again and carefully trim away the excess fabrics, leaving 4–5cm (2in) all the way around the hoop. If you are using a very small hoop, you may need to trim away slightly more.

5 Thread up an embroidery needle with a long length of buttonhole thread and tie a knot in the end. Stitching through both layers of fabric, work running stitches all the way around, about 1cm (⅓in) in from the edge.

6 When you reach where you started, pull the thread tight and all the fabric will pull around the hoop to the back.

7 Work lacing stitches all the way around the hoop, making sure to pull tight as you go. Then anchor the thread. This will help prevent the embroidery from losing tension over time.

8 To finish of the back of the mounting, cut a circle of backing fabric that is about 2cm (¾in) wider than the hoop all the way around.

9 Pin the backing fabric to the fabrics that are now pulled to the back of the frame, turning the edge underneath and making sure to pull the backing fabric tight as you do so.

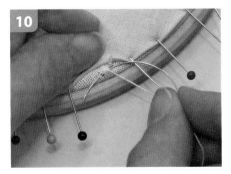

10 Using a curved needle and a length of buttonhole thread, anchor the thread into the fabrics that have been pulled to the back and hidden underneath the backing fabric.

continued on the following page…

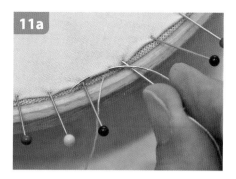

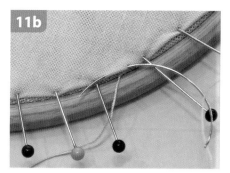

Then work slip stitches (*see* Mounting over Mount Board instructions) all the way around the hoop – first stitching into the fabrics at the back of the hoop, right next to the wood of the hoop, then through the fold of the backing fabric.

Work in this way all the way around the hoop till you reach where you started. Then anchor the thread, hiding the stitches under the backing fabric as best you can. Remove all the pins and your embroidery is successfully mounted and backed in an embroidery hoop.

GETTING YOUR EMBROIDERY FRAMED

Having your finished embroidery framed is the final finishing touch that will protect and preserve your embroidery for generations to come. It will protect it from dust, dirt and – if quality glass is chosen – even light damage, which causes fading and yellowing. Picking the right frame and mounts can be a long process as there are so many options to choose from, but it is important to make the right choices for each specific piece of embroidery. The frame and mount need to enhance the embroidery, not detract from it. Again, using blue in varying shades will help brighten your whitework embroidery, but other colours will work well too. Like when choosing the backing fabrics, try to avoid yellows and creams that will make the whitework look dirty and faded.

One of the most important things is to pick a professional framer who has had experience framing textiles before. That way, they will be able to help and guide you to make the right decision, but will also know and understand how to frame your embroidery correctly.

It is important to note that in most cases you will need to pick a deep frame. This is because the glass should not touch the surface of the embroidery at all. Choosing to have a coloured mount to surround the embroidery can also be helpful with this.

You can buy ready-made frames, but the options will be more limited as to depth, finish and quality. You will also have to mount your embroidery to fit the ready-made frame, which may not be the most aesthetically pleasing option. Bespoke ready-made frames are also available, but you can't try these out against your work before you buy them, and if they're not quite right you can't return them. If you visit a professional framer you will be able to test then pick the perfect combination for frame, mount and embroidery.

Even bespoke frames come with standardised depths and you may be limited in choice as to which frames are available with the right depth for your embroidery, but even if there is only a 5mm gap between embroidery and glass, that is enough.

MOUNTS

When having your embroidery framed, a window mount has many benefits. Most importantly it acts as an extra layer of protection between your embroidery and the frame and glass. A window mount will also create a void/space between the embroidery and the inner edge of the frame, which gives the embroidery space to breathe, rather than having your embroidery looking cramped and boxed in by the frame. Mount board comes in many different colours and textures, but always try to use mount board that is acid free. There are many variations too, from single to double mounts, or having the embroidery attached to the front of the mount so it seems to float within the frame.

Whichever colour and combination you choose, the aim is to enhance your embroidery and not detract from it. Varying shades of blue work well with pieces of whitework, but greens, pinks and even reds could work too. Think about the design and what backing fabrics you have used; the mount should blend in with these so you don't even notice it's there.

Finished whitework piece with two shades of blue mount board. See how the darker blue mount darkens the piece but emphasises the eyelets; whereas the lighter mount brightens the piece. Always try a few different mounts next to the embroidery to see how they work together.

FRAME

With the mount picked, it's now time to choose a frame. The most effective way is to lay the chosen mount combination on the embroidery at the top left corner. Then with a range of different frame styles, lay each on top until you find the one you like the best and is sympathetic to the embroidery and the mount. With whitework, simple and plain frames work best as a subtle background, allowing the embroidery to speak for itself. Pale woods and whites work well, but don't be afraid to choose a coloured or metallic frame if it works well with your embroidery. The most important thing is to make sure that the frame is deep enough.

When you have made a decision on the mount test out different frame options by placing them at the top left corner of the mount and embroidery to see which combination works best.

GLASS

Most framers will have a few different glass options available for you to choose from. The cheapest option will always be the standard glass. This will have a reflective surface which will create glare which can get in the way when looking at your embroidery. It also has very little to no anti UV properties. In the middle there are glass options available with non-reflective and anti UV finishes (True View for example) which are more expensive but make viewing the embroidery better as there is no glare with the added UV protection. When looked through at the right angle these types of glass seem to disappear. Finally there is the museum quality glass which is very expensive and not generally necessary.

Discuss with your framer what the best options are for your budget. The glass is usually the most expensive part of framing so just choose the best glass you can afford or are comfortable paying for.

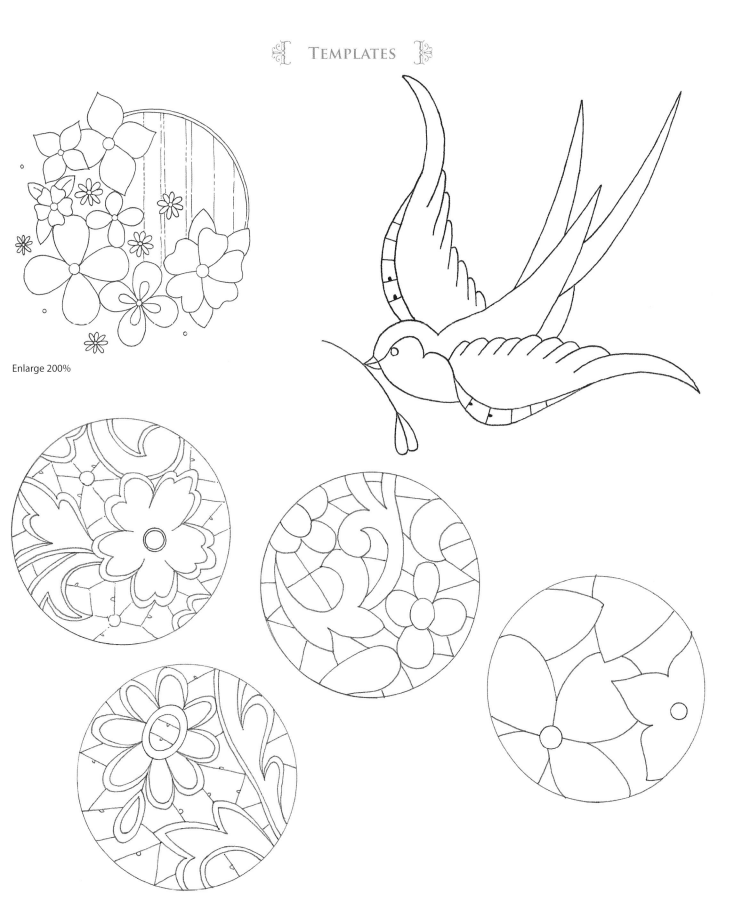

Enlarge 200%

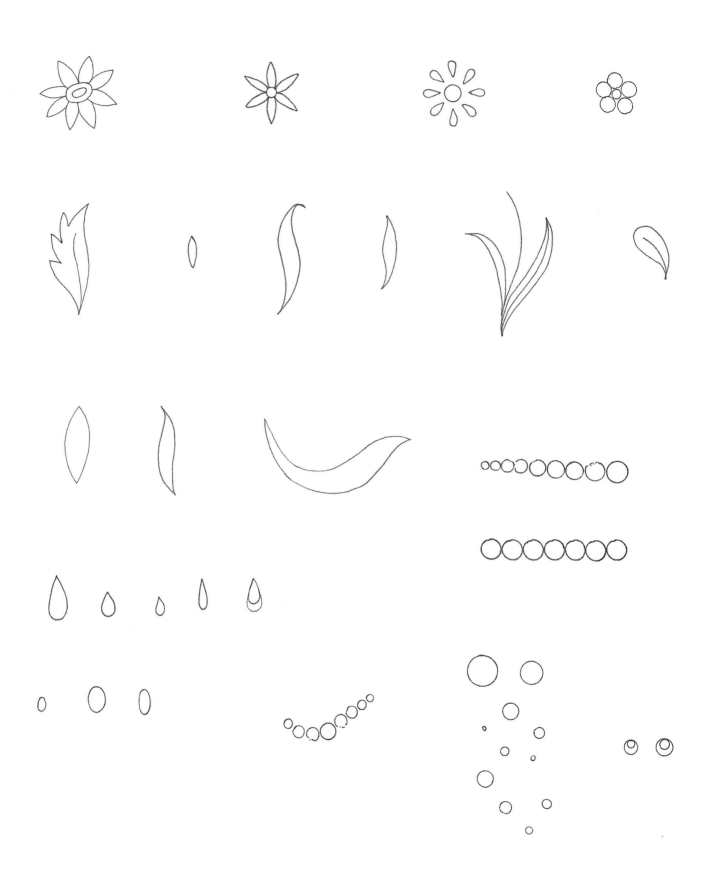

Crafty Ribbons
https://www.craftyribbons.com/

DMC
https://www.dmc.com/uk/

Jenny Adin-Christie
https://jennyadin-christieembroidery.com/shop

Jo Firth Lacemaking & Needle Craft
https://www.jofirthlacemaking.co.uk/

John James Needles
https://www.jjneedles.com/

Julie Barnes
https://www.fineartandframes.co.uk/

Lakeside Needlecraft
https://www.lakesideneedlecraft.co.uk

Lizzy Pye
https://www.laurelin.co.uk/collections/fabric

Love Crafts
https://www.lovecrafts.com/en-us/l/crochet/crochet-patterns

Restore Products
https://restore-products.co.uk/

Royal School of Needlework
https://royal-needlework.org.uk/

Whaleys Bradford
https://www.whaleys-bradford.ltd.uk/

Willow Fabrics
https://www.willowfabrics.com/

Zweigart
https://www.zweigart.de/?lang=en

Adin-Christie, J., *RSN: Fine Whitework: Techniques, Projects & Pure Inspiration* (Search Press, 2022)

Adin-Christie, J., *Fundamental Whitework Techniques*, spiralbound book created by J. Adin-Christie (n.d.)

Bryson, A.F., *Ayrshire Needlework* (Batsford Ltd, 1989)

Dawson, B., *White Work Embroidery* (Batsford Ltd, 1987)

De Dillmont, T., *Encyclopedia of Needlework* (Brustlein & Co., 1890), https://archive.org/details/encyclopediaofne00dill

Digges, M.-D., Fehd, D.N., Lawson, N. and Vogt, M.P., *Lady Evelyn's Needlework Collection* (Embroidery Research Press, Inc., 1988)

Fangel, E., Winckler, I. and Madsen, A.W., *Danish Pulled Thread Embroidery* (Dover Publications Inc., 2000)

Franklin, T.A. and Jarvis, N., *Contemporary Whitework* (Batsford Ltd, 2007)

Lansberry, L., *RSN Essential Stitch Guides: Whitework* (Search Press, 2012)

McNeill, M., *Pulled Thread* (HarperCollins, 1986)

Thomas, M., *Mary Thomas's Embroidery Book* (Wolfenden Press, 2015)

Toomer. H., *Embroidered with White: The 18th Century Fashion for Dresden Lace and Other Whiteworked Accessories* (Heather Toomer Antique Lace, 2008)

Toomer. H., *Fashionable White-Embroidered Accessories: c.1840 to 1900* (Heather Toomer Antique Lace, 2018)

Toomer. H., *White-Embroidered Costume Accessories: The 1790s to 1840s* (Heather Toomer Antique Lace, 2013)

First published in 2023 by
The Crowood Press Ltd
Ramsbury, Marlborough
Wiltshire SN8 2HR

enquiries@crowood.com
www.crowood.com

**British Library Cataloguing-in-Publication
Data**
A catalogue record for this book is available
from the British Library.

ISBN 978 0 7198 4229 0

Cover design by Sergey Tsvetkov

Graphic design and typesetting by
Peggy & Co. Design
Printed and bound in India by
Parksons Graphics

ACKNOWLEDGEMENTS

Most importantly, I would like to start by thanking my husband, Olly, not only for his never-ending support and encouragement, but also his understanding of my love for embroidery. We met the summer before I started my studies at the Royal School of Needlework so for him, at times, I am sure it has felt like embroidery has been a third person in our relationship. During the writing of this book, but also since the start of my career, he has listened to my ideas, shown interest and enthusiasm for my designs and pieces, and has also had to put up with late nights of stitching and the endless pins, needles and threads that I leave all over the house. He has also been cheerleader, tech support, photographer, teacher, tea maker and slate frame carrier, so without him I don't think this book would have been written.

I would also like to thank my family and friends for their support and understanding over the years, with special thanks to my parents who let me forge my own creative path in life and supported me all the way, even when they were not really sure what I was doing. An extra thanks to my Mum, who helped with the proofreading of this book. Even though she had no clue at the start, now I would like to think I have taught one of my family a little something about embroidery.

I would also like to thank the Royal School of Needlework. Without them, I would never have been able to turn my dream into a reality and become a professional embroiderer and embroidery teacher. In one way or another, everyone who works for the RSN has helped and encouraged me, but I would like to especially thank all the tutors I had during my training. There are too many to mention, but you know who you are. Thank you all, then and now, for being an endless source of inspiration and continuing to share your skills and knowledge with me. Without you I would still just be making it up as I go along.

Finally, a separate and heartfelt acknowledgement must be given to Jenny Adin-Christie. Many of the ideas and techniques in whitework that I was taught were researched and developed by Jenny, and she has made an invaluable contribution to the ideas and approaches that we now use as standard and are included in this book. I would particularly like to acknowledge and thank her for the techniques described in the preparation of pulled thread, drawn thread and cutwork, eyelets – the shaded teardrop in particular – shadow work, satin stitch and washing whitework.

I offer this book as part of the growing literature on whitework, which so many of us love and promote. I hope it will contribute to the advancement and use of the stitches, keeping them relevant and alive for generations to come.